The Political Economy of Turkey in the Post-Soviet Era

The Political Economy of Turkey in the Post-Soviet Era

Going West and Looking East?

Edited by
Libby Rittenberg

Westport, Connecticut
London

HF1583.4 .P65 1998

The political economy of
Turkey in the

Library of Congress Cataloging-in-Publication Data

The political economy of Turkey in the post-Soviet era : going West
  and looking East? / edited by Libby Rittenberg.
        p.   cm.
    Includes bibliographical references (p.   ) and index.
    ISBN 0-275-95596-6 (alk. paper)
    1. Turkey—Foreign economic relations.   2. Turkey—Economic
conditions—1960–   3. Turkey—Foreign relations—1980–
I. Rittenberg, Libby.
    HF1583.4.P65   1998
    337.561—dc21   97-26174

British Library Cataloguing in Publication Data is available.

Library of Congress Catalog Card Number: 97-26174
ISBN: 0-275-95596-6

First published in 1998

Praeger Publishers, 88 Post Road West, Westport, CT 06881
An imprint of Greenwood Publishing Group, Inc.

Printed in the United States of America

The paper used in this book complies with the
Permanent Paper Standard issued by the National
Information Standards Organization (Z39.48–1984).

10 9 8 7 6 5 4 3 2 1

To Naşit, Mim, and Nisa.

Contents

Figures and Tables

FIGURES

TABLES

Acknowledgments

I would like to express my heartfelt thanks to the contributors to this volume. Not only did they offer their particular professional expertise, but they were also instrumental in shaping the project as a whole. Their participation in a workshop on the issues covered in this volume contributed greatly to the cohesiveness of this endeavor. Colorado College provided generous support for the workshop and other aspects of this project. I am most grateful to Cathe Antonuccio for her excellent technical, editorial, and secretarial support from start to finish. I also wish to thank Pam Buick, Pat Collander, and Laura Dalros for their secretarial support.

Part I

Setting the Stage

Introduction: The Changing Fortunes of Turkey in the Post-Soviet World

Libby Rittenberg

Like the rest of the world, Turkey felt the reverberations from the sudden and unexpected collapse of the Soviet bloc in 1989 and of the Soviet Union itself in 1991. In a very short period of time, long-standing assumptions about who was friend and who was foe became an open question, alliances and relationships had to be re-considered, new challenges faced, and new opportunities explored. For Turkey, as a crossroads nation between the Eastern and the Western worlds, between the rich, industrialized and the developing worlds, and between the Christian and Muslim worlds, the new situation generated a number of special issues.

In the years following the Second World War, Turkey looked westward politically by becoming a member of the North Atlantic Treaty Organization (NATO) in 1952 and economically by becoming an associate member of what was then the European Community in 1963. Although it maintained generally decent relations with its so-called Eastern neighbors (i.e., with the former Soviet Union and Soviet bloc countries), Turkey's ties with the Western world were seen as its ticket to long-term peace and prosperity.

The dramatic events of 1989 and 1991 called into question the nature of this relationship, as other countries pushed ahead of Turkey in the queue to join the European Union (EU). At the same time, the reduction of political tensions with the Soviet bloc and the expected economic and political transformations of Turkey's neighbors (several with historical, linguistic, and cultural ties to Turkey) were viewed as an opportunity for Turkey to become a regional power. As Graham Fuller (1993a) wrote: "Located in geopolitical terms in the southeastern corner of Europe for so many decades, Turkey now lies at the center of a rapidly evolving new geopolitical region of Turkish peoples from Eastern Europe to Western China—in which it will be the central player" (163).

Others seem less certain about the centrality of Turkey's role. They note the precarious nature of Turkey's domestic economic and political situation, as well as its marginal position in Europe. Also, other countries with geographical proximity to Eastern Europe and the countries of the former Soviet Union, such as Russia, Iran, and China, will surely seek to assert their influence on the region as well.

The purpose of this book is to systematically examine how the political and economic fortunes of Turkey have changed in the aftermath of the Cold War. As one of the contributors to this volume mentioned, this exercise may be akin to putting the earth at the center of the solar system. While not implying a Turco-centric system, the articles in this volume describe and analyze the situation by looking outward from Turkey's perspective. Indeed, Chase et al (1996) argue that Turkey is one of a handful of pivotal states whose fortunes "could not only determine the fate of its region but also affect international stability" (33). Specifically, they argue:

"At a multifold crossroads between East and West, North and South, Christendom and Islam, Turkey has the potential to influence countries thousands of miles from the Bosphorus . . . A prosperous, democratic, tolerant Turkey is a beacon for the entire region; a Turkey engulfed by civil wars and racial and religious hatreds, or nursing ambitions to interfere abroad, would hurt American interests in innumerable ways and concern everyone from pro-NATO strategists to friends of Israel." (47–48)

The book analyzes how Turkey's foreign economic and political relations with Central and Eastern Europe and Eurasia have been affected by the collapse of the Soviet Union and Soviet bloc and the end of the Cold War. This puts the focus of the chapters on the 1990s and beyond. While Turkey's relations with countries of the Middle East, Far East, the Americas, and elsewhere have continued to evolve and develop, Turkey's relations with Europe, broadly defined, and with Eurasia have changed most markedly because of the historic events of the late 1980s and early 1990s.

Moreover, Turkey's potential new role in this region has been singled out for special attention. While the statements in 1992 by then prime minister (now president) Süleyman Demirel concerning a gigantic Turkic world stretching from the Adriatic Sea to the Great Wall of China and by then president Turgut Özal that the next century would be the century of the Turks are now generally dismissed as expressions of initial euphoria, the role that Turkey has played in the region in the 1990s, as we shall see, has been substantial and is likely to continue to grow as the region recovers and restructures.

Chapter 2 provides an overview of Turkey's economic situation and serves as a backdrop for viewing Turkey's foreign economic and political relations. Parts II and III of this volume examine Turkey's relations with Western Europe and with the former Soviet Union and Soviet bloc countries, respectively. Each part begins with a chapter that provides an overview of Turkey's political relationship with the respective region, followed by chapters that discuss more specific aspects of the politico-economic relationships.

OVERVIEW OF THE CHAPTERS

In Chapter 2, Faruk Selcuk explains the recent unstable macroeconomic performance of the Turkish economy, characterized by boom-recession cycles in the real economy, persistent and slowly increasing high inflation, high public sector debt, and deterioration in the balance of payments. Since 1989, the Turkish Central Bank has operated under a policy of limiting devaluations in order to control inflation. The government has failed to adopt or stick to complementary fiscal policies, Selcuk argues, and the resulting non-credible, exchange rate-based stabilization policy has had the effect of generating a U-shaped pattern of inflation and an inverted U-shaped pattern of real economic growth. The present fiscal policy, characterized by large public sector deficits, high real interest rates on both domestic and dollar-denominated public debt, and the inability of government to collect high seigniorage revenue in the presence of currency substitution, is not sustainable, he argues. With regard to the balance of payments, the external balance has been highly volatile for the last 10 years, due to fluctuations in the value of the Turkish lira, as a result of the inconsistency between monetary and fiscal policies, and increased reliance on erratic short-term capital flows. Due to these policies, a major success of the 1980 economic reform package—the placement of the Turkish economy on an export-led growth path—has been partly undone, as evidenced by the zigzagging on the export-import ratio in response to appreciation and depreciation of the Turkish lira.

The picture presented by Selcuk confirms earlier work on this topic that concluded that the liberalization/stabilization program begun in 1980 has not yet reached maturity. (See, e.g., Rodrik 1990 or, more recently, Öniş and Riedel 1993.) Rather, persistent, macroeconomic disequilibria and recurrent crises of various degrees provide as apt a description of the post-reform period as they did of the pre-reform period. Öniş and Riedel (1993) have explained this phenomenon in terms of key features of the political economy of Turkey with its strong statist tradition and a multi-party democracy that has produced various governing coalitions that perceive the need to maintain an excessively high rate of economic growth in order to stay in power. Such unsustainable macroeconomic policies inevitably generate macroeconomic crises.

Thus, in the same way that certain urban areas located along geological fault lines experience periodic tremors and await "the big one," so the Turkish economy seems to totter seemingly endlessly on the brink of disaster, while at the same time maintaining a considerable level of economic success and normalcy as it goes. Indeed, the ability of Turkish economic agents to cope with uncertainty and economic difficulties has at times been turned into a virtue that will, for example, give Turkish entrepreneurs an edge in the newly opened markets of Russia and Central Asia, where the macroeconomic situations in the recent past and for the foreseeable future are likely to be similar to the situation of Turkey.

The three chapters of Part II explore the recent evolution of Turkey's relations with the European Union. In Chapter 3, Atila Eralp argues that relations between Turkey and the European Union began to deteriorate prior to the end of the Cold War and that they have become increasingly problematic since. In the 1960s Turkey's eventual membership in the then European Community (EC) was viewed as the economic prong linking Turkey to the West, in the same way that membership in NATO linked Turkey militarily to the West. However, Turkey's inward-oriented industrialization strategy and economic difficulties in the 1970s, followed by the military intervention in Turkey in 1980, which came at a time when the European Community was placing greater emphasis on democracy and human rights issues, led to a reconsideration in what had previously been regarded as a likely outcome. In 1987 Turkey officially applied for membership, and in 1989 the commission of the EC responded that it was unwilling to open accession negotiations with Turkey but suggested the reactivation of the Association Agreement. This eventually led to the formation of a customs union in 1996 between Turkey and the EC. Of course, by this time, Western European attention had begun to shift towards Central and Eastern Europe. Throughout this period, Turkey has officially clung to the idea of eventual full membership, while Europe has moved away from linking the customs union to this issue. Thus, the creation of the customs union with the EC did not relieve the tension between the parties, and the divergence of opinion continues.

At the same time, Eralp cautions that Turkey should not give up its aspiration for full membership and that further marginalization of Turkey is in the interest of neither party. If Turkey is further excluded from Europe, Turkey and its neighbors are likely to experience increased instability. A stable Turkey can serve as a conduit for furthering Europe's relations of various kinds with the Middle East, Persian Gulf, and the Transcaucasus. Turkey, on the other hand, is strengthened in the region by having good connections with Europe. Even while the attainment of full membership for Turkey in the EU has become more difficult, he sees an opportunity for Turkey in the move within the EU toward flexible models of integration. For example, he suggests that Turkey seek to join as a full member some of the emerging European security institutions that will likely have close links to NATO, such as the Western European Union (WEU). Such alternative paths toward integration will serve to prevent further deterioration in the relationship between Turkey and the EU.

Canan Balkır provides a detailed analysis of the newly formed customs union between Turkey and the EC. Turkey is the only country to have concluded a customs union agreement with the EC without being a full member. Although a more comprehensive assessment of this unique arrangement on both parties will have to await the passage of time, Balkır concludes that its inaugural year in 1996 was disappointing for both sides. The salient negative features for Turkey from the arrangement were the loss of public revenues, as certain taxes had to be adjusted to fulfill the obligation of the customs union, the growing trade deficit with the EC, declining foreign investment in Turkey, the blocking of financial aid from the EC to Turkey, the fact that Turkey's chances of achieving full membership do not seem to have been enhanced, and perceived meddling by the EU in Turkey's domestic affairs. The EC has been disappointed with political developments in Turkey. There are complaints that Turkey's progress on human rights and democracy has been inadequate. The coming to power in Turkey in 1996 of a coalition government that included the pro-Islamist Welfare Party (RP), an outcome that, it had been argued, the customs union would preclude, left certain deputies in the European Parliament (EP) feeling cheated. Tensions with Greece, a full member of both the EU and NATO, around the Aegean and over Cyprus further increased the alienation that both sides felt. While recognizing that the benefits from the customs union are more likely to arise for Turkey in the medium and long terms and that Turkey's macroeconomic imbalances must be dealt with in order to realize maximum benefits, Balkır concludes that the arrangement has bound Turkey to Europe in a unique way and sees it as a positive step in the process of further deepening relations between the EU and Turkey.

Bahri Yılmaz's chapter deals with the narrower, but very critical, question of whether or not Turkish industry is ready to compete in the EU. The chapter provides a detailed analysis of the structure of specialization and international competitiveness of Turkish industry compared to the EU as a whole and to the poorer, southern members (Greece, Portugal, and Spain) in particular. He concludes that Turkey has markedly changed its export structure in recent years and has closed somewhat its development gap with Greece and Portugal. The next challenge for Turkish policy-makers, he feels, is to pursue policies that will move the structure of Turkish exports from the so-called labor-intensive category to the "easily imitable and difficultly imitable research-oriented goods" categories. But, he argues, Turkey can compete in the raw material, labor-intensive, and, to some extent, capital-intensive sectors. Indeed, he argues that Turkey's improvement in international competitiveness has been greater than Greece's or Portugal's in recent years, despite the benefits that the latter two countries have realized from full membership in the EU. He expects that, as the dynamic benefits to competitiveness of the customs union kick in and despite the challenges that that arrangement poses, Turkey will experience even further improvements.

The five chapters of Part III explore Turkey's emerging relations with countries that had been part of the Soviet Union or Soviet bloc. The section leads with the chapter by Gareth Winrow, who examines how Turkey's political role in the Black Sea region, the Transcaucasus, and Central Asia has evolved in the 1990s and speculates on how that role will continue to evolve in the near

future. The focus is primarily on official relations, as opposed to private rela-
tions, which are explored more fully in other chapters. In the early post-Soviet
years Turkey seemed to take full advantage of its geographical location. The
Black Sea Economic Cooperation (BSEC) project, which includes the six Black
Sea littoral states (Turkey, Russia, Ukraine, Georgia, Bulgaria, and Romania),
as well as five other nearby states (Armenia, Azerbaijan, Moldova, Greece, and
Albania) and seven other states with observer status (Poland, Slovakia, Italy,
Austria, Tunisia, Egypt, and Israel), demonstrated the "bridge" role that Turkey
hoped to play in the post-Cold War era. It is important to remember that the
government in Turkey viewed the construction of BSEC as a means of enhancing Turkey's prestige and thus as a means of improving prospects for admission into the EU, while at the same time building up hitherto minimal relations with the various countries in transition. Launched formally in Istanbul in
1992, BSEC has acquired many of the trappings of an official international
organization, with a secretariat, parliamentary assembly, and bank. While
BSEC may be responsible for strengthened ties with some of the involved
countries, it does not seem to have enhanced Turkey's prospects of entry into
the EU.

Turkey's efforts to augment relations with its Transcaucasian and Central
Asian neighbors have played into Russian concerns about developments in, and
relations with, its "near abroad," as well as Iranian interests in this area, which
Winrow argues seem to be mainly aimed at promoting its economic interests as
opposed to exporting its brand of an Islamic-based society. Thus, initial statements by prominent Turkish government officials suggesting the creation of a
larger Turkic world and efforts to exert leadership in these areas have been
scaled back over the course of the 1990s, although the official Turkic summits,
as well as other, unofficial summits, continue as forums for discussion. The
official relations that have emerged seem considerably less than what Turkish
governing elites initially envisioned. All three countries—Turkey, Russia, and
Iran—are kept somewhat at bay because of the possible contribution each could
make toward destabilizing the others. For example, Turkish support of Chechens in Russia or Azeris in Iran could be countered by Russian and/or Iranian
support for Kurds in Turkey.

Winrow concludes that the attitudes of future Turkish governments toward
the Black Sea region, the Transcaucasus, and Central Asia will depend on the
nature of the government in Ankara, as well as on the governments of the other
states in the region. He speculates that if a future Welfare Party government in
Turkey were "to place greater emphasis on the Turkic world at the expense of
Europe" and "to combine such a policy with its traditional interest in furthering
relations with Moslem states," then "that could set Turkey on a collision course
with Iran over leadership of the 'Islamic world,' with Russia over Moscow's
fear of the spread of radical, politicized Islam and with various regimes in
Central Asia and the Transcaucasus that are determined to maintain a secular
approach." Noting at the outset of the chapter that Turkey's defense coopera-

tion with Israel and the implementation of the customs union with the EU stayed on track under the Welfare-True Path coalition government in Turkey, the political situations both in Turkey and in the neighboring states make the likely evolution of relationships difficult to discern.

The following chapter by Serdar Sayan and Osman Zaim provides an in-depth analysis of the Black Sea Economic Cooperation project, especially its economic dimensions. Noting that at the time of its formation in 1992 all BSEC members but two (Turkey and Greece) were essentially centrally planned economies and that now these members are considered transition economies, the authors caution that traditional economic tools for analyzing the impact of economic integration are somewhat inadequate. Moreover, since the low level of trade between Turkey and Greece, on one hand, and the former Soviet bloc and countries that emerged with the breakup of the Soviet Union, on the other hand, was due primarily to structural factors resulting from different socioeconomic systems and sector-specific barriers rather than to high tariffs or quotas, the agreement is more appropriately aimed at facilitating the integration of the countries involved into the world trading system. The authors go so far as to argue that even in the complete absence of tariff and non-tariff barriers, trade volume would be constrained by poor transportation and communication links, a shortcoming that the BSEC project is trying to resolve. Thus, the whole project should be viewed more as an attempt towards regional economic cooperation than towards economic integration per se.

Sayan and Zaim then employ a gravity model to analyze trade flows between Turkey and the other members. While the empirical results for estimating Turkish exports to BSEC members did not fit a priori expectations, the authors argue that this may be due to the very success of BSEC itself. That is, Turkish exports to BSEC members have increased despite sharp declines in their gross domestic products (GDPs) during the transition period. The gravity model, however, provides a more conventional explanation of Turkish imports from BSEC members: Turkish demand for imports from BSEC countries increases with Turkish and partner-country GDP and decreases with distance between Turkey and the BSEC trading partners.

In the medium and longer terms, the authors predict that the gains from trade will increase. For the former communist countries, as they proceed with their structural transformations, relative price signals will become more important, and trade according to comparative advantage will likely increase. As this occurs, the authors believe that the existence of BSEC, in which Turkey played a leadership role, will be beneficial to Turkey as well as to the other members of the project.

In the next chapter Gülten Kazgan reports that relations between Turkey and Russia began to improve in the 1980s as "trade followed the flag." In the post-Cold War period this sequence was reversed to the extent that souring political relations beginning in 1993 (stemming from local armed uprisings and strengthening radical political movements in both countries, as well as compe-

tition over oil and natural gas pipeline routes) failed to put a damper on growing economic relations. The chapter provides an overview of the domestic economic situation in each country, a comparison of their economies, and a detailed historical analysis of their recent trade and investment flows. Complementary economic structures encourage strong and growing trade relations
between the countries. Turkey mainly exports services and consumer products
to Russia and imports from Russia heavy industrial products, including military
equipment, and fuels. In addition, unrecorded, so-called suitcase trade between
the two countries may exceed recorded trade. In contrast to booming trade relations in goods and services, capital flows have been quite modest, reflecting
capital shortages in both countries and risk. Cooperation in the field of science
and technology looks promising, as Russia's strong background in basic sciences complements Turkey's strength in the social sciences and in management
techniques. While political and economic uncertainties in both countries make
the future of relations between them difficult to predict, Kazgan argues that the
increased role played by private economic agents in both countries may serve to
temper intergovernmental rivalries, so long as barriers to trade are not raised,
cooperative solutions to common problems (such as the pipeline routes) are
sought, and macroeconomic stability in both countries is enhanced.

The chapter by Meliha Altunışık focuses specifically on the Eurasian oil market and pipeline routes. This "case study" provides a concrete example of how
initial euphoria over a perceived new opportunity for Turkey in due time gave
way to a more realistic understanding of Turkey's limitations in influencing
developments. As is well known, several Eurasian countries, specifically Azerbaijan, Kazakhstan, and Turkmenistan, have substantial, unexploited oil and
natural gas resources. She reports that the Turkish government had three desired policy goals in its active pursuit of production and transportation of Eurasian natural resources: the achievement of economic benefits, an enhanced
leadership role for Turkey in Eurasia and thus increased recognition of Turkey's importance in the post-Cold War era, and increased popularity of the
Turkish government, headed for most of the post-Soviet period by Tansu Çiller.
The pipeline issue has been a source of intense rivalry between Russia and Turkey and a place where politics and economics intertwine uneasily. The author
argues that because of Turkey's domestic political situation, Turkish policy-
makers were slow to recognize the implications of Russia's "near abroad" policy and thus were slow to emphasize that its pipeline proposals could be viewed
as complementary, and not rivalrous, with Russia's. To date, despite some minor gains, the role of Turkey in the Eurasian oil market has been rather limited.

In the final chapter, Gül and İlter Turan divide the post-Soviet period into
three stages. The first was marked by general optimism and great expectations
for the possibilities that could develop between Turkey, Azerbaijan, and the
Turkish countries of Central Asia. The second was a time when all sides discovered the limits of the relationship, while the third is described as a time
when the relationship has become more routine. During the initial euphoric

period, Turkey moved in quickly to help with transportation and communication links, to offer diplomatic support, and to develop cultural and educational ties. During this period, reference was often made to a Turkish model of development that the Turkic states might follow in their transitions from central planning to market-based systems. To support these developments, a number of institutions were created, including the Turkish Cooperation and Development Agency (TİKA), under the Turkish Ministry of Foreign Affairs, and the Foreign Economic Relations Board (DEİK), an association of non-governmental, bilateral business councils. The authors trace the beginning of the second stage to the Ankara Summit in October 1992. The lack of specificity contained in the declaration signed at the end of the summit was a clear signal that relations between Turkey and the Turkic countries formed in the aftermath of the Soviet Union would be tempered by other considerations, including commitments to the Commonwealth of Independent States and Russia, conflicts of interest among the Turkish states themselves, and desires by the newly emerging states to diversify their foreign relations and to assert their own leadership roles. Moreover, it became clear that Turkey's ability to extend assistance and support was marginal in comparison to what would be required to achieve the economic transformations in the Turkish states. On the flip side, progress in economic transformation turned out to be quite slow in these countries. Thus, during the third and current stage, the relationship has become more realistic. Though the development of economic relations has proceeded with the support of the Turkish government, the volume of trade and investment between Turkey and the Turkish states is still quite modest. It is not that Turkish businesses are losing to other foreign businesses; rather, the integration of the Turkic countries into the world economy has been slow. During this period, Turkey has tried to position itself as the leading partner country through which other countries should develop their economic relations with the Turkish states. Though there are some examples that this "bridge" policy may be working, the low volume of such endeavors makes a firm conclusion at this point hazardous. Throughout this stage, cultural, linguistic, and educational linkages have been promoted. Moreover, Turkey has become increasingly aware of Russia's security concerns and seems to be moving toward more cooperative policies with Russia in the Transcaucasus and Central Asia.

GENERAL THEMES

We may glean a number of general propositions about Turkey's political and economic relations with other countries as these relations have been shaped in the period following the collapse of the Soviet bloc and the breakup of the Soviet Union itself into constituent parts.

First, the decrease in the importance of Turkey to the West as well as its rise to prominence in the East were both initially exaggerated. Concerning Turkey, an initial reaction to the end of the Cold War was to assume that since Turkey's role as a front-line state to aid in the containment of the Soviet Union had disappeared, so had its geopolitical importance to the West. This line of thinking has been refuted. The neighborhood in which Turkey lives is potentially explosive, and a Western-oriented Turkey can help to calm the region. Turkey's role in the United States-led coalition against Saddam Hussein in Iraq in 1991, and Turkey's continued role in allowing the use of its İncirlik Air Base by the United States in its effort to protect the Kurds in Iraq, are the most prominent examples. In addition, in the 1990s, Turkey has broadened its economic and strategic ties with Israel and also contributed to the Middle East peace process (Gruen 1995). Agreements between Turkey and Israel allow Israeli pilots to train in Turkey and contain plans for cooperation on intelligence matters; a free trade agreement between the two countries is expected (Economist Intelligence Unit, 1997).

The *Economist* (14 December 1991 survey: 3) lays out a scenario that "leaves only one large stretch of the world notably liable to produce turmoil and mayhem on a large scale in the coming 15–20 years: the appropriately crescent-shaped piece of territory that starts in the steppes of Kazakhstan and curves south and west through the Gulf and Suez to the north coast of Africa." With such potential for turmoil, Turkey can serve as "an example to the region around it—a living demonstration of the proposition that a Muslim country can become a prosperous democracy, a full member of the modern world" (Ibid: 4).

On the other hand, while the political and economic links that Turkey has established with its "new, eastern" neighbors—the countries around the Black Sea, the Transcaucasus, and Central Asia—both through official and private channels, have been substantial, the creation of a Turkic-centered world does not seem imminent either. Initial euphoria has given way to more realistic analysis and appraisal of the situation. Other countries, especially Russia, have made it clear that they plan to be big players in the Turkic regions, as well as in other parts of the former Soviet Union and Soviet bloc. Also, Turkic peoples are not as homogeneous as this term suggests, and the expansion of economic, social, and political relations made possible by the post-Soviet period has served to point out some of the differences. Moreover, many of the so-called Turkic countries have large Russian populations. Finally, none of the Turkic countries, including Turkey, have the political or economic "reach" that would be required to create such a Turkic world.

Second, Turkey's full membership in the European Union has never been a given, even though pursuit of such membership has continued to be the policy of successive Turkish governments. This uncertainty is separate from the fact that some former Soviet bloc countries seem to have pushed ahead of Turkey in the queue to join the European Union. As mentioned earlier, Turkey's relations with Europe had deteriorated considerably before the Berlin Wall came down.

However, especially since 1980, when Turkey began its liberalization/ structural adjustment program, its economic ties with Europe have expanded and matured. As the chapter by Yılmaz shows, Turkey's competitive position vis-à-vis the European Union has improved even without full membership.

The two authors in this volume (Eralp and Balkır) who address the issue feel that the possibility for full membership should be kept alive and pursued strategically. Ironically, the end of the Cold War, which seems to have moved Turkey down in the queue of countries seeking to join the European Union, may offer a means of keeping this aspiration alive: because the countries seeking membership are at different stages in their transitions to democracy and to market-based economic systems, there is greater consideration given to more flexible models of integration over the near and medium terms. Both authors suggest ways beyond the recently formed customs union to further strengthen ties and integrate Turkey into Europe.

Turkey's frustration on the issue of EU membership became more pronounced in 1997. Government officials in Turkey have threatened to block the expansion of NATO and the use of NATO weapons by the Western European Union if relations with the EU continue to deteriorate (Economist Intelligence Unit 1997).

Third, the breakup of the Soviet Union and of the Soviet bloc afforded Turkey a special opportunity to pursue new initiatives at all levels—from the establishment of the Black Sea Economic Cooperation project at the official level, to the development of largely unrecorded suitcase trade between individuals and small businesses in neighboring states. In addition to the development and expansion of direct ties with the newfound neighbors, Turkey is often considered as a base from which multinationals may enter into the new markets or, in the case of natural resources, as a conduit for those resources. A recent survey of 50 multinational corporations doing business in Turkey found that 22 of them use their facility in Turkey to serve a region stretching beyond Turkey, and 8 of them are handling an increase in regional exports and cross-border services. Among explanations for this offered by the various executives of these companies were geographic proximity, good infrastructure in Turkey, ethnic ties to some of the countries, and Turkey's being in a customs union with the European Union (*Wall Street Journal,* 27 March 1997). So, despite some setbacks at the official level (such as in the area of oil pipelines), ties are progressing in an evolutionary manner and over time could have a large cumulative effect. Moreover, because of the growing strength of the private sectors in both Turkey and these partner countries, private relations seem very resilient, even when relations at the official level are at a standstill or are souring.

Fourth, the pace of development of these new relationships is limited, though, both by the pace of transformation in the partner countries and by Turkey's progress in creating a secure economic environment.

The countries with which Turkey is expected to have a comparative advantage in terms of developing new ties include those around the Black Sea, due to geographic proximity, and the non-Baltic countries of the former Soviet Union, stemming primarily from cultural and linguistic similarities. As pointed out by the de Melo et al. (1996) study for the World Bank on transition economies, these are the so-called low intermediate and slow reforming countries, some of which have been affected by war or other hostilities. Speculations as to why these countries have been slower to reform include the fact that, as a whole, they started from a lower level of economic development, had longer historical experience with communism and lack any historical experience with modern political and economic systems, and, since the end of the Cold War, have often been involved in territorial disputes, civil wars, and other hostilities.

While the political and economic transformations of the advanced reformers into modern democracies with market-based economies seems likely, the outcome for the slow reforms is much more uncertain. Przeworski (1991) argues that slow reform processes allow those against reform to organize more effective resistance and create opportunities for the non-reform-minded to gain the upper hand. This slow pace of transformation in the neighborhood of Turkey limits participation by all outside partners, including Turkey.

As shown in following chapters, Turkey's role in the transformation processes under way is quite respectable, given the limitation stemming from the slow reform process. Russia has become an important economic partner for Turkey, especially in certain sectors, such as natural gas, tourism, transportation, and construction. While such relations with Russia exceed in magnitude those with all the Turkic countries combined, Turkey's economic inroads into the Turkic countries are considered substantial, given the meager relations that these countries have developed with countries that were not previously part of the Soviet Union. Important for Turkey has been the development of regional hubs in Turkey's northeast, such as Trabzon. Thus, when the pace of change in these slowly transforming countries accelerates, Turkey seems well poised to move ahead and to become a major player in the region.

A caveat, though, could limit Turkey's participation. Turkey must complete its own structural transformation if it is to realize its ambitions in both Western Europe and in the newly opened countries of Central and Eastern Europe and Eurasia. Whereas in the early 1980s Turkey was considered a leader in economic reform within the developing world, it has since come to be viewed as a laggard (Lieberman 1996). Its macroeconomic instability, characterized by wide swings in the rate of economic growth and high inflation, has become a way of life. As pointed out by Saraçoğlu (1996), Turkey and Venezuela share the dubious distinction of having been able to maintain the longest stretches of high inflation (more than 15 years) without falling into hyperinflation.

Such instability warps economic decision-making processes away from activities that could yield long-term benefits and toward speculation and quick profit opportunities (Ferhatoğlu 1996). Seemingly endless delays in privatizing state-owned enterprises in Turkey forestall improvements in overall economic efficiency (Bayar 1996) and are a source of continual drain to the government's budget. The downgrading of Turkey's sovereign credit rating to sub-investment grade by Standard and Poor's and Moody's in 1994 may reflect the difficulty

Turkey has had in attracting its share of world foreign direct investment and capital flows (Toksöz 1996).

Domestic sources of investment funds in Turkey are an inadequate substitute. The national savings rate averaged just over 20% in the 1990s. Gavin et al. (1996), drawing on the experiences of East Asian countries, argue that to break out of the vulnerability caused by high exposure to, and reliance on, volatile international capital flows, government policy must be designed to create a stable and predictable economic climate that will give savers confidence that the value of their savings will be maintained and not eroded by the vagaries of inflation and/or a weak financial system. The short-term effect of such policies is likely to be a reduction in savings (until a period of sustained growth ensues), during what will hopefully turn out to be the transition to a high-growth, high-saving equilibrium (Gavin et al. 1996: 7).

If Turkey were to pursue such policies now, then conceivably, by the time the countries of Eastern Europe and Eurasia were ready to absorb increased trade and capital flows, Turkey would have generated internally the means to extend its reach from the rhetorical level to the financial level.

The dynamism of Turkey's private sector and its resilience under very unpredictable circumstances are often credited with keeping Turkey afloat despite the recurring vagaries of Turkey's political and economic crises (Yıldırım 1996). One can only imagine how much more effective the private sector could be in an environment of credible government policies.

In sum, Turkey's regional economic role can only strengthen as the neighboring countries are ready to absorb higher levels of contacts, and as its domestic house is put in order.

POSSIBLE FUTURE SCENARIOS

Figure 1.1 provides a schematic of four possible future outcomes based on the coherence and desirability of Turkey's economic and political policies and the policies of its potential regional partners.

Scenario 1 assumes that both Turkey and the other countries in the region pursue policies that are generally conducive to economic growth and prosperity. This scenario would mean growing economic clout for Turkey and for the region as a whole. In the same way that the Association of South East Asian Nations (ASEAN) was initially considered an ineffective organization but later gained prestige and influence as the Asian economies grew and prospered, so might new regional organizations, such as BSEC, gain importance in the world. Organizations outside the region, such as the EU, would seek increased contacts. Turkey could be perceived as an economic leader in this group, although there would be other major players as well, such as Russia and perhaps Ukraine and Uzbekistan.

Figure 1.1
Possible Future Scenarios

TURKEY

		More desirable policies	Less desirable policies
REGIONAL	More Desirable Policies	1	3
PARTNERS	Less Desirable Policies	2	4

The second scenario would lead Turkey to look even more toward Western Europe and to other countries outside the region. The markets of Eastern Europe and the former Soviet Union would be left to risk-takers, speculators, and small-scale traders. Strong entrepreneurial attitudes would give Turkey a major role in such a game; however, the payoff would likely be limited and volatile.

Scenario 3 envisions that Turkey's inflation comes down more slowly than that of its neighbors and that while Turkey's growth continues to oscillate, the growth of its neighbors starts to resemble that of the leading reformers in Central Europe. Such a scenario would seem to create serious problems for Turkey, as Turkey would be bypassed by, for example, multinationals that would choose Russia or other countries as bases of their operations. Either the organizations that Turkey helped create in the 1990s would wither, or Turkey would be forced to cede leadership to more successful countries in the region.

The fourth scenario represents the grand failure. Such a scenario would likely mean a highly unstable and unpredictable region. The outside world would probably react by trying to isolate the region in order to contain its problems within its borders.

The purpose of looking at these last two scenarios is not to bolster the image of economics as a dismal science. These scenarios do allow one, though, to see the consequences if opportunities are missed and to see the crossroads-like nature of the period.

Furthermore, the analysis does highlight the importance for Turkey of getting its domestic house in order. Continuing to muddle along is possible and does not necessarily have dire consequences in the short run. But at some point, Turkey may find that a historic opportunity has been lost, perhaps forever.

2

A Brief Account of the Turkish Economy, 1987–1996
Faruk Selcuk

In 1980, Turkey started to implement a substantial market-oriented reform package. It received wide-range support from several international financial organizations, including the International Monetary Fund (IMF) and the World Bank. The effects of this program became evident in Turkey's improved economic performance in terms of relatively higher economic growth and a "healthy" balance of payments situation in the early years of the 1980s. However, the overall appearance of the macroeconomic picture has been quite bleak since the end of the 1980s.

More recently, at the beginning of 1994, the economy experienced a major financial crisis, triggered by concerns over the sustainability of current macroeconomic policies. The financial crisis also had a spillover effect on the real economy; the gross domestic product (GDP) fell 4.7% in that year. On 5 April 1994, the government launched a stabilization program in order to rescue the economy. A standby arrangement was approved by the IMF two months after the program. Nevertheless, it soon became clear that the program was destined for failure. Although the economy did not experience another exchange rate crisis or higher inflation immediately, by the beginning of 1995 there was an implicit consensus among market participants that the 5 April stabilization program had finished. At the time of the writing of this chapter, the government had invited a delegation from the IMF for consultation on a new standby arrangement. The committee left the country after a short review of the current economic situation and with proposals by the government for the near future. The diagnosed prospects for the economy were not promising: "[T]he Fund, unwilling to trigger a confidence crisis toward Turkey, will wait and watch for some positive signals" (*Financial Times* 29 October 1996: 3).

What went wrong with the exemplary economy of the 1980s? The aim of this chapter is to provide an overall picture of the Turkish economy, with emphasis on development in the real sector and fiscal and external imbalances, particularly after 1987.[1] The first section summarizes the growth performance of Turkey after 1987 by analyzing the underlying driving forces in the economy. The second section presents an overview of the public sector deficit and examines how the deficit was financed. The same section also gives a brief account of public debt during the period under consideration. The third section investigates developments in the external balance, citing how the policies since 1987 have resulted in the permanent deterioration of the balance of payments.

REAL ECONOMY: BOOM-RECESSION CYCLE

Persistent and slowly increasing high inflation has probably been the most important characteristic of the Turkish economy during the past two decades. Although there were seemingly ambitious programs to fight inflation, in hindsight it is evident that the policy-makers never attempted to strengthen public finances, which undoubtedly accounts for the inflation. Not facing any serious shocks to the price level, the system has developed the means of coping with high inflation. Given the past failures of "stabilization" programs, the public has grown reluctant to assign any credibility to new or seemingly well-designed inflation stabilization programs.

By late 1988, however, the Turkish Central Bank initiated a lower rate of devaluation policy in order to control inflation. Since there were no major changes in the other areas of policymaking, this policy switch may be interpreted as the Central Bank's concern for its own short-term credibility.

The possible effects of a non-credible exchange rate-based stabilization policy can be analyzed within the framework of a model developed by Calvo and Vegh (1991). It is well known that there are two explicit effects of this kind of policy on the inflation rate of home goods. First, the lower rate of devaluation has a dampening effect on the inflation rate of home goods. Second, the aggregate demand increase pushes the inflation rate up. Due to this second effect, the fall in the inflation rate of domestic goods is less than the fall in the devaluation rate. Although inflation falls at the beginning, it begins to rise with the anticipation of a higher devaluation rate, imminent at the end of the program. The result is U-shaped inflation during the course of the program.

Given a degree of capital mobility, it is reasonable to expect that nominal interest rates in the economy would necessarily fall as well. Since the effective price of consumption (and investment) is relatively lowered, and since the program is perceived as temporary, the intertemporal allocation decisions of the optimizing agents come into play, and the aggregate demand jumps up immediately. The greater the public belief that a "lower devaluation policy" is temporary, the greater the jump in the aggregate demand. As a result, the economy experiences a boom during the early stages of the policy. As time passes, the aggregate demand eventually declines. If the program is adopted for a short time, the economy does not enter a recession prior to the end of the program. However, since the total output deviates from its long-run trend, it is inevitable that the economy will fall into a recession. The end result is an inverted U-shape representing the growth rate of the economy.

During the early stages of a lower-devaluation policy, the real exchange rate, defined as the relative price of non-traded goods in terms of traded goods, begins to increase; that is, the domestic currency appreciates. This is not surprising, as the inflation rate of home goods is always higher than the rate of devaluation. With an increase in the total demand stemming from inter-temporal substitution decisions, the trade account registers a large deficit. As time passes, the current account deficit increases, while the interest income on foreign assets decreases. In short, non-credible, lower-the-exchange-rate-based stabilization attempts will put the economy into a boom-recession cycle, bring about higher than average current account deficits, and give rise to a U-shaped curve for inflation and an inverted U-shaped curve for the real exchange rate.

The prediction contained in Calvo and Vegh's model is consistent with the stylized facts of both the Turkish economy and other high inflation economies (Vegh 1992). In Turkey, with the Central Bank's initial lower devaluation policy (1989–1990), the yearly change in the wholesale price index decreased to 44.1% (July 1990) from the pre-program peak of 80.9% (November 1988). Additionally, yearly changes in the consumer price index slowed during that period but were less pronounced than those cited for the wholesale inflation. That the Turkish economy has followed this pattern is reflected in Table 2.1.

The Turkish economy experienced a sharp increase in domestic demand as the model predicts. Private sector consumption increased in real terms 13.1%, and real private investment expenditure increased sharply by 19.4% during 1990. As a result, the yearly growth rate of the economy was 9.2% that year. The real exchange rate appreciated significantly during the program, and the external deficit registered a historical high of 4.3% of GDP in the same year.[2] As expected, the program was abandoned at the end of 1990, and the economy entered a growth recession in 1991.[3] Inflation was slightly higher than before the program, and the real exchange rate depreciated, albeit at a slower speed than it had previously appreciated.

The same policy was readopted in 1992–1993. The Central Bank, with a dominant position in the shallow foreign exchange market and with strong backing from the financial sector, started to slacken the percentage change in the exchange rate by the summer of 1992. The Turkish lira started to appreciate once again. Real private consumption increased by 8.4%, and real private investment increased by 35% in 1993, due to the perceived temporary nature of the program. The annual growth rate of GDP was 7.7%. The external deficit reached a new historical high at 5.6% of GDP.

Following a financial crisis at the beginning of 1994, the economy entered a depression.[4] The real gross domestic product fell 4.7%. Inflation was higher than before, and the Turkish lira depreciated in real terms immediately. On 5 April a stabilization program was announced by the government. However, it was clear at the beginning of 1995 that the program was doomed to failure. Nevertheless, policy-makers did not seem to learn from past experiences. Instead of designing a new program containing structural reforms, privatization, and fiscal tightening to correct the fundamental problems in the system, they instead returned to the alluring hot-money policy. The Turkish lira began to appreciate, and the real exchange rate returned to pre-1994 levels. Real private consumption and real private investment have continued to increase during the last two years. The external deficit was 4.6% of GDP in 1995. It fell somewhat in 1996, but was still high. It would not be surprising to witness a new recession and a real depreciation of the Turkish lira in the near future.

Table 2.1
Growth Rate of Real GDP and Its Components

	1988	1989	1990	1991	1992	1993	1994	1995
GDP	2.3	0.3	9.2	0.8	5.0	7.7	-4.7	7.5
Private Consumption	1.2	-1.0	13.1	1.9	3.3	8.4	-5.3	7.6
Government Consumption	-1.1	0.8	8.0	4.5	3.8	5.4	-3.5	6.7
Private Investment	12.6	1.7	19.4	0.9	4.3	35.0	-9.1	14.9
Government Investment	-20.2	3.1	8.9	1.8	4.3	3.5	-34.8	-16.9
Export	18.4	-0.3	2.6	3.7	11.0	7.7	15.2	6.7
Imports	-4.5	6.9	33.0	-5.2	10.9	35.8	-21.9	30.0

Source: State Institute of Statistics, National Income Accounts.

One of the side effects of real exchange rate appreciation is indicated in the national income accounts. Without any significant change in real production, the entire economy suddenly looks and feels richer than previously. The overall growth of real GDP between 1987 and 1997 is approximately 41% (an average of 3.9% per year) in Turkey. However, the nominal GDP in dollar terms in 1987 was $87.3 billion. It is expected to reach $180 billion in 1996, an astonishing 110% increase in only nine years. In order to avoid any misleading conclusions, the comparison of the dollar-based macroeconomic indicators across the years should take into account the real appreciation or depreciation of the currency.[5] Table 2.2 summarizes other aspects of the Turkish economy over the recent past.

Table 2.2
Some Economic Indicators*

	1988	1989	1990	1991	1992	1993	1994	1995	1996*
Wholesale Price Index	67.9	62.3	48.6	59.2	61.4	60.3	149.6	64.9	89.3
Consumer Price Index	63.0	64.3	60.4	71.1	66.0	71.1	125.5	78.9	83.0
Exchange Rate (US Dollar)	66.0	49.2	23.0	59.9	64.7	59.9	170.4	53.9	75.0
Money Stock (M3)	62.9	82.1	46.9	60.6	62.3	51.5	124.3	100.4	
Money Stock (M1)	48.2	95.9	49.9	48.2	66.8	71.9	84.1	75.7	
Reserve Money	84.3	61.6	42.6	54.4	67.6	64.7	84.3	86.0	
FX Deposits (by residents)	84.5	46.1	70.7	143.3	132.1	125.8	151.4	100.0	
TL Deposits (Total)	64.0	80.1	46.4	61.6	60.1	47.4	128.6	102.9	
Interest Rate (TL terms)	68.1	59.8	56.9	88.0	97.8	90.2	146.6	134.6	121.4
Interest Rate (dollar terms)	1.3	7.1	27.6	17.5	20.1	18.9	-8.8	52.4	26.5

*Yearly percentage changes with the exception of interest rates. Interest rates are the compounded
 yearly interest rates of average 3-month treasury bill rates.
Source: State Planning Organization, State Institute of Statistics, Turkish Treasury, and the Central
 Bank. 1996 figures are the author's estimates.

PUBLIC SECTOR DEFICIT AND DEFICIT FINANCING

National savings (NS) in an open economy by definition is equal to the sum
of private savings (PS) and government budget surplus (T-G). This aggregate
also equals the sum of net exports (X-M) and gross investment (I):

$$NS = PS + T - G = I + NX$$

At first glance, it may appear that an increase in the public sector deficit causes
a one-to-one decrease in the national savings. However, economic theory posits
that this result is not always warranted. For example, according to the
Keynesian approach, an increase in government consumption may lead to an
increase in the total output, causing an increase in private savings and total

taxes. As a result, the relative decrease in national savings would be less than the relative increase in government expenditure. Similarly, the permanent income hypothesis asserts that only permanent increases in the government deficit matter. If the deficit is temporary, the effect would be minimal, according to this hypothesis. The strictest approach to the relation between government expenditure and total savings is the Ricardian equivalence hypothesis pioneered by Barro (1974). It denies the predictions of both the permanent income hypothesis and the Keynesian approach. Since an increase in the public deficit today implies an increase in taxes tomorrow, rational consumers would change their saving plans accordingly. Consequently, private consumption falls one-to-one after an increase in government expenditures or a decrease in total taxes. The result will be constant national savings.[6] Table 2.3 gives the breakdown of Turkish GDP by sectors, from 1987 to 1995.

Table 2.3
Components of GDP (%)

	1987	1988	1989	1990	1991	1992	1993	1994	1995
Private Consumption	68.6	65.2	67.7	68.7	68.1	66.8	66.5	66.1	70.4
Government Consumption	7.9	7.8	9.6	11.0	12.3	12.9	12.7	11.6	10.9
Private Investment	14.5	17.6	15.6	15.6	15.6	15.4	18.2	19.0	19.5
Government Investment	10.4	9.2	7.9	7.3	7.7	7.4	7.0	5.4	3.8
Change in Stocks	0.9	-1.0	0.7	1.7	-1.0	0.4	1.1	-3.1	0.0
Exports	15.6	19.2	16.7	13.3	13.7	14.3	13.5	21.3	20.0
Imports	17.8	18.0	18.4	17.6	16.4	17.3	19.1	20.3	24.6
External Deficit	2.2	-1.1	1.6	4.3	2.8	2.9	5.6	-1.0	4.6
Total	100.0	100.0	100.0	100.0	100.0	100.0	100.0	100.0	100.0

Source: State Institute of Statistics, National Income Accounts

No clear-cut evidence explains the possible effects of government spending on national savings in the literature. Recently, McCallum (1993) found for the major industrial democracies (G-7) and Organization for Economic Cooperation and Development (OECD) countries that a relative increase in the government expenditure causes a decline in national savings as a percentage of GDP. Selcuk and Rantanen (1996) report the following estimation results using quarterly data for the Turkish economy between 1987 and 1994.

CN = 0.49 -1 .36 CG

and

$$CCA = -0.57 + 0.94\ CIG + 0.55\ CIP + 1.31\ CG$$

where C denotes the change over the same period of the previous year, N is the ratio of national savings to GDP, G is the share of government expenditures in GDP, IP and IG are the share of private and government investment expenditures in GDP and CA is the current account deficit as a percentage of GDP.

The first equation indicates that a one-percentage-point increase in government expenditures will result in more than a one-percentage-point decrease in national savings. The effect of an increase in the share of government expenditure strongly manifests itself in the current account deficit. According to the second equation, a one-percentage-point increase in government expenditures will increase the current account deficit more than one percentage point. This result implies that government expenditure in Turkey strongly crowds out net exports and does so more than investment. In summary, the findings of Selcuk and Rantanen (1996) show that public spending and private spending are complementary in the Turkish economy. An increase in government expenditure stimulates private spending and leads to a net fall in national savings.

Following the financial turmoil experienced at the beginning of 1994, the PSBR decreased to 8.3% in the same year and to 6.4% the following year. The decrease in the PSBR was a direct result of the measures administered in the 5 April program. Nevertheless, the medium-term outcome of the program was not a permanent improvement in the fiscal balance. This was due to the fact that the central government did not initiate an overall restructuring of public finances. The pillars of the program were premised on a drastic cut in real public sector investment expenditures and reliance on temporary tax increases.[7]

Once the program was abandoned, it was definite that the PSBR would assume its previous position. It jumped from 6.4% of GDP in 1995 to 9.6% of GDP in 1996.

If the Ricardian hypothesis can be rejected on empirical grounds, developments in the public sector deficit deserve more prominence in the economy. The public sector deficit in Turkey consists of the deficits of the consolidated budget, state economic enterprises, local administration, revolving funds, social security organizations, and extra budgetary funds. Table 2.4 provides a picture of Turkey's public finances over the last ten years. The public sector borrowing requirement (PSBR), as a percentage of gross domestic product, shows a rapid deterioration starting from 1987. After increasing from 3.8% in 1986 to 10.3% in 1991, the ratio hit a record level of 11.8% in 1993. This worsening fiscal situation was primarily caused by sharp increases in consolidated budget expenditures, unmatched by an increase in overall public sector revenues.[8]

There was a secular negative trend in public investment expenditure as a percentage of GDP between 1987 and 1993. The 5 April program caused a further fall in public investment expenditure. In 1994, the real investment expenditure by the public sector was 42% less than in the previous year. The following year registered another 20% decrease in real terms. Preliminary figures and forecasts reveal that there is no significant change in (real) government investment expenditures during 1996.

Table 2.4
Public Finance in Turkey (as a Percentage of GDP)[a]

	1987	1988	1989	1990	1991	1992	1993	1994	1995	1996[c]
PSBR[b]	6.1	4.8	5.4	7.5	10.3	10.7	11.8	8.3	6.4	9.6
Financing										
Domestic Debt	2.9	2.2	4.4	6.5	8.1	7.6	8.3	7.8	7.7	
Foreign Debt	2.7	2.1	0.8	0.9	0.5	1.5	1.5	-1.0	-2.2	
CB Advances	0.5	0.5	0.2	0.1	1.7	1.6	2.0	1.3	0.9	
Public Debt										
Domestic	5.8	5.7	6.3	6.2	6.8	11.8	12.8	14.1	14.7	18.0
Foreign	38.7	38.1	32.8	25.1	26.3	25.4	24.1	37.6	33.2	37.0
Total Debt	4.5	43.8	39.1	31.3	33.1	37.2	36.9	51.7	47.9	57.0

(a)The effect of real exchange rate appreciation shows itself specifically on the ratio of foreign debt to GDP. The total foreign debt of the public sector reached US $39.7 billion in 1991, whereas it was US $33.8 billion in 1987. This increase in the net burden on the economy does not indicate itself clearly on this table. See Table 2.5 for more details.
(b) Public Sector Borrowing Requirement.
(c) Author's estimate.

Source: Turkish Treasury.

Another development in the composition of public sector expenditure is that interest payments on existing government debt have increased to extreme levels. The bulk of this payment has been made to domestic T-bill and bond holders. By 1991, total interest payments (in real terms) were 50% higher than they were in 1987. There was an explosion in interest expenditures after 1991, that is, a 100% increase in two years and another 50% increase in the following three years (in real terms). As of August 1996, the yearly real interest payment in the consolidated budget had quadrupled since 1987.

From an "infinitely lived, identical individuals' macroeconomics" point of view, this may seem to pose no problem to the economy. The government continues to collect resources (in the form of taxes) from residents and provides the same resources back to residents (in terms of interest payments). However, it is usually not the same group of people who pay taxes and who collect interest payments. In *A Tract on Monetary Reform*, Keynes (1971) points out the social problems arising "when the State's contractual liabilities . . . have reached an excessive proportion of the national income. The active and working elements in no community, ancient or modern, will consent to hand over to the *rentier* or bond-holding class more than a certain proportion of the fruits of their work" (Keynes 1971: 54, quoted in Spaventa 1987).

Galloping interest payments in real terms seem to be a combination of several factors. In order to understand these factors, it is essential to see the way a given fiscal deficit was financed in the past. During 1987 and 1988, domestic and external borrowing had a close to equal share in financing the fiscal deficit. Domestic debt on average accounted for 47% of the PSBR while foreign financing accounted for 44%. The remaining 9% was from the Central Bank resources (printing money). After 1988, there seems to have been a significant policy change in terms of financing the deficit and conducting monetary policy. With no attempt from fiscal policy-makers to correct existing imbalances, the monetary authority initiated implementation of a policy of monetary discipline in the economy. During 1989 and 1990, the share of Central Bank financing of the PSBR decreased to 2%, while the share of domestic borrowing increased to 84%. This shift in policy, coupled with an upward trend in the PSBR, resulted in a rapid increase in the domestic debt stock. By the end of 1990, the outstanding domestic debt reached $8.3 billion, twice the 1988 stock amount of $4.1 billion. Rolling over the existing debt and extra borrowing requirements of the public sector raised the domestic government debt to unprecedented level. The debt stock hit $17.6 billion by 1993, double that of two years earlier.

It is often argued that as long as the primary deficit (deficit net of interest payments) is negative, developments in the debt stock should not be a concern in the economy. This naive approach to debt dynamics ignores the fact that the difference between the real interest rate and the real growth rate of the economy is another important source of change in the debt stock. More specifically, the debt stock as a percentage of GDP will necessarily evolve according to the following equation (Selcuk and Rantanen 1996):

$$d_T = d_0 f^T + \textit{Summation } (j = 1 \textit{ to } T) \ (p_j - m_j) \ f^{(T-j)}$$

$$f = (1+r)/(1+g)$$

where d_T is the debt-GDP ratio at time T, d_0 is the initial debt stock-GDP ratio, p_j is the primary deficit as a percentage of GDP, and m_j is seigniorage revenue (as a percentage of GDP). The real interest rate r and the real growth rate of GDP g are assumed to be constant.

It is clear from the given equation that if the real interest rate paid on the existing debt deviates from the real growth rate of the economy, it is not sufficient to have a primary surplus in order to label the fiscal policy "sustainable." It can be argued that the seigniorage revenue places the policy into a sustainable path. However, it can be shown that the government cannot collect a high seigniorage revenue as a percentage of GDP if the economy is experiencing some degree of currency substitution (Selcuk 1996b).

The real interest rate paid on the existing domestic debt was negative in 1989 and 1990 in Turkey. Coincidentally, the interest rate on domestic debt in dollar terms jumped up during these years. Afterward, the real interest rate in domestic terms and the real interest rate in dollar terms have been very high. It is therefore appropriate to call the fiscal policy after 1987 "unsustainable."

It was obvious also to the market participants during the early years of the 1990s that the prevalent path of macroeconomic policy was unsustainable. An ever-increasing PSBR and worsening current account position in 1993, combined with poor handling of the extremely fragile system by policy-makers increased impatience in the market. As in any other fragile market where the currency is vulnerable to attacks, early 1994 saw a run on the Turkish lira after a small shock.

Data on public debt are provided in Table 2.5. Although the outstanding government debt decreased slightly in real terms in 1994 due to an increase in the price level and real depreciation, it began to accelerate in the following years. As of September 1996, government bonds and T-bills amounted to $28 billion and are estimated to reach $30 billion worth at the end of the year. Two and a half years after a major financial crisis with a spill-over effect on the real economy, the current macroeconomic indicators are no better than at the end of 1993. As a result, increasing nervousness, especially in financial markets, continues.

Table 2.5
Public Debt in Turkey ($ Billion)

	1988	1989	1990	1991	1992	1993	1994	1995	1996[a]
Domestic (DD)[a] $ billion	4.1	6.2	8.3	8.5	15.0	17.6	14.5	20.2	27.9
Foreign $ billion	34.6	35.2	37.8	39.7	40.3	43.5	49	56.3	58.0
TOTAL	38.7	41.4	46.1	48.2	55.3	61.1	63.5	76.5	85.9
Interest Rate on DD.									
TL terms (real), percent	3.1	-2.7	-2.2	9.9	19.2	11.2	9.4	31.1	21
$ terms, percent	1.3	7.1	27.6	17.5	20.1	18.9	-8.8	52.4	26.5

(a) as of September 1996. Interest Rates are calculated as $[(1+r)/(1+p) = (1+I)]$ where r is the yearly compounded average interest rate of 3 month treasury bill, and p is the yearly percentage increase in consumer price index or TL/$ exchange rate.

Source: Turkish Treasury.

EXTERNAL BALANCE

The most acclaimed success of the 1980 reform package was placement of the Turkish economy on an export-led growth path. The degree of openness in the economy increased dramatically during the 1980s. This was achieved through a liberalized trade regime, increased productivity, and a competitive real exchange rate policy.

However, there was a significant change in the real exchange rate policy in 1989, as mentioned in the first part of this chapter. The new policy became very influential in financial circles and had its intellectual adherents among the more elite technocrats in the government. Rüşdü Saraçoğlu, later the governor of the Central Bank, succinctly described the new approach in a paper on the role of the exchange rate in inflation stabilization, presented at a colloquium at the World Bank in 1985: "[A]n overvalued domestic currency may not be an inappropriate policy choice as long as foreign borrowing is readily available" (Saraçoğlu 1985). The behavior of the real exchange rate is shown in Figure 2.1.

Figure 2.1
Real Exchange Rate (Yearly Percentage Change)[a]

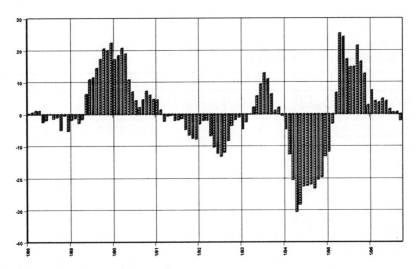

(a) An increase indicates appreciation.

Source: Data is from Reuters. The figure itself is compiled by the author based on the data.

Beginning in 1989, "the overriding goal of the Central Bank was to restore control of its own balance sheet. To achieve this goal, a monetary program was announced . . . Combined with lax fiscal policy, this resulted in high real interest rates and an appreciating real exchange rate, with consequences for interest costs of the public debt and external competitiveness" (OECD 1995: 21).

A useful framework to study the long-run relationship between an independent fiscal authority and a not-that-independent monetary institution is the "unpleasant monetarist arithmetic" analysis developed by Sargent and Wallace (1981). In this framework, an independent fiscal authority determines the primary deficit, and a not-that-independent monetary authority adjusts its policies, sooner or later. Given a constant primary deficit, if the monetary authority picks up a lower rate of inflation today, it triggers higher inflation in the future. Then the question remains: Why does a central bank pick up a low inflation rate? There might be two answers to this question. The Central Bank may believe that the fiscal authority, having access to lump-sum taxes, will adjust its policies in the future. Another possibility is that policy designers at the Central Bank heavily discount the future in the Central Bank's utility function (Winckler, et al. 1996).[9]

Beginning in 1989, the capital account of the balance of payments, the behavior of which is described in Table 2.6, was liberalized and the Turkish lira was made fully convertible. This new policy provided a necessary condition for a real exchange rate appreciation policy, namely, that "foreign borrowing was readily available" for the economy. For the first time since the 1980 program, the Turkish lira started to appreciate quickly. The total appreciation between January 1989 and December 1989 was 22%. That year can be marked as Turkey's first brush with "hot money." This appreciation continued in 1990, albeit at slower speed than experienced in 1989.

Table 2.6
The Capital Account in the Balance of Payments ($ Million, Net)

	1987	1988	1989	1990	1991	1992	1993	1994	1995	1996[a]
Direct Investment	106	354	663	700	783	779	622	559	772	440
Portfolio Investment	282	1178	1386	547	623	2411	3917	1158	1724	1450
Other long-term	1453	-209	-685	-210	-783	-938	1370	-784	-79	-460
Other short-term	50	-2281	-584	3000	-3020	1396	3054	-5127	2305	6160
Total	1891	-958	780	4037	-2397	3648	8963	-4194	4722	7590

(a) January–September.
Source: Turkish Central Bank.

A brief look at the capital account in the balance of payments reveals that short-term (net) foreign capital movements became the dominant player in the economy. During the last 10 years, there has not been a significant change in foreign direct investment. The portfolio investment item, mainly credits obtained abroad by bond issues of the government, decreased in 1990 and 1991 as the direct result of the switch in the deficit financing preference of fiscal authority. Nevertheless, the item increased later, whenever the government was able to borrow from abroad.

The short-term capital movements item, on the other hand, shows greater variation. Although it had a yearly average of negative $134 million between 1987-1995, the standard deviation of short-term capital movements is $2.9 billion. This high standard deviation indicates vulnerability in the capital account and justifies the claim that the economy became heavily dependent on "hot money" after 1989. Because of this dependence, the proponents of the new policy have claimed that the capital account of the balance of payments is more important than the current account for the economy. The entire economic policy according to this approach should be designed to ensure that there is a constant inflow, or at least not an outflow, of foreign capital:[10] "[F]or example, if the macroeconomic policies designed to increase total yearly exports from $15 billion to $23 billion adversely affect the capital inflows-outflows by ten percent, your *loss* from capital movements would be approximately $20 billion" (emphasis added; Kumcu 1995).

The current account situation of the economy from 1987 to 1996 is shown in Table 2.7. As can be seen, it worsened immediately as a result of the real appreciation of the lira in 1989.

The behavior of the export-import ratio is shown in Figure 2.2. The export-import ratio fell below 0.60 by the end of 1990. The ratio had slightly increased between 1981 and 1989, reaching its maximum (0.87) in 1988. Despite the fact that the trade balance was substantially worsening, the current account yielded a surplus in 1989, thanks to a sudden increase in workers' remittances that year. The real effect of the "lower-the-devaluation" policy of 1989 was evident in the following year. The $1.0 billion current account surplus in 1989 turned into a record $2.6 billion current account deficit in 1990. A small depreciation, followed by a contraction in domestic demand, halted the process, and the current account yielded a surplus in 1991.[11]

Without any support from the fiscal authority to fight inflation, the Central Bank returned to a "higher interest rate-lower exchange rate depreciation" policy in the summer of 1992, and the Turkish lira started to appreciate again. The total appreciation during the seven-month period (August 1992–March 1993) was 18%. Once again, the export-import ratio began to fall, decreasing to 0.53 on the average in 1993. Other components of the current account did not register any improvements at that time. As a result, the current account deficit reached a historical high of 4% of GDP ($6.4 billion) in 1993.

Toward the end of 1993, poor handling of macroeconomic imbalances by policy-makers increased nervousness in the market. In January 1994, concerned about sustainability of the prevailing policies, the international credit-rating agencies, Standard and Poor's and Moody's, lowered Turkey's sovereign debt rating to below investment grade. This triggered a panic rush in the market.

The government, already preoccupied with an upcoming local election campaign, did not take any significant action for three months with the exception of increasing overnight interest rates. Between 20 January and 5 April, the overnight interest rate was never less than 120%, occasionally reaching very high levels. At one point it was a recorded 700%. A number of banks with short positions in foreign currency had a chance to close their positions during that period. As a result, the foreign exchange reserves of the Central Bank were depleted. In November 1993, the total foreign exchange reserves of the Central Bank amounted to $7.2 billion. In April 1994, the amount stood at $3 billion. Incidentally, the short positions of the commercial banks at the same period decreased from around $5 billion at the end of 1993 to $1 billion in April 1994.

Table 2.7
The Current Account in the Balance of Payments ($ Billion)

	1987	1988	1989	1990	1991	1992	1993	1994	1995	1996
(1) Exports	10.3	11.9	11.8	13.0	13.7	14.9	15.6	18.4	22.0	23.5
(2) Imports	13.6	13.7	16.0	22.6	21.0	23.1	29.8	22.6	35.2	41.9
Trade Balance (1-2)	-3.3	-1.8	-4.2	-9.6	-7.3	-8.2	-14.2	-4.2	-13.2	-18.4
(4) Other Goods and Services (Credit)	4.2	6.0	7.1	8.9	9.3	10.4	11.8	11.7	16.1	20.5
(5) Other Goods and Services (Debit)	4.2	4.8	5.5	6.5	6.8	7.3	7.8	7.9	9.7	10.9
(6) Total Goods and Services (3 + 4 -5)	-3.2	-0.6	-2.6	-7.1	-4.8	-5.0	-10.2	-0.5	-6.8	-8.8
(7) Others (Workers' remittances, etc.)	2.4	2.2	3.6	4.5	5.1	4.0	3.8	3.1	4.5	4.4
Current Account Balance (6+7)	-0.8	1.6	1.0	-2.6	0.3	-1.0	-6.4	2.6	-2.3	-4.4

Source: Turkish Central Bank.

On 5 April, one week after the local elections and three months after the first run in the financial markets, a seemingly ambitious stabilization program was announced. The Turkish lira was depreciated in real terms by 30% between December 1993 and April 1994. An extremely high level of interest rates on three-month T-bills (yearly compounded 406% in nominal terms) right after the 5 April program helped the government to borrow from the market and to roll over the existing debt stock. The foreign exchange reserves of the Central Bank began once again to increase. There was a sharp contraction in total imports. In the meantime, total exports increased dramatically. The export-import ratio rose above 0.8 in the third quarter. The current account registered a surplus of $2.6 billion in 1994.

Figure 2.2
Export-Import Ratio

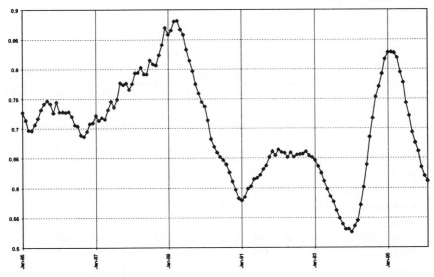

Source: State Institute of Statistics.

Nevertheless, it was clear by the end of 1994 that the stabilization program was defunct. There were no permanent changes in fiscal policy, and inflation did not respond favorably to the onetime, temporary corrective measures taken in the 5 April program. The initial real depreciation was reversed, and the Turkish lira appreciated by 22 % between April 1994 and December 1994. In order to prevent a collapse in financial markets, policy-makers raised interest rates and further slowed the nominal depreciation. The alluring hot money policy was implemented once again at the beginning of 1995. Consequently, the export-import ratio began to fall, and the trade deficit increased to the 1993 level immediately. However, the current account deficit was not as large as in 1995 ($2.3 billion, 1.3% of GDP), this time thanks to some questionable, long-standing accounting practices by the Turkish Central Bank.[12] The current account deficit of only $4.4 billion (2.5% of GDP) in 1996 is again the result of the Central Bank accounting practice of considering an unknown foreign current flow to the economy as current account income. This practice is justified as a reflection of unregistered exports, or so-called suitcase trade, with the countries of the former Soviet Union.

With no reserve depletion in the economy, some analysts are put at their ease on the external balance position of the economy. However, the current situation gives the impression that the equilibrium is unstable. As was mentioned before, the Turkish economy has become dependent on short-term capital inflows. The total short-term capital inflow in 1995 was $2.3 billion, roughly the same as the current account deficit for that year. This scenario seems to have been repeated in 1996. Developments in the "net errors and omissions" item in the balance of payments give further support to the claim that the external balance situation of the economy has become dependent on unreliable sources. The level as well as the variation of this item continue to increase over the years. The high degree of currency substitution in the economy might be a contributing factor to this phenomenon. Nevertheless, it bears little relevance whether the hard currency leaving the system is channeled into domestic residents' portfolios or into non-residents' portfolios.

In summary, the external balance of the Turkish economy has been volatile during the last 10 years, due to the real exchange rate policies preferred by policy-makers. Recurrent appreciation of the Turkish lira is causing a worsening current account balance situation. In the meantime, extremely high levels of interest rates in dollar terms attract short-term capital and delay the inevitable correction to macroeconomic fundamentals. Unless Turkish policy-makers adopt a well-designed stabilization program to address the underlying issues in the economy, it will be no surprise to see "corrections" repeated in the future.

These persistent macroeconomic imbalances cannot but affect the role that Turkey can play in the re-structuring of Central and Eastern Europe and Eurasia. That is, any new role for Turkey will be limited if it does not get its domestic house in order.

NOTES

1. See Öniş and Riedel (1993) and the references therein for a detailed account of the Turkish macroeconomic experience during 1951–1987. Tezel (1994) is one of the main reference studies of Turkish economic history up to 1950.

2. Data on the external deficit are given in the national income account information presented in Table 2.3. The balance of payments statistics may yield slightly different results. See the third section of this chapter.

3. The end of the program coincides with the Gulf War. As in any other unsustainable program, the arrival of bad news was blamed for the failure of the strategy by some critics. See Dornbusch, et al. (1995) for more details.

4. Standard & Poor's delivered the "bad news" this time. Some analysts still believe that if it had not been for that bad news, policy implementation could have continued unhindered.

5. This pronounced effect of appreciation was labeled as "a perpetual motion machine" by the main opposition leader of that time, who is the current president of the Republic, Suleyman Demirel. See Selcuk (1997).

6. The argument rests on the crucial assumption, among others, that "there is no liquidity constraint" in the economy. Note that there is another plausible explanation for an increase in national savings after an increase in the budget deficit: if there are strict government controls on domestic credit and capital flows, a decrease in government savings (i.e., an increase in the budget deficit) reduces the available credit to the private sector, causing an increase in private savings (Easterly and Schmidt-Hebbel 1994). Although capital flows in Turkey were not strictly controlled during the period under consideration, the available evidence shows that the Turkish economy was credit-constrained in international markets. See Selcuk (1996b) for an empirical investigation of consumption smoothing and the current account in Turkey.

7. Developments in public sector expenditures explain the main cause of the public deficit in Turkey. Total tax revenues as a percentage of GDP fluctuated around 12–13% between 1987 and 1995.

8. It is interesting that the decrease in the PSBR/GDP ratio in 1994 (by 3.5 percentage points) was mainly generated from the decrease in the share of real investment expenditure by the public sector in GDP (2.6 percentage points).

9. In fact, if a central banker believes that he has a limited term, future inflation may enter his utility function with a positive sign. Note that the utility function in question here is the central banker's utility function, not the central bank's utility function.

10. It is noteworthy that some officials regarded the capital inflows as "income," but not as a liability for the economy. The vice governor of the Central Bank during that period wrote: "[T]he size of the capital flows *income* or capital flows *expenditures* is interesting: in 1992, 81% of the total balance of payments *income* was capital flows *income*. This number increased to 86% in 1993" (Kumcu 1995).

11. Total official aids and grants from abroad were $1.1 billion in 1990 and $2.2 billion in 1991. This item is usually under $1.0 billion. In order to glean a better understanding of the developments in the external balance situation, this source of income should be disregarded in any analysis.

12. According to the Central Bank, if a Turkish resident exchanges a foreign currency for the Turkish lira without reporting the source of money, the total amount is accounted among "the other income" in the current account. "The other income" item shows a dramatic increase in recent years: $6.3 billion in 1994 increased by 50% and amounted to $9.6 billion in 1995, almost 50% of the total exports. The balance of payments statistics for the first three months of 1996 shows $3.3 billion as "other income."

Part II

Turkey and the European Union

3

Turkey and the European Union in the Aftermath of the Cold War
Atila Eralp

INTRODUCTION

This chapter analyzes Turkey's relations with the European Community/Union in the changing post-war international climate by focusing on the nature of these relations in the post-Cold War context. I show that Turkey's relationship with the Community was rather cooperative during the Cold War years when both the Community and Turkey acted with security imperatives. I argue that with the decline of the Cold War relationship, for Europe during the 1970s there was a rise of problems first in the economic sphere around the customs union issue, then in the political arena around the issue of democracy in the 1980s. These tensions seem to have continued in the aftermath of the Cold War as Turkey's application for full membership is frozen, and the European attention is turned toward Central and Eastern Europe.

I show in the analysis of Turkey-European Community/Union relations that Turkey is facing difficulties in the process of adjustment to the changing international climate. The Turkey-European Community/Union relationship in the post-Cold War context reflects these growing difficulties. Turkey's relationship with the Community was less problematic when the international system was viewed within the East-West context and when security considerations dominated the political agenda. As the East-West axis became less determinant of the relations of the international system, and as security issues were intertwined with political, economic, and cultural factors, Turkey-European Community/Union relations increasingly became more problematic. We have witnessed increasing divergence between the dynamics of European integration and the Turkish case. This trend, which started during the 1970s and 1980s, accelerated with the end of the Cold War.

Turkey and the European Union in the Aftermath of the Cold War
Atila Eralp

INTRODUCTION

This chapter analyzes Turkey's relations with the European Community/Union in the changing post-war international climate by focusing on the nature of these relations in the post-Cold War context. I show that Turkey's relationship with the Community was rather cooperative during the Cold War years when both the Community and Turkey acted with security imperatives. I argue that with the decline of the Cold War relationship, for Europe during the 1970s there was a rise of problems first in the economic sphere around the customs union issue, then in the political arena around the issue of democracy in the 1980s. These tensions seem to have continued in the aftermath of the Cold War as Turkey's application for full membership is frozen, and the European attention is turned toward Central and Eastern Europe.

I show in the analysis of Turkey-European Community/Union relations that Turkey is facing difficulties in the process of adjustment to the changing international climate. The Turkey-European Community/Union relationship in the post-Cold War context reflects these growing difficulties. Turkey's relationship with the Community was less problematic when the international system was viewed within the East-West context and when security considerations dominated the political agenda. As the East-West axis became less determinant of the relations of the international system, and as security issues were intertwined with political, economic, and cultural factors, Turkey-European Community/Union relations increasingly became more problematic. We have witnessed increasing divergence between the dynamics of European integration and the Turkish case. This trend, which started during the 1970s and 1980s, accelerated with the end of the Cold War.

The problematic relations between the European Union and Turkey crystallize around the issue of Turkey's aspirations for full membership in the European Union. Turkey's relationship with the European Community was shaped in the Cold War context on the expectation of its full membership in the Community. This chapter shows how the issue of Turkish full membership has become a contentious one between the European Union and Turkey in the post-Cold War context. The chapter concludes by examining the prospects for a new relationship short of full membership between Turkey and the European Union in the post-Cold War context.

TURKEY AND THE EUROPEAN COMMUNITY IN THE COLD WAR CONTEXT

With the establishment of the Republic, modernization in Turkey was increasingly defined as Westernization in Turkey.[1] In the post-Second World War system and particularly in the Cold War context, Westernization specifically meant belonging to the Western institutional structure, the so-called Western Alliance. With that main goal, Turkey sought to be included in the international institutions set up in the wake of the Second World War (i.e., the North Atlantic Treaty Organization (NATO), Marshall Plan, the Organization for Economic Cooperation and Development (OECD), Council of Europe), the institutions that cemented this alliance. It was thought that belonging to the Western Alliance would lead to the inflow of external funds and promote the economic development of the country as well as incorporate Turkey into the democratic club of Western nations. Westernization thus became a foreign policy orientation as well as an identity and a social project. It was recognized that Westernization could not be realized unless there was cooperation with the United States and Western Europe.

Seeking closer relations with the European Community (EC) was a logical extension of this approach to foreign policy. The EC was regarded by the Turkish policy-makers as the economic axis of the Western Alliance, supplementing and cementing this political pact. (See Eralp 1993; 1994.) Europeans on their part also viewed relations with Turkey mainly in the framework of the Western Alliance. The Cold War prompted the members of the EC to act with strategic considerations in mind toward Turkey as well as toward Greece and to welcome their applications for associate membership. Both Turkey and Greece were front-line states in the containment policy vis-à-vis the Soviet Union, and their economic strengths, thought to be crucial for political stability for Europe, needed to be bolstered.

Although the EC signed several association agreements with other countries over this time period (such as with Malta and Cyprus), only in the cases of Greece and Turkey were there clauses in the agreements that envisaged the ultimate full membership of the two countries.

Turkey and the EC signed the Ankara Agreement, regulating Turkey's association with the community on 12 September 1963, two years after the Athens Treaty, which set out the terms of Greek association with the EC.[2] The Ankara Agreement encompassed three stages, consisting of a preparatory period followed by transitional and final periods. The preparatory stage proceeded smoothly enough, and Turkey took the necessary steps to initiate the second stage of the association agreement by applying to the Community in May 1967. But the issue of transition to a customs union proved to be thorny, and not until July 1970 was a Supplementary Protocol setting a revised timetable finally agreed on at the EC-Turkey Association Council meeting. Ratification of the agreement took even longer and had to weather not only misgivings felt by both parties but also the military intervention in Turkey in March 1971.

TENSIONS BETWEEN WESTERNIZATION AND DEVELOPMENT PROJECTS IN THE 1970s

Previously smooth relations changed in the early 1970s as Turkey increasingly began to see association with the EC in terms of economic development strategies rather than as a matter of foreign policy, that is, belonging to the Western Alliance.[3] The possible negative impacts of a customs union with the EC on Turkey's industrialization were a fear that industrialists began to voice during this period. As economic difficulties, particularly balance of payments problems, increased, especially after the 1973 oil crisis, industrialists started to complain that the transition period specified by the Supplementary Protocol was too short for the restructuring of the Turkish industry. Even in the originally pro-EC institutions, such as the Istanbul Chamber of Industry and the Economic Development Foundation, a strong opposition to the idea of the customs union began to be mounted. Industrialists went so far as to ask the government to abandon the idea of the customs union altogether and seek ways of formulating new forms of association with the EC. These demands of the industrialists echoed well in the State Planning Organization, which, in line with industrialists' demands, emphasized the detrimental effects of the customs union on Turkey's industrialization and its development policy of import-substituting industrialization. While the Ministry of Foreign Affairs maintained its traditional position of the importance to Turkey of accession to the EC and argued for the primacy of political and foreign policy considerations, the State Planning Organization viewed the relation with the EC in terms of economic considerations and within the context of Turkey's industrialization. In this period, thus, we witnessed the emergence of different positions vis-à-vis the EC among key government agencies. In brief, it would not be too unfair to say that the 1970s witnessed the emergence of a tension between two of Turkey's national projects—Westernization and development—which had hitherto seemed quite compatible.

At the end of the 1970s, the difficulties involved in implementing tariff reductions of the customs union agreement finally compelled then prime minister Bülent Ecevit to present a plan to revise the terms of the Association Agreement and ask for a five-year period in which Turkey hoped to honor its tariff-reduction obligations. This resulted in the freezing of the terms of the Association Agreement in October 1978.

Turkey's association with the EC was very much colored by increasing economic difficulties during the 1970s. However, the 1970s were also a decade during which concern with political issues acquired increasing weight within the Community. The move toward inclusion of some Mediterranean countries within the structure of the Community brought in its wake new political attitudes that emphasized the promotion of democracy as a foreign policy issue. Such considerations were apparent in the Greek case as the Community froze all relations with that country when the Junta was in power. The belief that membership in the Community would strengthen democratic regimes guided the Community's response to the Greek, as well as to the Portuguese and Spanish, applications.[4] This greater emphasis on political issues even outweighed the new economic burdens that inclusion of these countries in the Community would bring.

It was this shift in emphasis that Greek policy-makers assumed in their decision to forge ahead with their bid for full membership in 1975 (Verney 1987). By contrast, the Turkish policy-makers emphasis on the problems of the customs union agreement served to create a gulf between Turkey and the experiences of those southern Mediterranean countries that sought to establish closer links with the EC.[5] While southern Mediterranean countries (Greece, Spain, and Portugal) were becoming parts of the EC, Turkey's relations with the EC were entering a more problematical period.

THE ISSUE OF DEMOCRACY IN TURKEY-EC RELATIONS IN THE 1980s

The 1980 military intervention in Turkey further complicated Turkey's bid for incorporation in Europe and thus ushered in a more tense period in Turkish-EC relations. In the aftermath of the military intervention, the focus of attention in Turkish-EC relations shifted from economic to political matters as the issues of democracy and human rights gained a central place on the political agenda (See Da 1997). While the European Community regarded democracy as a sine qua non for inclusion into Europe, Turkish leaders continued to regard it as an internal problem. European insistence on democracy, publicized by a number of reports attesting to inhuman practices in Turkish courts and jails, was interpreted as unwarranted interference in a sovereign country's internal affairs. Furthermore, Turkish leaders saw democracy in relative, rather than absolute, terms and believed that relations would resume a smooth course once Turkey was able to announce a timetable of transition to a democratic regime. Thus, the relationship between the European Community and Turkey during much of the 1980s continued to unfold in terms of competing definitions of democracy. The inability of Turkish policy-makers to assess correctly the importance placed by Europe on the question of democracy, even in view of the Greek, Spanish, and Portuguese examples, served to escalate tensions between Turkey and the EC.

The community regarded the 1984 local elections as constituting the first steps toward the establishment of a parliamentary democracy in Turkey, rather than the 1983 general elections, which the then Turkish government depicted as making the transition to democratic rule. In these local elections those parties banned from participation in the general elections were allowed to take part for the first time. In this climate the EC changed its earlier stance and started a process of reactivating the Association Agreement, albeit without easing the pressure on the question of democracy.

In circumstances under which normalization of Turkey-EC relations were still debated, the decision taken by the then prime minister Özal to apply to the Community for full membership on 14 April 1987 came as a surprise to many observers inside and outside Turkey. With hindsight one could say that there were serious problems with the timing of the Turkish application. Turkey's application had come at a point when the EC itself was facing important problems of consolidation and had turned inward. The addition of six new members to the Community in the 1970s and 1980s had slowed down the pace of European economic and political integration. Larger membership has also made the process of decision making longer and more complicated. The difficulties of independent nations, operating in the world economy in an environment of increasing global competition from the United States and Japan had finally prompted the Community to take decisive steps toward reforming its constitution. These attempts specifically aimed at creating a more integrated structure, were crystallized with the adoption of the Single European Act in 1986. Apart from a number of clauses designed to speed the process of decision making, the Single Act accepted as a concrete, short-term strategy the creation of a single market within Europe by the end of 1992. It is fairly obvious that the Community would be rather reluctant to welcome the application of a new country at such a stage.

As a result of this conjuncture, it took more than two and a half years for the commission of the EC to prepare a report on Turkey (Commission of the European Communities 1989). Compared with the Greek, Spanish, and Portuguese applications, this seems rather a long period, suggesting that the Commission was trying to postpone the declaration of its rather negative opinion about Turkey. The commission in its report assessed the situation of European integration and the specific case of Turkey and reached the conclusion that because of internal problems of consolidation, accession negotiations not only with Turkey but with any country should not start before 1993. In addition to this general assessment, the Commission stated that the specific analysis of the economic and political situation of Turkey showed that it would be hard to cope with the adjustment problems with which it would be confronted, if it acceded to the community. The commission, based on this analysis, concluded that it would not be useful to open accession negotiations with Turkey. The commission also suggested the reactivation of the Association Agreement, which had been dormant for a long time, and proposed a set of measures toward increasing interdependence between the Community and Turkey. These proposals included measures in four areas: the completion of the customs union, the resumption and intensification of financial cooperation, the promotion of industrial and technological cooperation, and the strengthening of political and cultural links. The Council of Ministers of the EC endorsed this report of the commission.

It should also be noted that important changes in the international climate at the end of the 1980s also led the Community to give less attention to the issue of Turkey's membership. As the European Community was facing important problems of integration following the adoption of its strategy on the Single European Act and single market, dramatic changes in Eastern Europe and the Soviet Union began to shake the very basis of the post-war international system. The dissolution of the socialist regimes in Eastern Europe and the ending of the Cold War and the division of Europe forced the Community members to focus their attention on these historical changes.

POST-COLD WAR CLIMATE AND TURKEY-EUROPEAN UNION RELATIONS

The relationship between Turkey and the European Community was shaped within the Cold War context in which security considerations were dominant. With the relaxation of tensions in the international climate in the 1970s, the Community started to act not only with security imperatives but also with economic and political concerns. As was pointed out in the preceding pages, we have witnessed the rise of economic problems centering around the issue of the customs union in the 1970s and political frictions revolving around the issue of democracy in the 1980s. While the Community began to shift its attention to such issues, Turkey continued to act with security considerations and in general within Cold War parameters. As a result, we have witnessed increasing divergence between the dynamics of European integration and the Turkish case. This trend, which started during the 1970s and 1980s, accelerated with the end of the Cold War.

During the Cold War years, for the Turkish governing elites, the West had largely meant Western Europe and the United States, undifferentiated as the Western Alliance. At the end of the Cold War, Turkish elites belatedly realized that the West was no longer an undifferentiated entity. Cooperation with the United States did not ensure a smooth relationship with the European Community as in the Cold War years. It was seen that Turkey's relationship with the

United States was running rather smoothly, while relations with the Community were increasingly becoming conflictual.

In the Cold War context, Europe was the central orientation of Turkish foreign policy, and all other regional policies were considered in relation to the European policy and in general within the context of the East-West conflict. The dramatic changes in the international climate prompted Turkish policy-makers to develop new options for integration in the emerging international system. Efforts were directed to the formulation of a new type of strategic importance that would emphasize that importance in relation to Turkey's role in its immediate region rather than in terms of the East-West conflict. Particularly, the dissolution of the Soviet Union and the ensuing independence of Central Asian Republics were thought to present Turkey with a viable option of regional foreign policy orientation. There was an unprecedented drive to increase economic, political, and cultural links with the newly-independent Central Asian states.

The coincidence of this climate with the EC's negative attitude on Turkey's full membership increased anti-European tendencies. These sentiments were fashioned and utilized by those with nationalist and religious political orientations and led to a feeling that Turkey did not need Europe as in the Cold War years. As a result, we have witnessed the distancing of Turkey from its traditional policy of Europeanization during the period from 1989 to 1992. The Gulf crisis reinforced this tendency as Turkish policy-makers began to voice the concept of strategic cooperation to emphasize the development of special relations between the United States and Turkey that would locate the strategic importance of Turkey in relation to its role in its region rather than in terms of the East-West conflict. Based on his close cooperation with the United States, the then president Özal increasingly pointed out that Turkey provided a model for the countries in its region. Özal believed that the Turkish example, which aims at wedding Islamic identity and aspirations to Western modernity, could be a viable option to be emulated by other countries in the Middle East and Central Asia and thus needed to be supported by the West (meaning, increasingly, the United States).

This euphoria of regionalism, however, did not last long. It was soon realized that expectations were set too high, and Turkey did not have adequate resources and expertise in regional matters to fulfill such high expectations. As Turkey started to establish increasing economic, political, and cultural links with countries, from which it had been cut off for a long period of time, it was seen that it needed more time to develop this new regional orientation. It was also realized that Turkey had crucial and traditional economic and political links with European countries that could not be forsaken easily. In this context, Turkish policy-makers began to think that new regional orientations should not be thought of as alternatives to the traditional policy of Europeanization. Rather, these links could be functional in Turkey's relations with the Community: an influential Turkey in its region would have a better place and a greater role in Europe as well. As a result, after 1992, we witnessed increasing attempts to strike a balance between new regional orientations and the traditional European policy. The European Union also realized that there was a need to pursue new patterns of cooperation with Turkey, even if these were short of full membership. With the convergence of these new orientations of both parties, we started to see attempts to establish a working relationship after 1992.

In this climate, the dormant Association Council started to convene, and there were efforts to normalize relations between Turkey and the European Union (EU) within the context of the Association Agreement and the package of cooperation formulated by the commission and the Council of Ministers of the Community. (See Economic Development Foundation 1996: 45–48.) For both Turkey and the European Union, the customs union arrangement emerged as the lowest common denominator in their relationship. Thus, the Association Council focused its attention to reactivate and complete the customs union arrangement.

The discussions on the issue of the customs union in the last three years showed the process of politicization of what was once considered an economic issue. (See Eralp 1994.) It was seen in the heated debates how the economic aspects of the customs union remained rather secondary, and political matters such as the Cyprus or the human rights issues gained the upper hand on the agenda of Turkey-European Union relations. When the issue of the customs union was first considered in the 1970s, the discussions revolved around the policy of industrialization. In recent debates, however, political and economic matters are so intertwined that it is nearly impossible to disentangle them. Recent discussions on the customs union also show that many problems remained unsolved from the 1970s and 1980s, and these problems come on the agenda of the discussion of any issue and adversely affect the relationship between Turkey and the European Union.

It was thought initially that the decision of the Association Council on 6 March 1995 to complete the process of the customs union would be a turning point in the relations between the European Union and Turkey. The tense relations between Turkey and the EU that has been existing for nearly 20 years would give way to a better working relationship between Turkey and the EU. However, it was soon realized that there were some major divergences in the views of the two parties, and it would not be easy to establish a smooth relationship. While the Turkish side believed that the customs union should be thought of as part of a comprehensive package that would eventually lead to full membership, European Union officials viewed the customs union as the basic mechanism to improve cooperation between the Union and Turkey and did not like the idea of linking the customs union with the issue of full membership.

These divergences of opinion increased resentment toward the customs union arrangement in Turkey, as reflected in frequent statements that a customs union alone without linking it to full membership was not politically acceptable for Turkey. The customs union was increasingly viewed as a mechanism of compensation for full membership and as a means to marginalize Turkey in Europe. While Eastern European and Mediterranean countries were considered candidates for membership, the attitude of not mentioning Turkey further increased resentment toward the customs union arrangement with the European Union. The decision of the EU to invite some eastern European and Mediterranean countries but not to invite Turkey to the opening of the Inter-Governmental Conference in Turin in March 1996 accelerated hard feelings toward the European Union.

It seems that changes in the international climate in the aftermath of the Cold War as well as in Europe make Turkish aspirations for full membership in the European Union more difficult to attain. As is well known, Turkish foreign policy has stressed Europeanization, which specifically meant the attainment of the customs union which would eventually lead to full membership in the European Union. Within the present context of the process of European integration, this objective is becoming largely politically unfeasible. In this development not only the problematic nature of Turkish-European Union relations but also the transformations within the union play a critical role. The analysis of the present stage of the process of European integration shows that in the post-Cold War context the EU has to focus on two critical issues of widening and deepening together and find an optimal political solution for both problems. While not leaving the ideal of further integration, the Union should also be inclusionary and aim to become the institution of the whole of Europe, that is, a truly European Union. However, this is not an easy task. Both the number of new applicants (around 12) and the nature of their economic and political structures (i.e., their differences from the existing members) make the question of membership a difficult puzzle for the policy-makers of the EU. Attention has recently focused on this major puzzle, and we have witnessed the rise of different projects, such as two-speed, multi-speed and variable geometry projects, that all aim at more flexible ways of integration than the present situation.[6] These projects aim both to preserve the ideal of integration and also to incorporate new applicants into the EU gradually. It is pointed out in these projects that the new applicants would face major problems of adjustment if they participated in all mechanisms of the EU. The Union itself would also face major problems in its decision making with such large numbers of members. It is proposed in these projects that if countries are unable to participate in all mechanisms of the EU, then they should not have equal representation and say in the institutions and in the decision-making structure of the EU. These discussions and proposals indicate that the issue of full membership is under consideration in the Union.

It seems from this analysis that Turkey's aspiration for full membership would face more difficulties within the context of flexible integration. As the EU is focusing on formulating new mechanisms of cooperation short of full membership, it will be difficult to fulfill Turkey's expectations of full membership. Thus, in addition to the political and economic problems between Turkey and the EU, the present climate of European integration and the possibility to move toward more flexible models of integration make the attainment of full membership more difficult.

However, it should also be pointed out that flexible integration projects, while making the attainment of full membership more difficult, open up new opportunities to go beyond the customs union relationship for Turkey. When, in the present state of European integration, pillars other than the economy are being developed, and new applicants are trying to be incorporated into these pillars at different speeds, Turkey should take advantage of this climate and try to link itself to other pillars in addition to the economic one. As the main economic relationship between Turkey and the EU (the customs union arrangement) is viewed by a large section of governing elites as politically unacceptable, Turkish policy-makers should find ways to go beyond the customs union agreement and deepen Turkey's relations with the EU. Rather than complaining about Turkey's exclusion and marginalization in Europe, this opportunity should be taken, and new points of convergence of interests with the EU should be sought.

The traditional area of security seems to be one of those areas where there is a possibility for more cooperation and new patterns of linkages with the EU. (See Karaosmanoğlu 1996a, b.) In the flexible integration projects, it seems that countries may have more differentiated roles in different mechanisms: while they have a less important role in the economic sphere, they may have a greater role in the security area. Turkey is one of those countries which may have a say in the emerging security architecture of Europe. It is envisaged that the European security institutions, such as the Western European Union (WEU) or the Common Security and Foreign Policy within the European Union, should have close links with NATO. In the short and medium terms, NATO emerges as the central institution in security matters, as reflected in the discussions of development of the European security architecture not only in the European security institutions but also within NATO. Turkey, being a full member of NATO, should take this opportunity and play a more active role in this linkage between NATO and the emerging European security architecture. Turkish policy-makers should emphasize more Turkey's intentions to be part of the emerging European security institutions in addition to NATO. Turkey should not limit itself to the status of associate membership in the WEU, but seek full membership in that organization. It may be possible within the new projects of flexible integration for countries that are not at present full members of the EU to attain full membership status within the WEU. It seems that Turkey, which has a traditional role in NATO, has a chance to play an effective role in the emerging European security architecture. However, it should also be pointed out that Turkey, as it links itself more to the security pillar of the EU, should not fall into the same limited relationship with Europe as in the Cold War years. In the Cold War period, Turkey's relationship with Europe remained mainly at the security field. In the present climate, when the security issues are getting more complex and intertwined with political and cultural issues, it seems essential that Turkey's security relations with Europe should not remain in the same form and level as in the Cold War period. It is an imperative that security relations should be enriched by mechanisms of political dialogue as well as through contacts of non-governmental actors.

PROSPECTS IN TURKEY-EUROPEAN UNION RELATIONSHIP

This analysis of Turkey-European Community/Union relations shows that Turkey is facing some major problems in adjusting to the changing international climate, particularly to the dramatic changes in the aftermath of the Cold War. Turkey's relations with the European Community were rather cooperative during the Cold War years, when security considerations were the common denominator between the two parties. As the Cold War context changed, and as economic, political, and cultural dimensions gained some significance, the Turkey-European Community/Union relationship became more problematic. These problems, which started around the issue of the customs union in the 1970s, continued with competing definitions of democracy in the 1980s and accelerated in the aftermath of the Cold War, when European attention began to shift to Central and Eastern Europe.

Based on the analysis of the preceding pages, it could be pointed out that Turkish aspirations for full membership in the European Union are more difficult to attain in the aftermath of the Cold War. Since Turkish governing elites are geared toward the idea of full membership, this development creates major tensions in Turkey-EU relations and increases resentment toward the EU. The traditional policy of Europeanization and Westernization makes it extremely difficult to give up the idea of full membership. However, it has become largely unfeasible to implement this idea in the immediate political context; thus, the idea of full membership should be reconsidered and reformulated both by Turkey and by the European Union as soon as possible. It is essential that the idea of full membership should be retained as the long-term goal of Turkish foreign policy. It would affect Turkish foreign policy rather adversely if the idea is given up altogether, since it has been such a long-standing cornerstone of Turkish foreign policy. However, Turkey and the European Union have to formulate a working relationship short of full membership in the short term.

There are two possible options in the Turkey-European Union relationship in the present context. The first option is the possibility of Turkey's exclusion from the emerging European project. The increasing marginalization of Turkey in the aftermath of the Cold War as well as the increasing anti-European feeling in Turkey both point to this trend of exclusion from the European Union. As the analysis of the preceding pages indicates, Turkey's relationship with the European Community has become increasingly conflictual since the middle of the 1970s. Tensions that started in the 1970s on economic issues continued in the 1980s on political matters and accelerated after the Cold War. Based on that trend, Turkey's marginalization and exclusion in the European Union are highly possible, if Turkey and the European Union do not formulate a working relationship as soon as possible. If the issue of full membership remains on the table as in the present context, and if the European Union neither responds to Turkish demands nor formulates a working policy toward Turkey, it would be rather difficult to change this trend in the Turkey-EU relationship.

While the marginalization of Turkey is more viable in the present context, it should be pointed out that this possibility is to the advantage of neither the European Union nor Turkey. It is evident that the stability of Europe is linked to the situation in the Mediterranean and Middle East regions. It would be difficult for Europe to maintain a stable economic and political system if instability reigns in these adjacent areas. Turkey's role is rather crucial in the promotion of such stability, primarily because Turkey is one of the few countries of the region that have been tied to the Western system for a long time and maintained a relatively stable system in comparison to other countries of the region. If Turkey is excluded from the European system, this would lead to a more unstable situation in Turkey as well as in its region. In addition to the promotion of stability, Turkey has some crucial roles to play in the linkage of trade, transport, and energy routes of the Middle East, Persian Gulf, and Transcaucasia to Europe. Both Europe and Turkey share the common interest of a free flow of oil at reasonable prices. For Turkey, the European link is also essential. It is important not only economically but as a wider civilizational project. As stated in this chapter, Turkey has followed a policy of Westernization since the establishment of the Republic. In the aftermath of the Cold War, it is evident that Turkey's options are increasing in its region, and many argue that Turkey does not have to rely solely on Europe. However, it should be pointed out that the European link would not adversely affect Turkey's new regional orientations. Rather, Turkey would be stronger in its region if well connected to Europe. Thus, it seems that there are mutual interests of Turkey and the European Union to formulate a working relationship.

This working arrangement should aim to go beyond the customs union agreement and incorporate political and security considerations.[7] Turkish governing elites would like to take an active role within the emerging security architecture of the European projects. Within the framework of flexible integration, there is more room for the incorporation into different pillars of the European Union at different speeds. It seems that there is more possibility for Turkey to cooperate in the security pillar of the European Union. Turkey, being a full member of NATO and an active country of the European Security system for the last 50 years, could play a greater role in the linkage between NATO and the emerging European security architectures. As NATO emerges as the central institution in security matters, and as European security architecture develops in linkage with NATO, Turkey's role in the security field cannot be overlooked. In addition to NATO, however, Turkey's links with the emerging European institutions need to be strengthened. Turkey should be made a full member of WEU as well as linked to the emerging Common Foreign and Security Policy of the European Union. It is essential that Turkey take part not only in the phase of implementation of security policies but also in the formulation of such policies. Since flexible integration models create an environment conducive for incorporation in different pillars at different speeds, Turkey should take the initiative and be active in the emerging European security architecture. These Turkish efforts need to be supported by the European Union if a working relationship is to be established.

CONCLUSION

The analysis of Turkey-European Union relations shows that Turkey and the European Union need to establish a special arrangement that will go beyond the customs union relationship. This arrangement should give a greater role to Turkey in the emerging security architecture of Europe if Turkish aspirations for full membership are not to be fulfilled in the foreseeable future. The creation of such a relationship seems to be politically feasible within the context of new projects of flexible integration, but both sides need to focus on the formulation of this working relationship before it gets too late. If they are unable to formulate such an arrangement, it will be quite difficult to change the trend toward Turkey's marginalization and exclusion from the emerging European Union project.

It could be concluded that Turkey's foreign policy in relation to the European Community was able to operate rather effectively when the international system was centered around the security imperative, and the East-West conflict was the dominant axis. It also seems that Turkish foreign policy is facing major problems of adjustment to the changing international climate when old ties of security are being intertwined with increasing political, economic, and cultural links. Turkey is in need of supplementing its traditional ties of security with the European countries and the union with new economic, political, and cultural exchanges primarily between non-governmental actors.

It should be noted that Turkey's traditional policy of Europeanization is in need of reconciliation with new regional orientations. Turkey's incorporation into the European Union as a full member, even if it were feasible, will take a longer time than expected in the changing international climate. It also seems that the dramatic changes in the international system are offering Turkey new regional opportunities. As a result, Turkey is in need of balancing the traditional Western policy with new Eastern orientations. As Turkey is involved in this attempt at reconciliation of its Western and Eastern orientations, it has to enrich security relations with political, economic, and cultural links not only with Europe but also with regional neighbors.

NOTES

1. See Eralp (1993) and Balkır and Williams (1993) for a more comprehensive analysis of Turkey's relations with the European Community during the Cold War period.

2. For a comprehensive and detailed examination of Turkey and European Community relations see Balkır and Williams (1993), Birand (1985), and Tekeli and İlkin (1991).

3. For a more comprehensive account see Eralp (1990) and Balkır (1993a).

4. For a detailed analysis of the Greek, Spanish, and Portuguese incorporation into the European Community, see Tsoukalis (1981).

5. For an examination of the effects of the Mediterranean enlargement on Turkey, see Eralp (1988).

6. For a comprehensive analysis of this issue see Nugent (1992, 1995) and Hughes (1996).

7. For analyses on arrangements that go beyond the customs union relationship, see Leicester (1995) and Kramer (1994).

4

The Customs Union and Beyond
Canan Balkır

INTRODUCTION

On the signing of the Ankara Agreement, Turkey became an associate member of the European Community (EC) in 1963. The second stage in the process of association was established by the Additional Protocol, which came into effect in January 1973. The final stage was to start after the parties had fulfilled the requirements of the preceding stages. The association between the two sides went smoothly until 1976, after which the timetable of the transitional stage was upset by the recession of the mid-1970s, and the relations became strained due to problems stemming from both sides. However, with Turkey's 1980 Stabilization and Structural Adjustment program, which aimed to integrate the domestic economy with the world economy, Turkey brought radical changes in its economic structure through the implementation of more liberal domestic and foreign trade policies, and the success achieved on this front was thought to enhance Turkey's possibility of accession to the EC. This led the government to apply for full membership in 1987.

After the refusal, at least for the time being, of the full membership application in 1987, a customs union looked like the only viable option, and from that moment on, Turkey used every means to make it clear that it was ready to fulfill its obligations regarding a customs union. For Turkey, the formation of the customs union with the EC has become a must in its process of integration with the market-based, liberal democracies of Europe.

However, since the signing of the Ankara Agreement, the nature of the Community and its rules of association have been changing. The Single Market Programme has reshaped economic relations within the Community, while the Maastricht Conference has reshaped the social rights and the rules of the political union. After the second enlargement process of the EC political considerations became the primary criteria for membership, and the Community has had serious concerns about the issues of democracy and human rights in Turkey. Hence, after long debates and bargaining between the parties, the Association Council meeting of 6 March 1995 made the decision concerning the implementation of the final phase of the customs union.

While Turkey was striving for a customs union, the breakup of the Soviet Union had afforded Turkey a special opportunity to pursue new networks of international relationships. Improvement in relations with the Balkan countries, close ties with the Central Asian Turkic Republics, the initiation of the Black Sea Economic Cooperation Project (BSEC), and the reactivation and enlargement of the Economic Cooperation Organization (ECO) are among the most important. But these have not stopped Turkey from trying to intensify its ties with the EC, since it perceives its role as a bridge of both stability and trade among these different regional arrangements.

However, these dramatic changes in the Soviet bloc and Eastern Europe diverted the Community's interest away from its oldest associate. In the process of reconstructing Europe, the place of Turkey became uncertain. The political transformation in Eastern and Central Europe put these countries in front of Turkey in the queue for financial assistance and full membership.

Under these circumstances the customs union began. The first year of the customs union has been disappointing for both sides. On the Turkish side, the immediate results were economic disadvantages, such as public revenue loss due to the abolition of tariffs and a growing trade deficit vis-à-vis the Community. The Community, on the other hand, did not see in Turkey the necessary determination for the enhancement of democracy and human rights. There was also growing tension in the Aegean and in Cyprus.

It is very early to make a comprehensive assessment of the customs union. However, it is evident that the economic benefit for Turkey will depend on the stability in its macroeconomic policies, as well as the establishment of a more comprehensive democratic system that complies with the contemporary democratic norms of the European Union. Even if the customs union is a success, or more so, Turkey will still strive toward full membership, since the customs union has never been considered as desirable for itself but as a temporary stage in the process to full membership.

The aim of this chapter is to provide an overview and general assessment of the relations between Turkey and the Community before and after the customs union. The first part of the chapter presents background information on the customs union, discussing the chain of events that led to the Decision of 6 March 1995. The subsequent parts deal with the coverage of the customs union and the obligations arising from its enforcement, the economic effects of the customs union, the political implications, and an appraisal of the first year under the customs union from the Turkish perspective.

BACKGROUND TO THE CUSTOMS UNION

Turkey's relationship with the European Community[1] has been long-lasting in terms of diplomacy, military power, and trade. Since 1923 Turkey has adopted European legal, social, and political norms and participated in most European institutions. Turkey became a member of the Council of Europe in 1949, took an active part in the military organization of the North Atlantic Treaty Organization (NATO), and was one of the founding members of the Organization for European Economic Cooperation (OEEC) which later became the Organization for Economic Cooperation and Development (OECD). Turkish policy-makers wanted to be included in almost all of the institutions of the Western alliance. Thus, when the economic and political difficulties experienced after the mid-1950s forced the Turkish government to look for policy alternatives abroad, it was logical that Turkey applied to the European Economic Community in July 1959. Having already signed a treaty of association with Greece, being careful to balance its relations between these two countries, and not underestimating the role of Turkey for security concerns, the community welcomed this application. Turkey gained the status of associate membership with the signing of the Association Treaty, namely, Ankara Agreement, on 12 September 1963. The objective of the Ankara Agreement was to promote a constant and well-balanced intensification of trade and economic relations between the contracting parties with the aim of establishing a customs union. Article 28 of the agreement went even further and foresaw the possibility of an eventual full membership for Turkey if and when it was able to perform the necessary obligations arising out of the treaty establishing the Community.

The Ankara Agreement envisaged the economic association's developing in three stages, namely, the preparatory, the transitional, and the final stages. The second stage aimed at setting the timetable toward the establishment of a customs union between the parties. Hence, the customs union between EU and Turkey reflects a process that started in 1964 with the signing of the Ankara Agreement and was reaffirmed in 1973 with the entry into force of the Additional Protocol to that agreement, which laid down the conditions and timetables for implementing the obligations of the transitional period. The principle of the progressive setting up of the customs union over a period of 22 years is preserved in those texts and is legally binding on both parties.[2]

The section entitled "Principles," Article (2)2 of the Ankara Agreement, provides that "a customs union shall be progressively established." The agreement also lays down in Article 12 that "the Contracting Parties agree to be guided by Articles 48, 49, and 50 of the Treaty establishing the Community for the purpose of progressively securing freedom of movement for workers between them," in Article 13 that they "agree to be guided by Articles 52 to 56 and Article 58 of the Treaty...for the purpose of abolishing restrictions on freedom of establishment between them," and in Article 14 that they "agree to be guided by Articles 55, 56, and 58 to 65 of the Treaty...for the purpose of abolishing restrictions on freedom to provide services between them."

On the free movement of persons and services, Article 36 of the Additional Protocol stipulates that "freedom of movement for workers between Member States of the Community and Turkey shall be secured by progressive stages in accordance with the principles set out in Article 12 of the Association Agreement between the end of the twelfth and the twenty-second-year after the entry into force of that Agreement." Thus, the free movement of workers, one of the main pillars of the association, was expected to be established by 1 December 1986, and the Association Council was to decide on the rules necessary to that end.

In trade of manufactures, the obligations derived directly from the Additional Protocol include elimination of all customs duties and quantitative restrictions, alignment by Turkey on the Common Customs Tariff (CCT), elimination of protective measures between the parties, and the treatment of matters such as right of establishment and workers' rights. The EC would abolish all customs duties and equivalent taxes on industrial imports from Turkey, with the exception of certain sensitive products such as cotton yarns, cotton textiles, and machine-woven carpets. Petroleum products were subject to tariff reductions within quota limits. The Association Council was the governing body to oversee the timely implementation of the other complementary measures, too. As the type of customs union specified was more than a usual customs union, coming closer to an establishment of a common market including free movement of workers, freedom of trade in services, and harmonization of rules of competition, Kramer (1995a: 205) points out that it is "an additional indication that the relationship was not intended to stop here."

By 1973, the EC had abolished all customs duties and quotas for Turkish manufactured products, with the exception of textiles and clothing, which later came under the so-called voluntary export restraint agreements concluded between the EC authorities and Turkish textile exporters. Concerning agricultural imports from Turkey, under the Ankara Agreement they were treated as imports from a third country and subjected to the Common Customs Tariff. However, from the beginning, the Community granted tariff concessions on agricultural imports and tried to protect its agricultural sector by the sophisticated non-tariff barriers of the Common Agricultural Policy (CAP). The concessions were broadened to the gradual elimination of duties by January 1987 on primary agricultural products having a regulated market in the EC. There are variable levies and additional duties for processed products.

Turkey was given a longer period of adjustment to make reductions to the customs tariff for imports from the EC within the framework of two separate lists with different time spans, taking into consideration the competitiveness of the industries concerned.[3]

Following the oil crisis of 1973 and the military intervention of Turkey in Cyprus in 1974, the relations between the two sides deteriorated. This deterioration was further moved along by the privileges granted by the EC to third countries under the General System of Preferences and the Lomé Convention and also under the Global Mediterranean Policy, which eroded considerably the preferences granted to Turkey. The southern enlargement of the EC, the failure to fulfill its obligations regarding free movement of persons, the freezing of the Fourth Financial Protocol, and the imposition of quotas on Turkish textile exports were the other factors that strained the relationship. It must be noted that the financial aid under three protocols, which was given to Turkey to ease the negative repercussions of the tariff reductions on the economy, amounted to a total of ECU 827 million, a negligible amount compared to what other non-member Mediterranean countries received as financial aid from the EC.

In return, Turkey reduced tariffs only twice, in 1973 and 1976, and when faced with grave economic problems, delayed further tariff reductions on EC manufactured products. It did not even commence the adjustment to the CCT. As regards the adaptation of its agricultural policy to the CAP, Turkey could not take steps sufficient enough to close the gap between its agricultural policy and that of the Community. Finally, in 1978, under great economic difficulties and frustrated by the EC's not responding to its demands, Turkey took the step of freezing the terms of the Association Agreement under Article 60 of the Additional Protocol, which allowed both parties to take requisite measures in case of regional or general economic disruption. One must note that the 1970s were also hard years for the Community. Internal economic problems resulted in the restructuring of certain industries and the introduction of new protectionist measures against non-members, such as the Multi-Fibre Agreement.

The relations of Turkey with the Community came to a standstill after the military intervention in 1980. The fourth financial protocol, which was ratified in June 1981, was blocked. In January 1982 the European Parliament (EP) passed a resolution suspending the Joint Parliamentary Committee. The free circulation of Turkish workers in the Community as of 1986 was put off. The volume of trade between the partners declined, while Turkey's trade relations with Middle Eastern and North African Islamic countries increased considerably. The decline in economic relations was accompanied by the emergence of diverging views on political issues. Promotion of democracy and human rights gained increasing weight in the Community agenda and remained central to the relations during the period. However, Turkey continued to perceive the Community as an economic entity, and the EC's insistence on democracy and the promotion of human rights was interpreted by Turkish policy-makers as interference in Turkey's internal affairs.

At the beginning of the second half of the 1980s circumstances changed. The economic reforms in Turkey had brought on a major transformation in the economy. The competitiveness of Turkish industry increased, the growth of industrial exports was spectacular, and foreign trade was liberalized to a large extent. Given the importance of the EC as a trading partner, the failure to proceed with the customs union under an outward-oriented program was puzzling. The western-oriented business community, frustrated also by the declining trade alternative of the Islamic countries in the Middle East and North Africa due to the reduction in oil prices and concerned about the impact of the second and third enlargements of the Community on Turkish exports, began to voice the idea of application for EC membership. This was also backed up in other circles, not only for economic reasons but also to protect the recently gained civilian democracy. Thus, on 14 April 1987, Turkey applied for full membership, although this application did not meet with approval of the EC, based on the reasoning presented in the official "Opinion" of the commission in December 1989. The report pointed out the difficulties in immediate full entry, stating that the Turkish economy was still insufficiently developed to compete within the EC's emerging single market. Other short-term constraints were the Greek veto over the Cyprus issue and Turkey's record on democracy and human rights. There was also the concern of the deepening process in which the EC was engaged. Therefore, the commission suggested the reactivation of the Ankara Agreement. In accordance with this, in June 1990, the Commission presented the "Matutes Package," which contained measures on trade relations, economic and industrial cooperation, financial aid, and even political dialogue. When this ambitious package was rejected by the EC Council due to the Greek veto, a customs union became almost the only mechanism to rescue the relations. At the Ad Hoc Committee meetings in 1988 a new timetable for tariff reductions and adoption of the CCT by Turkey was set. In line with this timetable, the cumulative reduction of tariffs was to reach 70% by 1992 for commodities under the 12-year list and 60% for commodities under the 22 year list; and as regards adoption of the CCT, the cumulative reduction rate for both groups would be 40%.

The Gulf War and the dissolving of the Soviet Union once more upgraded Turkey's geopolitical position, gave impetus to reshaping the relationship between Turkey and the EC, and resulted in the revitalization of the Association Treaty. Political dialogue started in February 1993, followed by the establishment of the Common Steering Committee to prepare for the completion of the customs union. At the meeting of the Association Council on 9 November 1992 both sides, seeing the customs union as the only realizable cooperation mechanism, agreed to reactivate the implementation of the provisions laid down in the Association Agreement. The result was a list of topics to be resolved before the establishment of a customs union in 1995.

The establishment of a customs union was no longer just an abolition of customs duties and taxes having equivalent effect between the two sides and the implementation of the CCT on third countries by Turkey. For Turkey it also meant the abolition of all non-tariff barriers such as import levies (including the Mass Housing Fund), application of all the preferential trade agreements concluded by the EU with third countries, and adaptation of trade agreements to the respective EC position, which meant granting trade preferences to a number of countries that are competitors of Turkey in the Community market. It also meant admitting rules of competition that are compatible with those of the EC.

Although Turkey had taken enormous steps in liberalizing its trade regime in the 1980s, the concern was that the customs union would still create problems with regard to protected sectors such as automotive, pharmaceuticals, processed agricultural goods, and even textiles and clothing. Concerning the regulatory framework of competition, such as state subsidies, antitrust law, and the law concerning industrial and intellectual property rights, Turkey was to bring its legislation in line with that of the EC. The trade in agricultural products was to be excluded from the customs union, as Turkey has not adapted its domestic agricultural policy to the CAP. The EC, on the other hand, had to end its restrictions on textile and clothing imports from Turkey by abolishing the voluntary export restraint arrangement, which had always been contrary to the stipulations of the Additional Protocol.

The discussions on the issue of customs union were clear enough to show the difference between the two sides in defining the customs union. Turkey concentrated on the economic aspects, while the EC placed utmost importance on the question of democracy. The significance of this issue is depicted by the 1991 political conditionality clause, which placed the protection of human rights as one of the main objectives of the EC's external relations. Being critical toward the domestic politics of Turkey, the EC asked Turkey to enhance the democratization process. While Turkey was expected to take steps in this direction, the stripping of eight former deputies of the pro-Kurdish Democracy Party (DEP) of their parliamentary immunity by the Turkish Parliament strained relations overnight.

After long debates on both economic and political issues, the 36th Turkey-EC Association Council on 6 March 1995 took the decision on the customs union, which was to enter into force on 31 December 1995, although the conditions set forth by the EC in connection with the realization of the customs union, such as a radical change in the Kurdish policy and the improvement of the democratic conditions in Turkey, seemed to be extremely difficult to be fulfilled. However, to much surprise, Turkey took some concrete steps in the enhancement of democracy, such as the amendment of Article 8 of the antiterrorism law and the release of prisoners held under this article. Article 8 previously automatically condemned as terrorism "any written or spoken propaganda, meeting, demonstration, march, etc. which impaired the integrity of the state . . . , irrespective of the methods, motives or intentions of those concerned." The removal of the last part beginning with "irrespective" gave way to the consideration of the intentions involved, and the immediate result of this change was the release of 82 persons, including two imprisoned DEP members.

Both the EP and the council welcomed the legal and constitutional reform measures introduced on 23 July 1995 as sincere steps toward the improvement of the democratic situation in Turkey.[4] The Turkish government's message was that the drive for these reform measures did not stem from the requirement of the EC for the customs union but from the acknowledgment that they would enhance the quality of its citizens' lives.

The Association Council meeting of 30 October 1995 confirmed that Turkey had met the conditions set out in the Decision of March 6, by adapting its laws and taking steps to bolster democracy and the rule of law. Thus, the customs union was not only an economic issue but also a political link for Turkey to the market-based, liberal democracy of the West. It was feared that without the customs union, a strong anti-Western, particularly anti-European, sentiment could win the upper hand in Turkey.

The intense lobbying campaign of the Turkish government, with some support of U. S. diplomats in Community circles, resulted in the EP's positive decision on 13 December 1995 on implementing the final phase of the Customs Union, the commencement date being in line with the timetable of the Ankara Agreement and the Additional Protocol. Of the 528 European deputies who participated in the European Parliament session, 343 voted in favor of establishing a customs union between EC and Turkey, 149 voted against, and 36 abstained. As it was voiced by Pauline Green, the leader of the Socialist Group in the EP, the ones who voted in favor of Turkey wanted to encourage the democratic evolution in Turkey "in favor of individual and minority rights." They believed that it was the right way to support and encourage democratic forces in Turkey.

On 1 January 1996, the enforcement of the customs union started.

CUSTOMS UNION: COVERAGE AND OBLIGATIONS

Turkey is the first country to conclude a customs union with the EC without being a full member. However, the aid and the support mechanisms in the Community are designed in line with the full membership approach. In the case of Turkey, being a non-member country, it is forming a customs union without the necessary financial support mechanism and also without being part of the decision-making process.

The customs union stipulated in the Ankara Agreement and the Additional Protocol was limited to abolishing customs duties and taxes having equivalent effects and imposing common customs tariffs on third countries. As this no longer met the current needs with respect to the evolution of the *acquis communautaire* and the changes in the international arena, such as the stipulations of the Uruguay Round, the Generalized System of Preferences, and other preferential trade agreements of the EC, the concept of customs union underwent vital changes. Thus, the agreement on the current form of the customs union stipulated measures related to competition rules, industrial and intellectual property rights, harmonization of legislation, and other measures designed to bring the Turkish economy in line with that of the Community.

The legal framework (Decision 1/95), which set the coverage and implementation schedule of the customs union, was approved by the EC-Turkey Association Council on 6 March 1995. The Association Council agreed also on two more documents. The first document was the Resolution of EC-Turkey Association Council on the development of the Association. It is a kind of action plan calling for cooperation in matters such as macroeconomic dialogue, social issues, and institutional dialogue. In accordance with this, on 30 October 1995, the Association Council decided on the detailed rules to be applied within the context of institutional cooperation.

The second document is the Community Declaration concerning Financial Cooperation. Under the context of the unilateral declaration of the Community concerning financial cooperation, between the years 1996 and 2001, Turkey is to receive funds from four sources: the sum of ECU 375 million from the Community budget; ECU 300 million to 400 million from the European Investment Bank (EIB) loans available under the 1992–96 new Mediterranean policy for the financing of infrastructure projects[5]; from the EIB, loans over a five-year period starting in 1996 for improving the competitiveness of the Turkish economy, the amount of which can reach a maximum of ECU 750 million; and in cases of need an "exceptional additional medium-term macroeconomic financial assistance linked to the execution of the IMF approved programs." Thus, the overall aid over a five-year period is expected to be around ECU 1.5 billion.

The Decision 1/95 of EC-Turkey Association Council defined the timetable for the elimination of customs duties and charges having equivalent effect and the elimination of quantitative restrictions or measures having equivalent effect and also set the rules for the commercial policy, common customs tariff, preferential tariff policies, and the approximation of laws including competition rules of the customs union, and, finally, institutional provisions.

According to the Decision, Turkey is expected to fulfill the following conditions: (1) elimination of customs duties and charges having equivalent effect applied to the Community-manufactured products; (2) elimination of quantitative restrictions or measures having equivalent effect such as the Mass Housing Fund levy; (3) in relation to third countries, aligning itself with the CCT[6]; (4) aligning itself progressively with the preferential customs regime of the Community within five years; (5) incorporating into the legal order instruments to remove technical barriers to trade; (6) elimination of customs duties on processed agricultural products not under the agreed lists; (7) implementation of the commercial policy regulations, the Community's competition rules, protection of intellectual, industrial and commercial property rights; and (8) elimination of state aids and incentives that are incompatible with the proper functioning of the customs union.

With third countries, for limited product groups,[7] Turkey can retain customs duties higher than the CCT until January 2001. Turkey is also obliged to conclude preferential trade agreements with the countries with which the EU has preferential agreements. Article 16 states that Turkey shall gradually align itself with the preferential customs regime of the Community over a five-year period. "This alignment will concern both the autonomous regimes and preferential agreements with third countries."[8]

Trade in agricultural products was excluded from the decision, although the Association Council reaffirmed the intention concerning the move toward the free movement of agricultural products, conditional upon Turkey's adoption of CAP measures. Concerning processed agricultural products, Turkey was allowed to apply tariffs on imports from third countries for listed goods with agricultural components. The calculation of the agricultural component is stipulated in Article 18 bis.

The EC's removal of textile and clothing product quotas is made conditional upon Turkey's adoption of the EC's textile policy, both as regards commercial policy, including the agreements and arrangements on trade in textile and clothing, and with respect to state aids granted to this sector. The council expressed its wish to conclude the negotiations for the free movement of European Coal and Steel Community (ECSC) products in 1995.[9]

Concerning the implementation of the competition rules of the EU, Turkey is to establish a National Competition Authority and harmonize its state subsidy policy with the present regulations in the EC within a period of two years. There are exceptions to this provision in the areas of regional development policy and structural adjustment necessitated by the establishment of the customs union, for which a transition period of five years is granted, with the reservation that it does not adversely affect trade relations.

The institutional part of the decision requires Turkey to harmonize its legislation, as far as possible with Community legislation, in areas of direct relevance to the operation of the customs union. Should Turkey be unable to keep in step with EC policy, the customs union Joint Committee will work to find a mutually acceptable solution. Turkey also agreed to the inclusion of a clause stating that the provisions of the decision on the customs union will be interpreted in line with relevant decisions of the Court of Justice of the European Communities (Article 64).

ECONOMIC IMPACT OF THE CUSTOMS UNION (BENEFITS AND COSTS)

Trade and investment have been the two key factors in Turkey's relations with the EC. Integration with the Community was always perceived as the economic dimension supplementing Turkey's inclusion in other European organizations. Although the member countries of the EC were an important source of foreign investment and trade before the Ankara Agreement, their share has increased substantially over the years. In 1963, exports to the EC represented 38% of Turkey's total exports, and imports from the Community represented 28.5% of total imports, whereas in 1995, the Community accounted for 47.2% of Turkey's imports and 51.2% of its exports. The volume of trade, $336 million in 1963, increased to $28 billion by 1995. While the trade volume grew, the trade deficit with the Community also increased during the years to reach $6 billion in 1995. These figures demonstrate clearly the Community's priority position in Turkey's external trade. In addition, Turkey's exports to the EC previously consisted of agricultural goods but changed fundamentally in the 1980s, and today exports consist of 19% agricultural products and 80% manufactured goods. Textile and clothing, iron-steel products, food industry, electrical and electronic products, leather products, fruits, and industrial crops are the main export items. The main import items are machinery, vehicles, iron and steel products, chemical industry products, and electrical and electronic goods. The imports are closely correlated with the foreign investment and joint ventures in Turkey that originate in the EC.

Turkey's principal trading partner in the Community has been Germany (18%). The other important trading partners are Italy (7%), France (5%), the United Kingdom (5%), and Holland (3.3%).

As discussed in the preceding section, the intense trade and investment relations between Turkey and the EC are not coincidental but rather are the result of more than 30 years of close association. One must add to this picture the fact that over 2 million Turkish workers are employed in the member countries of the EC, and their remittances are an important source of foreign exchange.[10] Tourism revenue in Turkey is also mainly generated by the tourists from member countries of the EC.

The economic impact of the customs union on the Turkish economy concerns the overall economic fitness and the economic competitiveness of the major economic sectors. The structural disparities in both industry and agriculture, noted by the EC Commission in 1989 in its reply to the application for full membership, are still valid to a lesser extent. Purchasing power in Turkey is almost one-third of the EC average, the share of agriculture in GDP is 15% compared to EC's 2.8%, and also 46% of the active population is employed in agriculture compared to the EC average of 5.8%.

The macroeconomic imbalances in Turkey, including the high level of inflation, gross debt/GDP ratio and high long-term interest rates, are still problematic. These are summarized in Table 4.1. However, the level of protectionism in industry has been reduced substantially due to the tariff and non-tariff reductions required for the establishment of the customs union.

The most intensely discussed cost and the immediate challenge to the Turkish economy have been the diminishing public income due to the dismantling of customs duties and the abolition of the Mass Housing Fund levy, which is collected from industrial product imports to finance housing projects in Turkey. This is estimated to be a loss of around $2.5 billion annually, which, according to the World Bank estimate, is equal to 1.4% of GDP (Harrison et al. 1996: 14). The application of the CCT for third countries is also expected to have an impact on public income.

How this revenue loss will be replaced has been an important topic of discussion in Turkey. Everyone agrees that this revenue loss should be replaced by either reducing expenditure or increasing revenue; otherwise, the fiscal deficit will significantly increase. The reduction in the expenditure can be obtained by reducing subsidies and incentives given by the state, while the revenue can be increased by a replacement tax. Since the reduction in subsidies and incentives needed time, the proposals under consideration were either increasing the percentage of the value-added Tax (VAT) or a special consumption tax on a limited range of products.

Table 4.1
Maastricht Criteria and Turkey, 1995 (%)

	Inflation 1995	Gross Debt/GDP 1995	General Government Balance/GDP 1995	Long-term Interest Rate
				August 1996
Turkey	78.9	60	-4.0	100.0
Worst Member State	9.3	133.5	-9.2	14.2
Best Member State	1.0	47.2*	-1.6*	6.3
Maastricht Criterion	2.9	60	-3.0	9.2

*Not including Luxembourg with exceptionally low rates (Gross debt/GDP - 0.4; General government balance/GDP 6.3).

Source: IMF World Economic Outlook (October 1996); and State Institute of Statistics, Turkey.

Another important economic impact of the customs union was expected on trade relations. First of all, there is an expectation of an increase of the total two-way trade. Second, the trade gap for Turkey is expected to widen in the short run for several reasons. Turkey, not the Community, is dismantling barriers to trade, since the Community abolished all tariff and non-tariff barriers in 1973, with few exceptions. Therefore, it is natural that imports from the EC will increase first. The fact that the growth rate in Europe does not allow a booming market for Turkish products is another reason. Also, a large percentage of Turkey's imports is raw materials and investment goods needed for increasing manufacturing capacity, with the potential of ultimately increasing exports. Finally, with the dismantling of tariffs under the customs union, it is natural that imports are oriented toward the EC, a trade diversion effect in favor of the Community. The experiences of Spain and Greece verify this, as both had increased foreign trade deficits after accession to the EC. Spain's foreign trade deficit, $4.8 billion at the end of 1985, increased to $30.4 billion in 1992. Table 4.2 provides a summary of Turkey's trade with the EC.

The immediate advantages to Turkish industries include the removal of remaining restrictions on exports of manufactured goods to the EC, simplification of border procedures, improved access to the third-country markets with which the EC has preferential trade agreements, and lower prices on imported inputs. According to the World Bank estimates (Harrison et al. 1996), summarized in

Table 4.3, the impact on Turkey's GDP is expected to be 1.1–1.5% of its GDP per year, depending on the adoption of the complementary policies.[11]

Table 4.2
Turkey's Export to and Imports from the EC

	Exports (fob) to EC		Imports (fob) from EC	
	US $ billions	% of Total	US $ billions	% of Total
1967-80(average)	0.7	48.5	1.3	46.6
1980-84 (average)	1.9	36.3	2.7	29.8
1985-89 (average)	4.4	44.5	5.2	37.0
1990	6.9	53.3	9.4	41.9
1991	7.1	51.8	9.2	43.8
1992	7.6	51.7	10.0	43.9
1993	7.3	47.5	13.0	44.0
1994	8.3	47.7	10.3	47.0
1995	11.1	51.2	16.8	47.2

Source: State Planning Organization, Turkey.

The benefits to Turkey may be hard to visualize in the beginning, as they are expected to be more noticeable in the medium and long run, when the economy adjusts to the economic standards of the EC and gains international competitiveness. The customs union will be the big impetus for the modernization of the economic structure and restructuring of the state and the private sectors, resulting in the increased international competitiveness. The harmonization of the economic system with the EC will lead to the adoption of a legislative framework that is conducive to the globalization of the economy.

Agriculture, not being covered under the customs union, will become a highly protected sector relative to industry, and as the EC imposes no restraints on subsidies on agricultural exports, this might encourage resources to flow toward the agricultural sector, which will continue to receive subsidies.

Also, certain sectors, such as the automotive sector, have been considered sensitive sectors in the customs union by both sides. With the commencement of negotiations, the Turkish press heavily emphasized the customs union's expected adverse impact on the automotive industry. According to the Decision of 6 March, Turkey can maintain, vis-à-vis third countries, customs tariffs higher than those of the CCT, which gives the vehicles in Turkey or the EC exports to Turkey a preference over those of third countries. In return, Turkey has agreed to cooperate in devising a statistical monitoring system for the importation of Japanese cars and even, if necessary, the construction of Japanese cars in Turkey. Concerning the other sensitive sector, pharmaceuticals, Turkey has to adopt legislation or, if possible, revise the existing one for the patentability of pharmaceutical products and processes before January 1999 (Article 5 bis).

Table 4.3
Disaggregated Welfare Effects of Customs Union

	Welfare Gain	
	As % GDP of 1990	As % of Total Gain
I. Impact of All Changes (=II + III)	1.5	100
II. Impact of Required Changes	1.1	73
(=1+2+3+4+5+6)		
1. Preferential Access to Third-countries	0.5	33
2. Improved Access to EU	0.3	20
3. Tariff Reduction	0.1	7
4. Harmonization of Product Standards	0.1	7
5. Reduced Trading Costs	0.1	7
6. Elimination of Subsidies for Export to EU	0.0	0
III. Impact of Additional Changes (=7+8+9)	0.4	27
7. 50% Reduction in Agricultural Import tariffs	0.0	0
8. Elimination of Remaining Export Subsidies	0.1	7
9. Replacing Sector-specific taxes with VAT	0.3	20

Source: Harrison et al. *Economic Implications for Turkey of a Customs Union with the European Union*. Washington, D.C.: World Bank, 1996. Model simulations.

PROS AND CONS FOR THE EC

The benefits of the customs union to the EC are substantial. Turkey is its seventh biggest trading partner, with which it has a trade surplus of more than $10 billion. Turkey proceeded slowly with trade liberalization until 1988, after which tariffs were reduced in line with the anticipated entry into the customs union. The complete dismantling of tariffs and non-tariff barriers such as levies will increase EC exports to Turkey, for which some experts anticipate a doubling of figures in the first five years.

Under the customs union, due to the harmonization of economic legislation and the application of the Community case law, the growing and dynamic Turkish domestic market becomes a more secure environment for European firms for both investment and trade purposes. It can also be a potential base for the EC initiatives and exports to the Black Sea region, Central Asian Turkic Republics, and the Middle East. Compared to these advantages, the cost of the customs union to the EC is minimal, a total of ECU 1.5 billion financial aid, which will be spread over five years.

From the outset, the Decision of 6 March 1995 looks more favorable to the EC's interest than to Turkey's. While safeguarding European interests in sensitive sectors such as textiles and clothing, agriculture, iron and steel, and motor vehicles, it imposes new obligations on Turkey with respect to trade with third countries, intellectual property rights, competition law, and regulations regarding the technical trade barriers for manufactured goods.

ECONOMIC IMPACT OF TRADE RELATIONS WITH THIRD COUNTRIES

The customs union not only brings the dismantling of tariff and non-tariff trade barriers for manufactured goods between the two partners but also creates common trade barriers vis-à-vis third countries, since Turkey will also apply the CCT of the EC. This application involves a reduction of tariffs against imports from third countries. As the EC has also granted trade preferences to many third countries through either bilateral trade agreements or unilateral decisions, the application of the CCT will oblige Turkey to give preferential access to its markets to the countries to which the EC has given or will give preferential access. Turkey will have to negotiate these trade agreements by 2001, and, as most of these agreements will be negotiated reciprocally, Turkey should also gain from having preferential access to these markets. According to the World Bank estimates, "Improved access to these markets would result in a gain in Turkish welfare of 0.5%" (Harrison et al. 1996: 24). However, Turkey not only will have to harmonize its foreign trade policy with respect to preferences but also will have to apply the protective measures for imports from third countries and negotiate agreements on a mutually advantageous basis with the countries concerned (Article 12-16).

The tariff reduction to third countries due to the application of CCT can be expected to reduce the trade diversion costs of the customs union[12], if these countries have export similarity with the EC. The customs union does not impose any restraints on the subsidies on exports to third countries, and this might divert resources to sectors and products oriented toward these countries.

As to Turkey's obligations arising from its membership in Economic Cooperation Organization (ECO) and the Black Sea Economic Cooperation (BSEC) project, they will be subject to consultations with the Association Council. Article 52 of the decision stipulates the waiver of sovereignty into areas that are of direct significance for the functioning of the customs union, such as the agreements with third countries that constitute "a commercial dimension for industrial products."

POLITICAL IMPLICATIONS OF THE CUSTOMS UNION

In the preamble of the Decision 1/95 of the EC-Turkey Association Council, it is stated that "the Customs Union represents an important qualitative step, in political and economic terms within the Association relations between the Parties."[13] Although Turkey has concluded the customs union without full membership, the decision refers to the objectives set out by the Ankara Agreement and in particular by its Article 28, as maintaining their significance at present.

Article 28 states that "as soon as the operation of this Agreement has advanced far enough to justify envisaging full acceptance by Turkey of the obligations arising out of the Treaty establishing the Community, the Contracting Parties shall examine the possibility of the accession of Turkey to the Community."

The customs union is the final stage of the transitional phase, during which the two parties fulfill their reciprocal obligations. For Turkey, it is also considered as the first step of an irreversible chain of events leading to full membership. This was almost the same logic behind the official application for full membership by Turkey on 14 April 1987. The Turkish government, being aware of the difficulties with regard to carrying out the obligations, still wanted to remove the uncertainty surrounding EC-Turkey relations and open the path leading to full membership.

Since 1993, the EC has kept Turkey out of the list of the candidate countries for membership. "Among all the possible candidates, Turkey is the only country which has entered a customs union with the EU, which is the only NATO member among them having contributed to Europe's security, with the fastest developing economy among the candidates—and a growth rate higher than those of the EU members themselves for the past 10 years. So how come Turkey is still not on the list of the candidate members?" asked Undersecretary Öymen of the Turkish Ministry of Foreign Affairs in a press interview (*Turkish Daily News* 4 January 1997).

For the Turkish public there is no credible explanation for this situation, since beginning with the full membership application, it has used all means to make it clear that it will fulfill its obligations regarding the association. It is obvious that the tension in the relations arises not out of economic issues but because of Turkey's domestic politics concerning democratization and its struggle against terrorism, which have led to criticism with respect to human rights in Turkey. The large-scale military operations in the southeastern region of Turkey against the separatist Kurdistan Workers Party (PKK) affect relations adversely, and until the dividing line between legitimate fight against terrorism and violations of human rights is made explicit, this will affect Turkey-EC relations.

Another sensitive issue has been the Cyprus question.[14] In the renewal of ties with Turkey, Greece formed a link between the Cyprus issue and the customs union negotiations with Turkey. When the European Council promised to undertake open accession negotiations with Greek Cypriots six months after the conclusion of the Intergovernmental Conference, Greece withheld its veto. This enabled the Turkey-EC Association Council to reach an agreement on finalizing the customs union. Turkey reserved its right to achieve a similar integration with the Turkish Republic of Northern Cyprus, if the EU opens accession negotiations with Cyprus before a negotiated settlement is reached in Cyprus. The fact that Turkey's special economic ties with the Turkish Republic of Northern Cyprus would not be affected by the customs union was also stated in a joint declaration on 28 December 1995 by the president of Turkey and the president of the Turkish Republic of Northern Cyprus. Turkey also argues that Cyprus' membership is still not possible under existing international agreements, which bar its membership in international organizations of which both Turkey and Greece are not also members.

In spite of the relatively unfavorable situation on these issues, Turkey's determined pursuit of the customs union must be seen as a way of keeping its place in the extending queue for full membership. Being in line with the Ankara Agreement of 1963, which stipulated the customs union as a main step toward membership, the Decision 1/95 is expected to commit the EC more to its obligations concerning prospective membership of Turkey and hopefully distinguish Turkey from the other candidates in line. Concerning domestic politics, the customs union was promoted as an assurance against ultranationalistic and religious political developments. It was also promoted as a process that would contribute to the improvement of relations with Greece and to a solution of the Cyprus question, whose admission into the Union before a negotiated settlement is reached will endanger the relations between Turkey and the EC.

THE DEBATE IN TURKEY

The debate concerning the customs union in Turkey has been between the defenders of the customs union, who believe that it will yield positive results in the long term, and the opponents, who argue that it will harm Turkey's interests. The Islamist circles have claimed that Turkey as a Muslim country will never be accepted as a full member in a Christian club. In the economic arena, this opposition is represented by the Independent Industrialists' and Businessmen's Association (MUSIAD), a pro-Islamic, non-governmental organization. However, irrespective of the political stance, there has been criticism concerning the attitude of the EC toward Turkey for not honoring its obligations, such as the financial cooperation and the free circulation of labor.[15]

The criticisms widely discussed in Turkey can be classified under three headings. The first is that the customs union, by imposing an obligation on Turkey to align itself with the present and future customs regimes of the union, in time, might create political complications due to conflicting interests and obligations arising from agreements with third countries and also Turkey's relations with the Turkish Republic of Northern Cyprus.

The second, widely criticized point arises from the fact that the provisions of the Decision 1/95 shall be interpreted "in conformity with the relevant decision of the Court of Justice of the European Communities" (Article 64). The argument is that of a country transferring national sovereignty to a court whose legal references are created by political engagement in which it is not part. Turkey's participation in the decision making is restricted to consultation of Turkish experts (Article 57) and their involvement in the work of a number of technical committees (Article 58). Concerning the settlement of disputes set forth in

Articles 59 and 60 of the decision, it is significant only in the case of disputes of a technical nature, such as a dispute relating to the scope or the duration of protection measures. The disputes arising due to the differences in the politics of the trade policy or any other area of harmonization are not covered under the aforementioned articles.

The third main criticism is that the political conditions put forward by the EP to give its assent are considered to be interfering with the domestic affairs of Turkey. The discussions in Europe voiced especially by European deputies such as Pauline Green, Claudia Roth, and Catherine Lalumiere on Turkey's compatibility with the Western standards of democracy, with respect to human rights and the rule of law, were considered humiliating by the Turkish public, whose attitude is that "our government should not be told what to do by the foreigners."

Basing its argument on any of these points, the pro-Islamist Welfare Party (RP) declared that it would renounce the customs union if it got into power. However, later, as a partner in the coalition government, Necmettin Erbakan, the leader of the party, declared that his party's intention is only to renegotiate the terms of the customs union, which at present are unfavorable.

A YEAR LATER—DISAPPOINTMENT

Following the favorable vote by the EP, the customs union entered into force on 31 December 1995. This date was in agreement with the timetable set by the Additional Protocol of 1973. As of 1 January 1996, the customs duties and the charges having equivalent effect and the quantitative restrictions were abolished, with the exception of the export of raw cotton to the EC. The voluntary export restraint agreements on textiles implemented by Turkish exporters were abolished. In July 1996, a free trade agreement on products covered by the ECSC Treaty was concluded. Concerning the institutional provisions of the decision, the joint Customs Union Committee has been set up and has met several times. A free trade agreement has been signed with Israel, and another one with Hungary, and these will soon be followed by others with Romania, the Czech Republic, and Slovakia. Other agreements with Central and Eastern European countries are under way, including initial contacts with Lithuania. These free trade agreements, which include trade of industrial goods, some agricultural products, and processed food items, are expected to bring Turkey in line with the EC terms of trade with third countries.

Turkey has not yet adopted the EC's generalized system of preferences, nor did it conclude comparable trade agreements with Mediterranean countries and others. The establishment of a board to supervise compliance with the competition law, the adoption by the Turkish Parliament of a new customs code aligned with the EC code, and the establishment of Consumer Courts are the measures that were not concluded in a year's time. A draft bill proposing changes to the law on preventing unfair competition in imports has been a long time waiting at a commission in the Turkish Parliament, although it is important for securing compatibility with EC trade laws. Overall, one can say that in the field of harmonization of legislation, 1996 was not as successful as the previous year.

The customs union of 1996 is more than the customs union envisaged by the Ankara Agreement of 1963. With the development toward political union, democracy and human rights have become the preconditions for the development of the relationship. Thus, the EP, to give its assent, has asked Turkey to fulfill the conditions regarding the rule of law, democracy, and the promotion of human rights (Resolution of 13 December 1995). However, due to the unstable political situation in Turkey, the pre-customs union constitutional reforms were not converted into laws, and the democratic reform process did not advance as pledged.

The EU public opinion was also affected adversely when a Turkish minister was kept in the cabinet despite harsh criticism against his inappropriate talk about three female EU parliamentarians. The death of a journalist, Metin Göktepe, while in custody in January 1996, and the hunger strikes in prisons in July 1996, which led to the deaths of 12 people, created great disappointment in the EP. Most important, the pro-Islamist Welfare Party (RP) as a coalition partner in the government created uneasiness in Europe. The deputies of EP on several occasions stated that they felt cheated because, during the discussions leading to the customs union, the main argument was that if the customs union were not approved, the Welfare Party would come to power at the 24 December 1995 general elections. However, later in 1996 the True Path Party, led by Tansu Çiller, who was the spokesperson for the preceding argument, joined in a coalition with the RP, which has been against the EC and the customs union. The two partners in the coalition, which ended in mid-1997, had different views on this most important issue, which will shape the future economic relations of Turkey. When in government, Erbakan, leader of the RP, qualified his statement about the EC, saying that the party is against a relationship where Turkey is treated as a second-class country and that the goal is to be partners with equal rights. In a press interview, he stated: "Turkey is against a 'We decide, you do it' kind of relation; we do not see it as a correct attitude. Turkey is a powerful country at the center of the world."[16]

After a decision on 16 December 1995 by the European Court of Human Rights ruling that Turkey should pay compensation to a group of villagers whose villages had been burned, the EP, citing human rights violations and failure to fulfill pre-customs union democratization pledges, froze the financial support that had been earmarked for Turkey.

The resolution of 19 September 1996 received a majority of 319 affirmative votes to 23 against, with 20 abstaining. It blocked the first part of EU financial aid to Turkey, and it also urged the commission to block all allocations set under the Mediterranean Economic Development Aid (MEDA) program. The EP demanded that Turkey explain clearly its position on four issues; human rights, democratization, the Cyprus question, and the Kurdish problem. Apart from repeating objections to the continuing imprisonment of former Democracy Party deputy Leyla Zana and the military operations in the southeast, the EP had two international issues on its agenda: the idea of a Turkish buffer zone in Iraq and the Cyprus question. Discussing the death of two Cypriots on the demarcation line of the island, the resolution stated that "it was more than necessary to open the negotiations on the accession of Cyprus six months after the completion of the intergovernmental conference in order to defuse an explosive situation."

The response from the Turkish side of the decision of the European Court of Human Rights on 16 September was voiced by Professor Mümtaz Soysal (Democratic Left Party parliamentary group deputy chairman), who said that the court ruling was unfair since the judicial authority of the court starts when all avenues of domestic appeal have been exhausted, and the court acted on the belief that it is not possible to file a lawsuit in Turkey due to the conditions in southeastern Turkey (*Turkish Daily News* 19 September 1996).

The reaction of the Turkish private sector to the resolution of the EP was voiced by Meral Eriş, the president of the Economic Development Foundation, accusing the European Parliament of being "prejudiced, biased and irresponsible" (*Zaman* 25 June 1996: 6). Both the Turkish government and the private sector felt that the tone of the resolution of the EP was harsh. The EP resolution was considered a decision that ignored the domestic and external difficulties Turkey is facing and gave no support of the democratic forces in the country. However, not everyone in the Community was of the same opinion. On 12 November 1996, appearing before the EP Foreign Relations Committee and speaking on behalf of the EU Commission, Hans van Den Broek said: "No one should forget that this country is located in a very sensitive region. To isolate Turkey and to sever all channels of dialogue and cooperation is in nobody's best interest." The United States, which has been a supporter of the customs union, also threw its weight behind Ankara by announcing that it was disappointed over the EP's decision on freezing of aid.

This event aggravated the already tense relations between Turkey and the EP, which had taken place earlier in the year, in January 1996, over the events in the Aegean involving the islands of Kardak/Imia, during which the EP, which had remained impartial at the beginning, later supported the Greek argument. As a result, the EC-Turkey Association Council did not meet for the whole year. The European Council was unable to attain the required unanimity to adopt the financial regulation for the special customs union budgetary aid of ECU 375 million. The European Investment Bank has also been unable to act on the invitation made by the council in 1995 to grant loans of up to ECU 750 million to Turkey. The disappointment concerning the financial aid was not a new issue, when one considers that since the signing of the Ankara Agreement the total sum of financial aid received by Turkey is only ECU 827 million. Therefore, Turkey was once more deprived of the financial aid necessary to facilitate the implementation of the customs union and especially to compensate the short-term revenue losses. The financial cooperation that had not functioned since the suspension of the Fourth Financial Protocol was still not operational under the customs union.

Thus, within the first year, complaints about how the customs union has been to the disadvantage of Turkey began to mount. As previously discussed, the Association Council could not meet even once a year, the institutional cooperation mechanism did not work, the Customs Union Joint Committee, which was set up in order to establish the smooth operation of the customs union, could meet only five times during the year, and the financial aid was blocked. The total relationship had soured, and it looked as if both sides had lost interest and enthusiasm. The disappointment in the business circle was voiced by Istanbul Chamber of Commerce chairman Mehmet Yıldırım: "Contrary to expectations, after the beginning of the customs union process, Turkey and the European Union relations paused and entered a cooling off phase" (*Turkish Daily News* 3 January 1997).[17]

Part of this disappointment was due to the fact that the customs union was presented as a cure-all that would impose discipline on the domestic market, correct the foreign trade imbalance, provide financial resources, and promote foreign investment. It was deemed important for improving the macroeconomic imbalances, since Turkey had entered the customs union before solving its domestic economic problems, including high inflation, a mounting budget deficit, and a generally unstable economic environment.

Before the second half of 1996, the complaints had already begun about trade relations. Contrary to the expectations raised incorrectly by the politicians that the customs union would generate an export boom to the EC countries, Turkish imports from the EC began to boom over the year. Although it is early to draw conclusions concerning the impact of the customs union on Turkey's foreign trade in the absence of official trade figures for the year 1996, the data available for the first quarter of 1996 suggest that Turkey's trade deficit went up by 88% compared with the same period in 1995. Exports increased by 16%, while imports more than doubled. For the January–August 1996 period, the non-official estimates are around $16 billion for exports and $27.5 billion for imports, resulting in an annual two-way total trade reaching $70 billion, an almost 30% increase from 1995. As for trade with the EC, the figure is expected to reach $36 billion, with the trade deficit against Turkey growing.[18] The volume of trade expansion in a year shows that the trade with the EC has grown at the expense of trade with third countries. An important factor affecting the trade deficit has been decreasing textile exports to the EC, due to the slow growth in many countries, including Germany, Turkey's main trading partner.

The high growth rate in Turkey and the real appreciation of the Turkish lira should also be taken into account in evaluating the increase in imports. Although there has been an increase in the imports of consumer goods, the real increase is in raw materials and capital goods, which are demanded by the private sector in order to strengthen its competitive position.

Another major disappointment was the declining foreign investment, which, based on the Spanish and Portuguese experiences, was expected to soar following the customs union. Foreign investment went down by 35.2% in the first 11 months of 1996 compared to the same period in 1995. The EC countries provided 69% in value, 1% less than in the previous period. This was perceived mostly as the result of political and economic instability in Turkey. Also, the foreign investors had waited a long time for the announcement of a clear set of economic policies by the coalition governments.[19]

These immediate effects would have upset the public less seriously if financial funds had been provided to the economy. Turkey has viewed the EC as a stable market for its products and as a source of funds and foreign investment. The first year was a failure in all these aspects. However, no bankruptcies, contraction of the market, or rise in the unemployment rate occurred as the direct result of the customs union in the first year.[20]

Being aware of the unavailability of funds from the EC and searching for outside financial resources, a decision taken by the government in October 1996 brought a new dimension to one of the most sensitive sectors in the customs union, the automotive sector. According to the decision taken, a Turkish worker who opens a one-year DM 50,000 account in Turkey will have the right to tax free importation of second-hand cars and machinery. The decision created unrest for the local car industry, although it is expected to have an impact on the upper end of the car market. The consumers, on the other hand, were excited to have wider choice and believed this decision would put pressure on the domestic car industry to meet global standards.

Turkey learned in a hard way that the customs union is not a cure-all. It had to live with the problems of the first year in the customs union without any financial support. Although there are some basic problems stemming from the EC side, Turkey must first put its domestic house in order by solving its structural economic problems, such as the huge budget and foreign trade deficits and inflation around 90%, and achieving the expected standards of democracy. In the coming years, Turkey has new obligations to fulfill. It has to sign trade agreements with third countries that are necessitated by the preferential relations that the EC has with these countries. The other important concern is the banning of the state subsidies,[21] with the exception of those with a social aim, before 1 January 1998 and adoption of EC regulations in lifting the technical barriers to trade, which have to be finalized in five years, during which time the technical regulations will be prepared, independent laboratories will be set up, and a national accreditation system will be established.

CONCLUSION—LACK OF CONSENSUS ON TURKEY'S PLACE IN EUROPE

The customs union has been a milestone in the relations between Turkey and Europe. It is a dynamic process that has bound Turkey in a unique way to the

European Community, in which, although it has no access to the decision-making activity of the EC, it still accepts EC's *acquis communitaire* with respect to the free movement of industrial products and common rules of competition and trade.

The declaration of the Madrid Summit in December 1995 described Turkey as a neighboring country with which the EU intends to continue dialogue and cooperation. Thus, Turkey, in a way, is omitted from the future construction of the European Union. This conclusion is strengthened by the fact that Turkey is not even listed among the countries to be briefed on the progress of the intergovernmental conference, a list that included even Norway, which has rejected EU membership.

This event clearly points out the difference in the perceptions of the two sides concerning the final goal of this relationship. For Turkey, the final goal is full membership, and the customs union is the necessary step leading to full membership. The Ankara Agreement is the type of association treaty aimed at accession, and under Article 28, Turkey has the right to ask for membership after the successful completion of the customs union, although there is no automatic accession.

For the EC, the customs union looked like a skillful way to keep Turkey in the periphery of Europe, while concluding a cooperation arrangement that is to the advantage of the Community member countries. The Community, by being disinterested in discussing the period following the customs union, is adding to the uncertainty that has governed relations for a long time.

The collapse of the Soviet Union and the emergence of the independent states led to a restructuring of the regional balance of power and put Turkey's geostrategic status in a new light, opening the way for Turkey to develop economic and social ties with its eastern and northern neighbors. The relations with Central Asian republics assumed importance for trade and investment opportunities, especially when the historic, ethnic, and cultural ties with these countries oriented them toward Turkey for assistance. For many of these countries in the process of trade liberalization and restructuring their economies along the lines of a market economy, Turkey, which has already dealt with these changes, serves as a role model. However, in time, Turkey's role in Central Asia has proved to be more limited than initially anticipated, as it could not play a pivotal function in many aspects.[22]

For Turkey, the easiest way to develop relations with these countries was through economic cooperation, and the successfully realized examples are the Black Sea Economic Cooperation (BSEC) and Economic Cooperation Organization (ECO). Turkey became the initiator of the BSEC, which is a loose, regional, economic integration with the objective of creating a free trade area in a region with a population of more than 400 million. The economic value of BSEC was promoted by basing the argument on the complementarity of the economic structure of Turkey, which exports consumer goods and construction services, and the economic structures of some of the ex-Soviet countries, which have abundant raw materials and energy resources that Turkey needs. However, BSEC was perceived not simply as an economic cooperation but also as a regional arrangement that could contribute to the maintenance of peace and stability in the region. The predominant role of Turkey within the region was expected to increase its bargaining power and strengthen its position vis-à-vis the Community. None of these projects were considered an alternative to the EC but rather represented complementary initiatives reinforcing the process of rapprochement of European countries. For example, the possibilities of establishing a free trade agreement between the EC and the BSEC or of having the three Mediterranean members of the BSEC serve as a link between BSEC and the Euro-Mediterranean partnership were envisioned. All these options are oriented toward establishing a larger economic plan of Europe.

The collapse of the Soviet bloc presented new opportunities and challenges not only for Turkey but maybe more so for the EC. Feeling that it cannot afford to exclude the Central and Eastern European countries in the reshaping of the Europe, the Community concluded agreements with them with the possibility of eventual membership. Most of the countries emerged as applicants for full membership with a better chance than Turkey, and the cost of enlargement to include these countries was never even put on the agenda, while the financial cost of integration has always been emphasized in the debates concerning Turkish membership.

Today, Turkey-EC relations are focused on the successful implementation of the customs union. The full membership dream is getting more and more distant as the Community gets wider and deeper. However, considering the limited number of member countries that would be able to join the European Monetary Union (EMU) by 1999, flexible integration might be on the agenda sooner that expected. This will allow the non-EU members to participate in certain policy areas of the union, while refraining from others. It might give a chance for Turkey to go beyond the customs union and deepen relations.[23] The European security and defense arrangements can be one of these deepening areas. The Gulf crisis already served to show Turkey's commitment to the stability in the region, and this should not be underestimated. Turkey is also on the transportation and energy routes of the Middle East and Transcaucasia. Another option for deepening the relations beyond the customs union could be joining the European Economic Area, which would mean a step further toward the Single Market and would bring Turkish economic and social policy more in line with that of the Community's. All these options would bring Turkey closer to the final step of expanding its efforts toward the political accession, and target full membership.

NOTES

1. In the chapter, I mainly refer to the EC and not to the European Union, primarily because in the customs union relationship between Turkey and the Community, the EC is the main institutional mechanism in the legal text.

2. For the text of the Ankara Agreement see *Official Journal of the EC* (29 December 1964). For the text of the Additional Protocol, see *Official Journal of the EC* (27 December 1972).

3. For detailed assessment of trade relations see Balkır (1993: 100–139).

4. Some of the important changes can be listed as follows:

The age of right to vote was lowered to 18.
Turkish citizens living abroad were given the right to vote in general elections.
Political parties were permitted to set up wings for women and youth, to recruit members among students and university faculty, to establish links with trade unions or other associations, and to open offices abroad.
Decision to dissolve a political party must be based on objective criteria, and the political party should be given the right to organize its defense before the court.
Civil servants can negotiate collective agreements.

5. Turkey is to be a beneficiary of the budgetary component of the EC's cooperation policy with Mediterranean countries (MEDA funds) and the EIB loans component. The financial assistance under this budget was the subject of an Indicative Program agreed between the Community and Turkey and included a number of cooperation projects, whose aim is to facilitate the implementation of the customs union and to help Turkish small enterprises to face European competition. However, the projects on administrative cooperation and the information network for small and medium enterprises were the only projects approved as of October 1996.

6. February 1995 decision states that "Turkey shall progressively align itself with the Common Customs Tariff over a period of five years."

7. These products are leather and fur production, footwear, paper and paper products, refined petroleum products, non-metallic minerals, and motor vehicles and spare parts.

8. The autonomous regimes referred to in Article 16 are:

the Generalized System of Preferences;
the regime for goods originating in the Occupied Territories;
the regime for goods originating in Ceuta or Melilla;
the regime for goods originating in the Republic of Bosnia-Herzegovina, Croatia, Slovenia, and the territory of former Yugoslav Republic of Macedonia.

The preferential agreements referred to in Article 16 are:

the Europe Agreements with Bulgaria, Hungary, Poland, Romania, Slovakia, and the Czech Republic;
the Free Trade Agreement with Faroe Islands;
the Association Agreements with Cyprus and Malta;
the Free Trade Agreements with Estonia, Latvia, and Lithuania;
the Agreement with Israel;
the Agreements with Algeria, Morocco, and Tunisia;
the Agreements with Egypt, Jordan, Lebanon, and Syria;
the Free Trade Agreement with Switzerland and Liechtenstein;
the Agreement on the European Economic Area.

9. Under the Free Trade Agreement for Iron and Steel between the EU and Turkey, the customs duties and quantitative restrictions on imports of most steel and iron products will be eliminated immediately.

10. Nearly 2.7 million Turkish citizens live in the EU. In the early 1960s, these people went to the member states of the EC as unskilled workers. Today, however, most of them have an average monthly household income of around DM 3,300, and some have established businesses. According to a survey, there are 49,000 Turkish enterprises in the EC with an annual total turnover of DM 9.5 billion. See Şen (1995).

11. The general equilibrium model used for computing the economic implications of the customs union is a static model, ignoring the dynamic gains from trade.

12. The orthodox theory of customs union analyzes the effects of customs union on resource allocation in terms of trade creation and trade diversion. Trade creation refers to a union-induced shift from the consumption of higher-cost domestic products in favor of lower-cost products of the partner country. This can have a production effect by saving in the real cost of goods previously produced domestically as the domestic production is reduced or eliminated. It can also give rise to the consumption effect, which is the gain in consumers' surplus from the substitution of lower-cost partner country goods for higher-cost domestic goods. Trade diversion refers to a union-induced shift in the source of imports from lower-cost external sources to higher-cost partner sources. It increases the cost of goods previously imported from third countries, owing to a shift from foreign to union member sources. The substitution of higher-cost goods results in the loss of consumers' surplus. Both of these effects of the customs union must be considered. Trade diversion costs are not expected to be high in Turkey's case since the third country tariffs are not high. See Robson (1987).

13. For the discussion on the political implications of the customs union see Kramer (1995b).

14. I do not intend to write a substantial analysis of the Cyprus question but content myself with discussing the implications of the issues concerning the EC-Turkey relations. According to Kramer (1995: b2), "EU's interlinking the realization of the Customs Union with the starting of the accession negotiations with Cyprus without first reaching a solution acceptable to all the parties in the island could create a self destroying dynamic in relations with Turkey."

15. Concerning the EC's not fulfilling its obligations to Turkey, Haluk Kabaalioğlu states that "the Association Agreement, according to the European Court of Justice in Luxembourg, is part and parcel of European law. It is binding on all the institutions of the European Communities and also on the member states. It is analysing this Association Agreement, taking into consideration the final aim of the Association Agreement, which will prepare Turkey for full membership." See Kabaalioğlu (1992: 173).

16. For the entire interview see *Turkish Daily News* (December 1996: 1).

17. For an assessment of the first year of the customs union concerning the fulfillment of obligations by Turkey, see State Planning Organization (November 1996).

18. See Turkish Industrialists' and Businessmen's Association (1996: 67).

19. In a press conference on 9 January 1997, Meral Eriş, the chairperson of Economic Development Foundation evaluating the foreign investment during the first year, stated that the political instability, uncertainty in the field of macroeconomic policies, differences of opinion with the IMF, and the resulting loss of confidence on the international markets all had a damaging effect on foreign capital investments during the first 11 months of the year. However, the continued dynamism of the Turkish

economy, despite an unstable environment, had started to attract foreign capital by the end of the year. (Unofficial data on foreign investment permits in December 1996 have changed the picture, suggesting increased foreign investment by 31% over the previous year). On the same issue the president of the Foreign Investment Coordination Association (YASED), Yavuz Canevi, also stated that the expectations concerning foreign investment were not fulfilled due to domestic political and economic instability. See *Sabah* (14 October 1996).

20. During the discussions before the customs union, it was always emphasized that the main burden of the customs union would fall on small- and medium-sized business, and it is the government's responsibility to take measures for getting them ready to face competition from the EC countries. Therefore, studies were made by the government and other bodies, such as Halk Bankası (state-owned bank), the Chambers of Commerce and Industry, and others, for ways of supporting these enterprises. The Economic Development Foundation (IKV) and the European Commission signed a financial cooperation agreement on 3 October 1996 for a joint project on the "Information Network for Small and Medium-Sized Enterprises" in Turkey.

21. Agreement Article 32 sets out the state aids considered compatible with the functioning of the customs union. They are (1) aid to promote the economic development of areas where the standard of living is abnormally low or where there is serious underemployment; (2) aid to promote the execution of a project of common European interest or to remedy a serious disturbance of the economy of an EC member state or of Turkey; (3) time-bound aid (five years) to accomplish the structural adjustments necessitated by the establishment of the customs union; (4) aid to facilitate the development of certain economic activities without adversely affecting trading conditions between the EC and Turkey; (5) aid to promote culture and heritage conservation; and (6) other categories of aid as may be specified by the Association Council.

22. See Sayan and Zaim, this volume. Also see Balkır (1993b) and Öniş (1995).

23. See Eralp, this volume.

International Competitiveness of Turkey with the European Union: A Comparison with Greece, Portugal, Spain, and the EU/9

Robt Yilmaz

INTRODUCTION

On 13 December 1995, the European Parliament approved the decision of the Association Council for Turkey's membership into a customs union with the European Community to begin on 1 January 1996. With this historical decision, Turkey finally entered into the first stage of the European integration process. The main lines of the customs union between Turkey and the European Union (EU), which covers only free trade of manufactured goods between Turkey and the EU, create new opportunities for Turkish industry in the EU market in all manufactured goods. However, at the same time, by participating in the customs union, Turkey will not only share and enjoy the full power and benefits of the Community's common commercial policy (CCP) for internal and external trade but also share its obligations. Though this agreement, Turkey opened its domestic market not only to the EU member countries but also to the former European Free Trade Area (EFTA) countries, which became new full members of the EU starting in 1995, the African, Caribbean, and Pacific (ACP) countries, and the non-member Mediterranean countries.

The main purpose of this chapter is to ascertain and evaluate the structure of specialization and the international competitiveness of Turkey before joining a customs union with the EU. I also try to compare the international competitiveness between Turkey and the three EU member countries that seem to be most comparable to the Turkish economy, namely, Greece, Portugal, and Spain. Table 5.1 gives a comparison of these four countries and of the EU as a whole on a number of basic economic indicators.

5

International Competitiveness of Turkey with the European Union: A Comparison with Greece, Portugal, Spain, and the EU/9

Bahri Yılmaz

INTRODUCTION

On 13 December 1995, the European Parliament approved the decision of the Association Council for Turkey's membership into a customs union with the European Community to begin on 1 January 1996. With this historical decision, Turkey finally entered into the first stage of the European integration process. The main lines of the customs union between Turkey and the European Union (EU), which covers only free trade of manufactured goods between Turkey and the EU, create new opportunities for Turkish industry in the EU market in all manufactured goods. However, at the same time, by participating in the customs union, Turkey will not only share and enjoy the full power and benefits of the Community's common commercial policy (CET) for internal and external trade but also share its obligations. Through this agreement, Turkey opened its domestic market not only to the EU member countries but also to the former European Free Trade Area (EFTA) countries, which became new full members of the EU starting in 1995, the African, Caribbean, and Pacific (ACP) countries, and the non-member Mediterranean countries.

The main purpose of this chapter is to ascertain and evaluate the structure of specialization and the international competitiveness of Turkey before joining a customs union with the EU.[1] I also try to compare the international competitiveness between Turkey and the three EU member countries that seem to be most comparable to the Turkish economy, namely, Greece, Portugal, and Spain. Table 5.1 gives a comparison of these four countries and of the EU as a whole on a number of basic economic indicators.

Table 5.1

Some Indicators of the Economic Structures of Greece, Portugal, Spain, Turkey, and the EU 12, 1992

Indicator	Greece	Portugal	Spain	Turkey	EU/12
Population(1991, in millions)	10.1	10.4	39.0	57.2	350.0
Budget Deficits/ GDP (%)	-14.9	-5.8	-4.5	-3.0	-4.7
Total Domestic Debt/ GDP (1991, %)	115.5	65.3	46.0	15.1	59.4
Inflation rate	16.3	9.0	6.4	62.1	4.4
Current Account/ GDP (%)	-4.2	1.1	-3.1	0.2	-0.3
Real GDP Growth Rates (1991, %)	0.5	0.7	2.0	2.5	1.3
GNP($ billions)	65.5	58.5	486.6	147.4	-
Per Capital Income (1990, in $)	6,529.0	6,378.0	12,655.0	2,643.0	-
Real GDP Per Capita (PPP, in $)	8,331.0	9,938.0	13,338.0	5,262.0	-
Trade with the EU Export(%)	62.9	80.9	73.4	51.7	-
Import(%)	62.4	76.5	63.6	43.9	-

Source: Orhan Guvenen 1993), "A Statistical Presentation of the New and Emerging Trends in Turkish-EC Cooperation" unpublished paper presented to Forum Europe, Brussels, 13–14 May, 1993;
   and United Nations, *Yearbook of International Trade Statistics*, various years.

The central point of this chapter is to examine the structure of specialization and the international competitiveness of Turkey in, main and sub-sector trade compared with the members—Greece, Portugal, Spain, and the EU/9.[2] In other words, I discuss economic "fitness" in terms of Turkey's ability to overcome the difficulties that might arise from the creation of the customs union in 1996, mainly in the field of foreign trade.

This chapter is divided into four additional sections. The section that follows discusses the importance of the EU countries for the Turkish economy. In this context, we give an overview of the economic relations between Turkey and the EU.

The next section describes the methodology for assessing Turkey's competitiveness with the EU, while the penultimate section provides the estimates which allow for an evaluation of the structure of specialization and industrial competitiveness of Turkey by comparing it to Greece, Portugal, and Spain and to the EC/9. This empirical analysis sheds light on the structural differences in main and sub-sector trade among the four countries and the extent to which such differences have increased or decreased between Turkey and the three since their membership in the EU.

The concluding section discusses the empirical results and considers the future position of Turkey within the EU as an integrated part of the customs union.

THE IMPORTANCE OF THE EU FOR THE TURKISH ECONOMY

Economic relations between Turkey and the EU and Organization for Economic Cooperation and Development (OECD) countries are very close. Both are Turkey's traditional markets, and this has not changed over almost 40 years. There is no question today that the EU plays a tremendously important role in the international economic relations of Turkey. The EU is that part of the world economy in which Turkey today is most strongly integrated, even though not a member of the Union. In fact with a trade volume with the EU of ECU 18.07 billion, Turkey is the 10th most important trade partner of the EU (*Eurostat* 1994, vol. 5: 14).

The share of EU countries in Turkish export revenues was almost 52% in 1996, whereas the Islamic and Middle Eastern countries' share stagnated at around 15% in that same year. The regional distribution of imports reveals the same picture. The share of EU countries in total imports of Turkey was 44% in the same year.

Not only has the volume of trade between Turkey and the EU increased very rapidly over the years, but also the export structure of Turkey has changed radically. Whereas Turkey was mainly an exporter of raw materials and agricultural products in the 1960s and 1970s, today manufactured production covers almost 70% of Turkish total exports (State Planning Organization December 1996: 57–61). The importance of markets of the industrialized countries increased remarkably after Turkey's switch of industrialization strategy from an import-substitution policy to an outward (or world market)-oriented development strategy in 1980.

Foreign direct investments to Turkey mainly originate in the EU countries. The EU share is about 60% with respect to total foreign direct investment. Most foreign firms operating in Turkey come from the EU states and are a quite important part of the export-oriented Turkish businesses that are involved with the member countries of the EU. Similarly, export-oriented Turkish firms are operating mainly in EU countries.

At present, the main channel for the transfer of technology has been foreign direct investments. Turkish firms signed 707 patent licenses and know-how agreements between 1980 and 1992, 88% of which were related to manufacturing. Germany's role in the transfer of technology by foreign direct investment has been very important. The three main donor countries in the transfer process are Germany (264 agreements), the United States (120 agreements), and the United Kingdom (60 agreements).

Almost 2 million Turkish workers are employed in the EU member countries. Remittances have reached the level of $2 billion annually. Additionally, tourists to Turkey come mainly from European countries and make an essential contribution to the Turkish balance of payments (State Planning Organization December 1996: 69).

METHODOLOGY

In order to estimate the competitiveness of the countries in question in different categories of trade, we use the following four indices:

1. "Revealed Comparative Advantages (RCA)," using different versions of Balassa's formula.[3]
2. "Comparative Export Performance (CEP)" formula (Donges 1982).
3. "Trade Overlap (TO)" formula (Finger and DeRosa 1979) for the calculation of the overall importance of intra-industry, in comparison with inter-industry, specialization in international trade, including the economy as a whole and the manufacturing sector for Turkey, Greece, Portugal, Spain, and the EU/9.
4. "Export Similarity (ES)" formula of Finger and Kreinin (1979), in analog to the TO index.

In calculating these indices, the manufacturing trade sector Standard International Trade Classification (SITC) values were divided also into five different groups or sub-sectors for the period between 1987 and 1994.[4] The Appendix provides more detail on the grouping:

- raw material-intensive goods [SITC 0, 2–26, 3–35, 4, 56]
- labor-intensive goods [SITC 26, (6–62, 67, 68), (8–87, 88)
- capital-intensive goods [SITC 1, 35, 53, 55, 62, 67, 68, 78]
- easily imitable research-oriented goods [SITC 51, 52, 54, 58, 59, 75, 76]
- difficultly imitable research-oriented goods [SITC 57, 7–(75, 76, 78), 87, 88]

Note that SITC "3–35" means all of SITC 3 except for SITC 35, and SITC "6–62, 67, 68" means all of SITC 6 except for SITC 62, 67, and 68, and so on.

EMPIRICAL RESULTS

Revealed Comparative Advantages

As a first step we attempt to measure the international competitiveness of Turkey and the other three countries using the RCA indices, looking at them both individually and comparatively. By considering exports and imports together, RCAs describe comparative advantages or disadvantages in international trade.

RCA indices have been calculated using the following formula (Balassa 1965):

$$RCA = \ln[X_i / M_i](\sum_{i=1}^{n} X_i / \sum_{i=}^{n} M_i) \times 100$$

where X and M denote exports and imports, respectively, and the subscript i refers to a group at the one- or two-digit SITC level. The higher (lower) the RCA index, the more (less) successful is the trade performance of the country in question in a particular area of industry.

The empirical results of the RCA-index calculations for the member countries—Greece, Portugal, and Spain—and Turkey are broad indicators of the international competitiveness (or comparative advantages) of the four Mediterranean countries and their positions in international trade.

It is cautioned that the results for Turkey as compared to the others could be distorted by trade policy interventions, especially in the form of tariff and non-tariff barriers on imports and export subsidies. Therefore, the results for Turkey should be interpreted carefully because the foreign trade regime of Turkey was designed to protect its goods from international competition and was promoted by different forms of export subsidies over the period under consideration. Even if in some industrial sectors, such as the export-oriented sectors like textiles, clothing, and manufactured food sectors, in which Turkey seems to be internationally highly competitive, the effective protection ratio for export sectors, in spite of a decreasing tendency, was still 71% in 1991 (1983: 298.3%). Similarly, the export promotion ratio for the same sector was at the level of 12.8% in 1991 (1983: 42.6%) (Togan 1993). With that precaution in mind, the results are summarized in Table 5.2.

The main conclusion to be drawn from the RCA indices of all four countries is that they specialized mainly in labor-intensive sectors, although they did so to different degrees. It is very interesting to notice that, except for Greece, the three others have disadvantages in the raw material-intensive sector. The three and Turkey appear to have comparative disadvantages, although to different degrees, in the "easily imitable research-oriented goods" and "difficultly imitable research-oriented goods" categories. Spain and, to a lesser extent, Turkey show some specialization in capital-intensive goods.

Turkey, Portugal, and, partly, Greece appear in broad terms to be in a strong competitive position with respect to the labor-intensive sector, and the Spanish economy has been maintaining position but with a decreasing tendency. As far as the capital-intensive goods are concerned, Spain has a comparative advantage, compared to the other three. Despite fluctuations observed in some years, it is obvious that Turkey's position in the capital-intensive sectors is better than that of Greece or Portugal.

Concerning the easily imitable and difficulty imitable research-oriented goods, all four countries appear to have comparative disadvantages. But Spain and Portugal performed relatively better and have decreased the degree of their comparative disadvantages in comparison to Greece and Turkey.

Table 5.2
Revealed Comparative Advantage Indices by Product Category, 1987–1994

Product Category/Year	Greece	Portugal	Spain	Turkey	EU/9
Raw Material-Intensive Goods /1987	-10.0	-55.2	-21.8	-16.9	-52.4
1988	-17.0	-30.6	-11.9	-5.5	-36.8
1989	38.2	-30.4	-16.4	-32.2	-37.0
1990	36.6	-37.2	-21.9	-28.8	-37.7
1991	39.2	-45.2	-23.5	-8.3	-33.1
1992	38.2	-44.2	-27.5	-11.8	-29.3
1993	34.7	-60.2	-33.3	-9.6	-23.2
1994	36.1	-53.9	-34.8	-21.5	-17.5
Labor-Intensive Goods/1987	86.2	107.0	66.9	155.8	-6.0
1988	74.1	101.6	55.5	144.4	-3.5
1989	61.1	96.0	37.3	156.4	-2.0
1990	58.8	91.3	27.6	146.7	-3.8
1991	61.5	90.9	7.8	138.9	-10.0
1992	60.2	88.9	4.8	136.3	-10.0
1993	71.0	86.3	7.5	130.7	-5.7
1994	50.8	88.8	13.5	120.1	-2.0
Capital-Intensive Goods/1987	2.5	-68.5	53.1	-17.8	24.7
1988	5.4	-76.1	49.4	8.8	15.2
1989	-11.8	-76.4	48.8	16.7	12.3
1990	-22.4	-66.9	54.3	13.5	10.8
1991	-27.1	-70.7	56.1	9.9	7.6
1992	-27.7	-73.3	56.2	-3.7	8.2
1993	-25.9	-78.8	52.5	4.9	15.2
1994	-16.6	-81.1	52.1	30.4	15.6
Easily Imitable Research-Oriented Goods/1987	-160.3	-60.5	-47.5	-121.9	6.8
1988	-180.0	-61.3	-45.4	-103.1	-3.9
1989	-159.8	-52.7	-49.2	-81.8	-5.9
1990	-171.5	-53.1	-49.8	-84.2	-8.1
1991	-170.9	-65.3	-51.1	-104.9	-8.9
1992	-149.2	-71.5	-44.1	-113.6	-9.2
1993	-125.5	-63.9	-45.7	-112.9	-2.5
1994	-146.7	-51.8	45.6	-132.2	-0.4
Difficultly Imitable Research-Oriented Goods/1987	-214.9	-66.8	-58.9	-91.3	30.2
1988	-235.5	-70.9	-60.6	-162.0	21.6
1989	-224.1	-57.3	-39.7	-201.0	19.6
1990	-205.4	-59.3	-33.3	-192.0	18.7
1991	-207.9	-54.1	-36.1	-186.9	17.2
1992	-148.1	-41.5	-19.1	-161.9	19.5
1993	-144.4	-28.4	-11.4	-174.6	27.5
1994	-118.0	-30.8	-18.6	-152.9	26.6

Source: United Nations, *Yearbook of International Trade Statistics*, various years.

Comparative Export Performance

As a second step we estimated the structure of international competitiveness for Greece, Spain, Portugal, and Turkey for 1970, 1982, and 1988 by looking at comparative export performance (CEP). The years chosen for calculating this index were dictated by data availability. This measure avoids the impacts of distorted results of RCA indices that could be caused by trade interventions. Since the RCA indices are based on actual export and import flows, trade policy interventions in the form of tariff and non-tariff barriers on imports can distort their calculation. The CEP index, based only on export shares, naturally omits this source of distortion. It also allows for comparison of findings between the two measures. For this analysis, the manufacturing trade sector has been broken down and simplified into one digit (SITC 0-9) and two-digit commodities (SITC 6 and 8).

For the estimation of CEP coefficients, the following formula is used:

$$CEP = (x_{ij}/X_{iw}) / (\Sigma x_{ij} / \Sigma X_{iw})$$

where the subscript j refers to the country in question, and subscript w to the world or the EC/9, respectively. Index values above (or below) unity mean that the particular sectors have a greater (lower) share in total exports of the individual country than they have in the world as a whole or EC/9 trade. Thus, the country in question possesses a relative advantage (or disadvantage) in the export of these products. The results for CEP are summarized in Table 5.3.

To begin with, Turkey appears to hold advantages in the export of agricultural products (SITC 0) and capital-intensive goods such as beverages and tobacco (SITC 1). Turkey was able to reduce comparative disadvantage in animal and vegetables oils (SITC 4) since 1970. Compared with 1970, Turkey has made essential progress in exports of manufactured goods (SITC 6 and 8), which are mainly considered labor-intensive goods. It seems that Turkey has advanced considerably in textiles (6.5) and in clothing (8.4), especially in trade with EC/9. As the results show, the Turkish economy has disadvantages in chemicals and machinery and transport equipment (SITC 5 and 7).

Greece and Turkey have generally the same export structures. The Greek economy has shown good export performance in exporting agricultural products (SITC 0), crude materials (SITC 2), animal and vegetable oils (SITC 4), and basic and miscellaneous manufactured goods (SITC 6 and 8). Greece also achieved a remarkable export performance in leather (6.1), textiles 6.5), non-metallic mineral manufactures (6.6), non-ferrous metals (6.8), and clothing (8.4). Concerning machinery and transport equipment goods (SITC 7), Greece has shown quite a low export performance.

Portugal possesses relative advantages in beverages and tobacco (SITC 1), crude materials (SITC 2), and some basic and miscellaneous manufactured goods (SITC 6 and 8) produced mainly by labor-intensive and capital-intensive

Table 5.3
Comparative Export Performance Indicators (1970, 1982, 1988)

	Turkey				Greece				Spain				Portugal			
	World			EC/9	World			EC/9	World			EC/9	World			EC/9
SITC	1970	1982	1988	1988	1970	1982	1988	1988	1970	1982	1988	1988	1970	1982	1988	1988
0	3.78	3.56	2.65	1.99	2.47	2.44	2.20	2.64	2.78	1.14	1.73	1.95	1.20	0.54	0.52	0.28
1	9.34	4.85	2.40	1.22	12.50	4.21	5.50	5.11	2.34	1.54	1.66	1.46	5.17	3.80	3.50	4.29
2	5.03	2.08	1.20	1.19	2.11	1.23	1.10	0.83	0.49	0.52	0.72	0.74	1.67	1.72	1.74	1.97
3	0.18	0.71	0.30	0.49	0.29	1.28	0.55	0.32	1.59	0.87	0.50	0.32	0.68	0.52	0.30	0.11
4	0.16	1.67	1.67	0.28	1.29	4.57	3.14	3.76	10.36	3.33	3.80	3.74	2.41	3.39	0.98	0.69
5	0.18	0.29	0.91	0.44	0.83	0.51	0.44	0.22	0.60	0.75	1.01	0.79	0.84	0.88	0.67	0.57
6	0.32	1.52	1.85	1.57	1.26	1.67	1.73	1.61	0.76	1.60	1.32	1.16	1.55	1.67	1.51	1.37
7	0.01	0.14	0.18	0.10	0.04	0.12	0.09	0.08	0.55	0.73	0.95	1.11	0.24	0.38	0.48	0.50
8	0.11	0.91	1.80	3.26	0.41	1.46	2.21	2.57	1.50	1.13	0.83	0.78	1.33	2.31	2.71	3.05
9	n/a	n/a	0.01	0.02	n/a	0.27	0.80	0.92	0.09	0.20	0.07	0.00	0.92	1.13	0.03	0.01
61	0.31	0.03	0.11	0.07	6.89	5.10	2.50	2.56	2.68	3.82	2.18	3.17	0.33	1.47	0.34	0.37
62	0.34	0.24	0.58	0.49	0.57	n/a	0.44	0.43	2.37	2.28	2.25	2.15	1.10	0.26	0.44	0.39
63	n/a	1.41	0.23	0.12	0.27	0.91	0.55	0.28	2.77	2.28	1.14	1.40	9.44	12.43	7.81	8.94
64	n/a	0.15	0.18	0.00	0.15	0.52	0.22	0.15	0.28	0.75	0.60	0.64	0.41	0.91	0.51	0.36
65	0.98	4.55	1.93	3.37	0.30	3.41	1.52	2.10	0.82	1.06	0.63	0.59	3.85	4.68	1.93	2.22
66	0.31	2.63	0.51	0.58	0.53	3.40	1.25	0.66	0.72	2.28	1.22	1.11	3.55	2.08	1.44	1.25
67	0.08	1.14	1.78	0.64	1.79	0.85	0.84	0.60	0.33	1.86	1.17	1.03	0.19	0.26	0.11	0.06
68	0.41	0.33	0.46	0.39	1.91	1.99	1.44	1.74	0.60	1.27	0.68	0.78	0.11	0.18	0.20	0.06
69	0.04	0.54	0.40	0.24	0.24	0.70	0.38	0.21	1.19	1.51	1.12	1.17	0.97	1.01	0.76	0.60
82			0.04	0.01			0.01	0.01			1.34	1.47			0.14	0.11
83			0.19	0.19			0.05	0.02			0.78	0.51			0.03	0.03
84			1.51	1.53			1.48	1.50			0.36	0.35			1.09	1.04
85			0.07	0.01			0.24	0.19			3.45	3.41			1.77	2.03

Source: United Nations, *Commodity Trade Statistics*, various years and OECD, *Microtables: Import/Export 1988.*

means. Export performance in SITC 6 is largely unchanged since 1970, whereas export performance in SITC 8 improved considerably. Export performance has declined in agricultural products (SITC 0) and animal and vegetable oils (SITC 4). Portugal's economy did not indicate any noticeable performance improvement in the export of investment goods such as machinery and transport equipment (SITC 7).

In the case of Spain, the results show that the country lost in terms of export performance in agricultural products, crude materials, and animal and vegetable oils (SITC 0, 2, and 4) and kept relative competitiveness in basic and manufactured goods (SITC 6 and 8) with a decreasing tendency. The country has been able to improve export performance with respect to manufactured products such as chemicals and machinery (SITC 5 and 7). Again CEPs also show that Spain, in fact, is the only country among the four that has completed the first stages of export substitution and export diversification processes. It has achieved a relative advantage compared to others in export of investment goods and chemical goods (SITC 5 and 7), especially in trade with the EC/9.

In short, the trade patterns for the four countries that was revealed with the RCA indices, based on import-export ratios, are generally confirmed by the CEPs. It can be argued that there is much similarity with regard to CEPs among the four economies in the main production groups (except for the investment goods category).

Turkey, Greece, and Portugal are more similar in their export structures than the three are to Spain. Spain still maintains its relative advantage in the "early industries" (such as furniture, footwear leather, etc.), while it has already achieved a favorable export performance in the world and the EC/9 trade in some "easily and difficultly imitable research-intensive goods." The other three countries have revealed a more favorable export performance mainly in the agricultural goods (with the exception of Portugal) and in labor-intensive goods.

Intra- and Inter-industry Trade (Trade Overlap)

As a further step, we consider the overall importance for Turkey, Greece, Portugal, and Spain, as well as for the EC/9, of intra-industry in comparison to inter-industry specialization in international trade. As is known, under monopolistic competition there exists two-way trade within the manufacturing sector. This exchange of manufactures for manufactures is called intra-industry trade and an exchange of manufactures for food, for example, is called inter-industry trade.

The intra-industry trade suggests how and to what extent the country in question is already integrated into the world market and the degree of liberalization that the economy has already realized throughout the economic development process. In order to calculate the coefficients of country-specific "trade overlap" (TO), the following formula has been used (Finger and deRosa 1979):

$$TO = 2\sum_{i=1}^{n} \min(X_i, M_i) / \sum_{i=1}^{n}(X_i + M_i)$$

where X_i and M_i refer to exports and imports, respectively, of each of the SITC 0-9 production sectors i, and "min" defines the magnitude of the total trade that overlaps in dollar terms. The coefficient can vary between 0 and +1. The closer it comes to unity, the more intra-industry specialization exists. A lower coefficient implies that trade takes the form of inter-industry specialization.

Aggregate TO Coefficients. The TO results for Greece, Portugal, Spain, and Turkey with the world are presented in Table 5.4. It is expected that the TO coefficients for EC/9 would be higher than for any of the four countries and come close to unity. This emphasizes that the EC/9 has already realized full intra-industry specialization in trade with the world.

Table 5.4
Trade Overlap Coefficients, 1987–1994

	Greece	Portugal	Spain	Turkey	EU/9
1987	0.63	0.51	0.69	0.41	0.88
1988	0.49	0.53	0.73	0.43	0.91
1989	0.53	0.55	0.75	0.45	0.92
1990	0.51	0.57	0.74	0.42	0.92
1991	0.52	0.57	0.72	0.40	0.93
1992	0.58	0.57	0.74	0.40	0.93
1993	0.56	0.79	0.79	0.53	0.92
1994	0.60	0.79	0.80	0.61	0.92

Source: United Nations, *Yearbook of International Trade Statistics*, various years.

Of the four countries, Spain's TO coefficients come closest to unity but are still below the TO coefficients for the EC/9. Spain seems to be in the best position as compared to others and seems capable of catching up with the EU in the next decades.

The TO coefficients for Turkey and Greece are much lower than for the others. However, Turkey has made an enormous improvement in closing the gap with the EC/9 and the other three countries since 1970, whereas the TO coefficients for Greece remain almost unchanged since 1970. For both countries, though, the TO coefficient suggests mainly inter-industry specialization.

The TO results for Portugal occupy an intermediate position, but Portugal still possesses and shows features of inter-industry trade with the world.

TO Coefficients by Sector. Table 5.5 contains estimates for the TO coefficients by sub-sector. As far as the sub-sectors are concerned, Turkey approaches intra-industry specialization only in capital-intensive goods. In the other groups of goods, Turkey shows the characteristic of inter-industry trade with the world.

Table 5.5
Trade Overlap Coefficients by Product Category, 1987–1994

Product Category/Year	Greece	Portugal	Spain	Turkey	EU/9
Raw Material-Intensive Goods: 1987	0.75	0.50	0.61	0.3	0.75
1988	0.66	0.57	0.66	0.32	0.85
1989	0.71	0.52	0.67	0.40	0.85
1990	0.68	0.51	0.63	0.40	0.85
1991	0.73	0.50	0.65	0.29	0.87
1992	0.75	0.49	0.64	0.29	0.89
1993	0.70	0.51	0.70	0.64	0.92
1994	0.76	0.56	0.71	0.77	0.95
Labor-Intensive Goods/1987	0.65	0.58	0.83	0.38	0.98
1988	0.67	0.66	0.93	0.44	0.98
1989	0.71	0.65	0.95	0.43	0.98
1990	0.70	0.71	0.91	0.52	0.98
1991	0.72	0.74	0.84	0.54	0.98
1992	0.86	0.75	0.81	0.49	0.98
1993	0.87	0.80	0.89	0.68	0.99
1994	0.83	0.77	0.95	0.56	0.98
Capital-Intensive Goods/1987	0.99	0.36	0.91	0.67	0.87
1988	0.49	0.33	0.94	0.76	0.89
1989	0.51	0.40	0.96	0.78	0.91
1990	0.44	0.41	0.91	0.67	0.91
1991	0.40	0.38	0.84	0.72	0.93
1992	0.47	0.37	0.91	0.72	0.93
1993	0.45	0.44	0.88	0.71	0.89
1994	0.54	0.45	0.86	0.97	0.89
Easily-Imitable Research-Oriented Goods/1987	0.18	0.54	0.59	0.35	0.96
1988	0.13	0.50	0.58	0.45	0.99
1989	0.17	0.57	0.55	0.49	1.00
1990	0.13	0.55	0.56	0.40	0.99
1991	0.13	0.49	0.57	0.37	0.99
1992	0.17	0.46	0.58	0.34	0.99
1993	0.19	0.50	0.64	0.29	0.98
1994	0.18	0.56	0.66	0.34	0.97
Difficultly Imitable Research-Oriented Goods/1987	0.15	0.51	0.54	0.45	0.84
1988	0.12	0.46	0.52	0.28	0.86
1989	0.13	0.55	0.59	0.19	0.87
1990	0.16	0.53	0.62	0.16	0.87
1991	0.16	0.53	0.63	0.18	0.88
1992	0.17	0.57	0.69	0.23	0.87
1993	0.17	0.64	0.8	0.17	0.83
1994	0.23	0.65	0.79	0.29	0.83

Source: United Nations, *Yearbook of International Trade Statistics*, various years.

The Greek economy indicates the features of intra-industry trade in raw material-intensive and labor-intensive goods, whereas in the other groups the Greek economy shows the typical industrialization pattern of developing countries.

It is interesting to notice that Portugal's trade in many industries or areas of production, with the exception of labor-intensive products, is largely of the inter-industry rather than of the intra-industry type and that this pattern has not changed much over the time period under investigation.

The TO results for the Spanish economy reflect mainly intra-industry specialization. In all groups of production, more than half of the value of its exports to the world is offset by similar imports. Especially in labor-intensive and capital-intensive products, the country has already caught up with the EU/9. In the other sectors, Spain occupies an intermediate position, and the TO results show higher product differentiation, but the extent is still less than the EU/9's average as a whole.

As is known, the relative importance of intra-industry and inter-industry trade depends on how similar the capital-labor ratios of the countries are. If they are different, there will be a relatively low level of intra-industry trade, and trade will be based more on comparative advantage. However, it must be remembered that models of imperfect competition can explain intra-industry trade but cannot by themselves explain why some countries are net exporters of certain manufactures and net importers of other goods. Therefore, the TO results must be combined and interpreted with the other results in order to explain the whole trade pattern.

Export Similarities

Finally, we calculate whether or not the exports of Turkey overlapped with each of the southern Mediterranean countries in the period 1987–1994. For this purpose, we calculate coefficients of "export similarity" (ES), using the following formula of Finger and Kreinin (1979), which is analogous to the previously discussed trade overlap index. The formula is:

$$ES(ab,c) = [\Sigma min(X(ac), X(bc))]$$

where X (ac) denotes the total exports of Turkey (a) to the world markets, and X (bc) represents Greece's, Portugal's, Spain's, and the EU/9's competing exports to the world market c. An index of 1 indicates perfect overlap and the greatest degree of similarity between two countries. On the other hand, 0 indicates no export similarity between the countries in question and no overlap at all.

The estimated ES coefficients reported in Table 5.6 suggest that the degree of export similarity between Turkey and Greece and Portugal with the world market is very high. This means that by a possible accession of Turkey into the EU or in the case of joining in the customs union, Turkish export industries compete, first of all, with export goods originating from Greece, and then Portugal, followed by Spain, but to a lesser degree. The main question here is whether Turkish export goods bear complementary or substitutive features.

Table 5.6
Export Similarity Coefficients, 1987–1994

Year	Greece	Portugal	Spain	EU/9
1987	0.91	0.82	0.77	0.66
1988	0.94	0.79	0.75	0.65
1989	0.89	0.81	0.74	0.66
1990	0.88	0.83	0.71	0.66
1991	0.89	0.8	0.69	0.64
1992	0.88	0.84	0.65	0.63
1993	0.88	0.80	0.68	0.64
1994	0.85	0.81	0.68	0.65

Source: United Nations, *Yearbook of International Trade Statistics*, various years.

CONCLUSION

The preceding interpretations of the RCA, CEP, TO, and ES results allow us to draw some essential conclusions from the past and to make some predictions for general tendencies regarding future trade relations of Turkey and the EU.

To different extents, Greece, Portugal, Spain, and Turkey specialized in foreign trade mainly in raw material-intensive and labor-intensive, as well as easily imitable, research-oriented goods. To a certain extent Spain is the only country, in comparison to the other three countries, that has been able to catch up and close the industrialization gap with the EU/9. The results indicate that this country had made some impressive progress to reshape its export structure since its accession into the EU from labor-intensive goods to capital-intensive or difficultly imitable research-oriented products.

It seems that Portugal has lost its initial competitiveness in raw material-intensive goods, but it has established competitiveness in labor-intensive goods. Portugal seemed to have taken the advantage of full membership into the EU to restructure its export industries. Greece did not take advantage of the EU membership to change its structure. The results indicate that Greece's export diversification remained unchanged, even though its membership in the EU has been longer than that of Spain or Portugal.

The results further show that Turkey has radically changed its export structure and increased export revenues compared with the earlier years. Another interesting observation is that Turkey has been able to close the development gap with Greece and Portugal throughout the 1980s and beginning of the 1990s.

For a long time Turkey's trade policy was based on the uninterrupted protection of the import substitution industries. There was no intention by policy-makers in Ankara to shift trade strategy from an inward to an outward orientation until 1980. In the 1980s Turkey changed its trade policy so that import liberalization was selective and aggressively followed, and export promotion measures were put in force to encourage domestic producers to export their products. In other words, Turkey's earlier protection policy was quite comprehensive, and too little attention was paid during that period to the possibility of exporting manufactures to complement import substitution.

Now the question is how Turkey can realize step-by-step export diversification from labor-intensive to easily and difficultly imitable research-oriented goods. The first part of the answer is that Turkish governments should be determined to continue the export-oriented development strategy that has been interrupted in recent years. Second, policy-makers in Ankara have to take care of macroeconomic stability and not pursue populist macroeconomic policies that would cause an external debt crisis and hyperinflation. Third, Turkey should intensify the transfer of technology connected with capital inflows and foreign direct investments for renewing investment equipment in Turkey. These require that new reform measures be instituted, particularly in the field of education.

It is obvious that the establishment of the customs union will create and provide new dynamism and impulse for the Turkish economy. The Turkish economy has already accepted the serious pressure of international competition by abolishing tariffs and non-tariff barriers with the EU. There is a great challenge for the Turkish economy to recover and to integrate itself with the most advanced economies in the world.

The results of the study show that Turkey can compete in raw material-intensive and labor-intensive goods and partly in capital-intensive goods within the EU. Although Turkey is not a full member of the EU and only recently joined the customs union, the international competitiveness of Turkey in the observed period seemed to be better than that of Greece and Portugal. As a result of export similarities, Turkey would challenge not only Greece, Portugal, and Spain but also the EU/9 concerning raw material-intensive and labor-intensive goods. Turkey and the other three Mediterranean countries so far have comparative disadvantages in the difficultly imitable research-oriented goods and partly in easily imitable research-oriented goods.

As far as long-term impacts and perspectives are concerned, one can be more optimistic for a simple reason: it is theoretically well known that customs unions have some interesting dynamic effects such as increased competition, stimulation of technical change, and stimulation of investment. It is assumed that as tariffs are removed and the market expands, competition will increase. Monopolistic and oligopolistic market structures will become exposed to outside pressures. The experiences of Spain and, partly, Portugal lead to the conclusion that there are advantages to the opening of the markets to foreign competitors.

APPENDIX

Standard International Trade Classification (SITC)

Raw Material-Intensive Goods:
  SITC 0 Food and Live Animals
  SITC 2 Crude Materials, inedible
  SITC 3 Fuels, Lubricants, etc.
  SITC 4 Animal, Vegetable Oil, Fats, Wax
Labor-Intensive Goods:
  SITC 26 Textile Fibers
  SITC 6 Manufactured Goods
  SITC 8 Misc. Manufactured Articles

Capital-Intensive Goods:
  SITC 1 Beverages and Tobacco
  SITC 35 Electrical Current
  SITC 353 Dyes, Tanning, Color Production
  SITC 55 Essential Oils, Perfume, etc.
  SITC 62 Rubber Manufactures Nes
  SITC 67 Iron and Steel
  SITC 68 Non-ferrous Metals
  SITC 78 Road Vehicles

Easily Imitable Research-Oriented Goods:
  SITC 51 Organic Chemicals
  SITC 52 Inorganic Chemicals
  SITC 54.1 Medicinal Pharm. Products
  SITC 58 Plastic, non-primary form
  SITC 59 Chemical Materials Nes
  SITC 75 Office Machines and Adp Equipment

Difficultly Imitable Research-Oriented Goods:
  SITC 7 Machines, Transport Equipment
  SITC 87 Scientific Equipment Nes
  SITC 88 Photo Apparatus, Nes; Clock 5

NOTES

1. Comparative advantage is distinct from competitiveness. Two essential points can be singled out. First, competitiveness is related to the relative strength or weakness of a country for producing a given product, while comparative advantage is related to the relative strength or weakness of products of a given country. Second, competitiveness is often subject to macroeconomic fluctuations, while comparative advantage is structural. See Lafay (1992) for details.

2. Sweden, Austria and Finland did not become full members of the EU until January 1993 and, thus, have not been included in the empirical work

3. The methodology was originally developed by Balassa (1965) and refined later.

4. For more details see Hufbauer and Chilas (1974) and Klodt (1990).

Part III

Prospects for New Linkages

6

Turkey's Evolving Role
in the Post-Soviet World
Gareth Winrow

Turkish foreign policy-makers have had to adjust to unfolding events in today's post-Cold War era. Previously, membership in the North Atlantic Treaty Organization (NATO) had enabled Turkey to secure protection from the military threat posed by the Soviet-led Warsaw Pact and had also served to enhance Turkey's European and Western credentials. Officials in Ankara, though, were unable to secure full membership in the then European Community (EC). The prospects of joining the EC and, later, European Union (EU) appeared to diminish appreciably with the unraveling of the Soviet Union, as several former Council for Mutual Economic Assistance (COMECON) states interested in EU membership seemed to jump the queue ahead of Turkey. With the demise of the Soviet threat, the geo-strategic importance for the West of Turkey's position seemed to have been seriously eroded. However, conflict in the Balkans, the Transcaucasus, and the Middle East provided authorities in Ankara with an opportunity to underscore the value of Turkey as a regional stabilizing power. Turkish officials thereby hoped that this would boost the prospects of Turkey's eventually being admitted to the EU.

The emergence in the summer of 1996 of a coalition government in Ankara led by the Islamic Welfare Party (which ended in mid-1997) has led many commentators to question whether or not membership in the EU would remain a priority for Turkey. Interestingly, the first overseas trip of Necmettin Erbakan, the Welfare Party prime minister—excluding a brief visit to the "Turkish Republic of Northern Cyprus"—was to Iran, Pakistan, Malaysia, Indonesia, and Singapore. Apart from Singapore, these are predominantly Moslem states. Nevertheless, to date, close defense cooperation with Israel has remained intact, and the implementation of the Turkey-EU Customs Union—launched in January 1996—is proceeding.

Concerned to consolidate the new Republic of Turkey, Mustapha Kemal "Ataturk" had given little attention to the fate of Turkish and Turkic peoples in Eastern Europe and the Soviet Union. This policy was largely adhered to after the Second World War—an exception being the plight of the persecuted Turkish minority in Bulgaria in the 1980s—when throughout most of the Cold War era Turkey had only formal diplomatic ties and limited economic relations with the Soviet Union and other Warsaw Pact countries.

The breakup of the Soviet Union and the disintegration of the Warsaw Pact offered opportunities for officials in Ankara to establish relations on a new footing with the former Soviet republics and the newly democratizing states of Eastern Europe. The Turkish and Turkic peoples in these states were "rediscovered."

In the post-Cold War era Turkish governments have attempted to promote closer bilateral ties with former Soviet republics near to and around the Black Sea, Transcaucasus, and Central Asia. Ankara has also sought to expand links with Moscow, although the Turco-Russian relationship is a complex and multifaceted one. Turkish officials have also endeavored to make use of various international organizations and bodies and attempted to ensure that states respect certain international treaties and international law in general, in order to strengthen Turkey's influence in the post-Soviet world. This could be at the expense of other states interested in the post-Soviet world, particularly Russia and Iran. Turkey has also sponsored the formation of the Black Sea Economic Cooperation (BSEC) process and launched what appears to have become a regular summit meeting of Turkic heads of state.

The effectiveness of Turkish policy's relying on these multilateral mechanisms is only, in part, dependent on successful Turkish lobbying. The operational constraints and other shortcomings of these mechanisms must also be taken into account.

The future of the post-Soviet world is far from clear. Many policy-makers in Moscow seem eager to resurrect a Soviet empire "on the cheap" by seeking to deepen integration processes within the Commonwealth of Independent States (CIS). With a visibly ailing Boris Yeltsin at the helm in the Kremlin, it appears that in the not too distant future the nationalist and liberal forces in Russia are destined to clash.

The political situation in Turkey is also highly uncertain. For example, will the Welfare Party sweep the next elections and then form a government determined to reverse the traditional internal and external policies of secular, republican Turkey? The focus of this analysis is an examination of how Turkey's political role in the Black Sea region, the Transcaucasus, and Central Asia has evolved in recent years. The conclusion briefly speculates how this political role may evolve in the foreseeable future.

TURKEY AND THE BLACK SEA REGION

The term "region" in this context should be employed with caution. It is a point of debate whether or not there is a Black Sea "region" as such and, if so, the boundaries of this region are difficult to delineate.[1] In strict geographic terms there are six Black Sea littoral states, namely, Turkey, Russia, Ukraine, Georgia, Bulgaria, and Romania. The BSEC participating states also include Armenia, Azerbaijan, Moldova, Greece, and Albania, adding Balkan, Mediterranean, Caspian, and EU dimensions to BSEC. Poland, Slovakia, Italy, Austria, Tunisia, Egypt, and Israel are currently BSEC observer states giving a Central European, Middle Eastern, and North African slant. Moreover, Yugoslavia and Macedonia have applied for full membership of BSEC, and Bosnia, Croatia, Slovenia, Cyprus, Jordan, and Kazakhstan are seeking observer status. BSEC would thus include a Central Asian component.[2]

Most of the current BSEC participating states were previously republics of the Soviet Union or members of COMECON. These states are confronting serious problems along the path of transition from centrally planned to free market economies. In addition, the former Soviet republics are still heavily dependent on energy supplies from Russia. Economic difficulties could lead to heightened political instability and encourage the spread of ultra-nationalism or religious radicalism in the Black Sea region. At present there are interstate tensions between Russia and Ukraine over the Crimea and the Black Sea fleet, between Armenia and Azerbaijan over Nagorno-Karabakh, and between Greece and Turkey and Turkey and Russia over a number of issues. The Moldovan authorities have to contend with the breakaway Transdniester region, and the central government in Georgia is having to negotiate with groups seeking secession for South Ossetia and Abkhazia.

Cooperation between states neighboring and near to the Black Sea was possible only with the collapse of the Soviet Union and the elimination of Cold War divisions in the area. BSEC is a post-Cold War creation initially sponsored by Turkey. In December 1990 in Ankara, Turkish officials convened a preliminary meeting with delegates from Romania, Bulgaria, and the Soviet Union (the Soviet delegation included representatives from the republics of Azerbaijan, Armenia, Georgia, Ukraine, and the then Moldavia) to discuss the possibility of establishing a Black Sea Economic Cooperation scheme. When the project could have possibly remained stillborn due to the lack of enthusiasm of certain states and on account of the initial confusion caused by the breakup of the Soviet Union, Turkish officials continued to press for the project's adoption. Eventually, BSEC was formally inaugurated in Istanbul in June 1992 with the participation of by now 11 founder states. BSEC was less ambitious than the originally proposed Turkish scheme. At the Ankara meeting in December 1990 the delegates had agreed to consider proposals allowing the free movement of persons, goods, capital, and services. This was perhaps surprising, given Turkey's interest in joining the then EC. The Summit Declaration in June 1992 did not refer to a free trade arrangement but spoke rather of the reduction or the progressive elimination of obstacles to trade and referred to the free movement of only businessmen, rather than persons (Hale 1996: 59).

Turkish officials were eager to launch BSEC in order to demonstrate Turkey's importance as a regional stabilizing power. It also appears that policymakers in Ankara hoped that Turkey's prestige would be enhanced as a consequence, thereby possibly improving the prospects for Turkey's admission to the EC. Membership of BSEC was not meant to be an alternative to membership of the EC. On the contrary, it was believed that BSEC could complement the activities of the EC and be a part of the interlocking institutions of an increasingly more integrated Europe. Significantly, Turkey did not oppose Greece's entry to BSEC. This direct link with the EC was clear proof that BSEC was not intended to be a rival to the EC. Paragraph 7 of the Summit Declaration on Black Sea Economic Cooperation of June 1992 noted that economic cooperation would be developed so as not to prevent the formation of relations between participating states and third parties, including international organizations as well as the EC. The Bosphorus Statement released on the same day declared that BSEC constituted an effort that would facilitate the processes and structures of European integration.[3]

In the longer term Turkey could also benefit economically from the establishment of BSEC with its commitment to liberalize trade among the participating states. Many of these states are potentially important markets for Turkish consumer goods. BSEC's aims to promote governmental and nongovernmental cooperation in a number of technical fields, including transportation and communications and tourism and industry, could strengthen the Turkish economy. This cooperation may also help to promote political stability in the region by a "spillover" effect resulting from representatives of the BSEC participating states working together in more functional areas of activity. In turn, this could improve the quality of life for the Turkish and Turkic minority peoples in the Balkans and in Russia. With the democratization process under way in most of the former Soviet republics and in Eastern Europe after the end of the Cold War, officials in Ankara have now become much more concerned with the well-being of these minorities.

Although the launching of BSEC was the direct result of concerted Turkish lobbying, the BSEC "process" has, in reality, developed a momentum of its own. While not officially an organization, lacking the required statute or charter, BSEC has become much more institutionalized in recent years. By 1996 BSEC had acquired a Permanent International Secretariat, a Parliamentary Assembly (PABSEC) with three specialized committees, a BSEC Council (with business councils operating under it), and various technical working groups. A Black Sea Trade and Development Bank is scheduled to open in late 1997. The foreign ministers of the BSEC participating states meet regularly. BSEC has developed working links with the Central European Initiative, the EU, the Council of Baltic Sea States, and several United Nations (UN) agencies. Turkish officials themselves have ensured that BSEC should not appear to be under

Turkey's complete control. Thus, for example, it was agreed that the head-quarters of the Trade and Development Bank will be in Salonica in Greece. The current director of the Permanent International Secretariat based in Istanbul is a Russian ambassador.

Interestingly, on at least one occasion Turkey has attempted to involve BSEC in security issues in the Black Sea region. At the third meeting of PABSEC in Tbilisi in May 1994 the speaker of the Turkish Parliament, Hüsamettin Cindoruk, had pressed for BSEC to mediate between Armenia and Azerbaijan over the disputed territory of Nagorno-Karabakh. Cindoruk had appealed for the formation of a BSEC Consultation Committee, which could help to promote peaceful solutions to regional problems (*Turkish Daily News* 19 May 1994). Previously, the Georgian leader Eduard Shevardnadze had been calling for what, in effect, amounted to the establishment of a Black Sea collective security system. Not surprisingly, Cindoruk's initiative was never seriously considered. Russia is not prepared to allow BSEC to become directly involved in sensitive security matters. Nationalists in Russia are determined to make the CIS a collective security system serving Russian interests.

In spite of common membership of BSEC, Turkey is still confronted with a number of problems in its relations with Greece, Russia, and Armenia. In the case of Greece, this has even contributed to tensions between the two parties within BSEC. In May 1995 Greece belatedly applied for full membership of PABSEC. Turkish authorities attempted unsuccessfully to block Greek admission. Rasim Zaimoğlu, a prominent Turkish official in PABSEC, had accused Greece of conspiring with Russia, Bulgaria, Romania, and Armenia to set up an anti-Turkish grouping within BSEC and had thus argued for the exclusion of Greece from PABSEC (Ertan 1995: 11). This incident also appears to have been related to Ankara's opposition to the decision of the Greek Parliament to agree in principle to extend its territorial waters to 12 miles. Furthermore, Turkish officials were annoyed at the assumption made by Greek deputies that the Greek entry to PABSEC should be automatic and immediate.[4] The following year Ankara reacted vigorously to the conclusion of a military accord between Greece and Armenia. The spokesman of the Turkish Ministry of Foreign Affairs publicly declared that this was an example of a Greek policy that aimed to encircle Turkey and threaten peace and stability in the region (*Turkish Daily News* 20 June 1996). The continued friction between Greece and Turkey over these issues and others related to the Aegean and Cyprus in particular has, in part, hindered the prospects of Turkey's securing full membership in the EU. In practice, hitherto, the launching and development of BSEC do not seem to have strengthened Turkey's case concerning EU membership. The formation of a customs union between Turkey and the EU—which began to be implemented in January 1996—had been agreed upon two decades before the inauguration of BSEC.

Turkey has also strengthened bilateral relations with former Soviet republics around the Black Sea. The following section focuses more specifically on

Turkish policy in the Transcaucasus. With regard to Moldova, various agreements have been concluded, including a Treaty of Friendship and Cooperation. Ankara is satisfied with the treatment of the Gagauz Turks in Moldova. Visiting Moldova in June 1994, President Süleyman Demirel referred to the Gagauz Turks as "blood brothers" who formed a bridge of friendship between Turkey and Moldova (*Turkish Daily News* 3 June 1994).[5] Demirel has also stated that the Crimean Tatars—another Turkic people—returning back from Central Asia to their former homelands in the Crimea, formed an "indispensable bridge for friendship and cooperation" between Turkey and Ukraine (*Turkish Daily News* 31 May 1995). The Turkish president promised to provide support to settle the Tatars. A project is on the drawing board to transport oil from the Middle East to Ukraine through the construction of a pipeline from the Turkish Mediterranean port of Ceyhan to Samsun and then probably by tanker to Odessa *(Cumhuriyet* 10 September 1996). This could reduce Ukraine's energy dependence on Russia, while Turkey would benefit from the royalty fees and transportation costs for delivering the oil. Turkey's policy toward the Transcaucasus is also heavily influenced by pipeline politics.

TURKEY AND THE TRANSCAUCASUS

As well as forming part of the Black Sea region, the Transcaucasus—that is, the territory covered by Armenia, Azerbaijan, and Georgia—is connected physically, demographically, and economically with the area to its immediate north, the northern Caucasus, which is a part of the Russian Federation. The Transcaucasus is a potentially important corridor for the transport of oil and gas from the Caspian Sea and Central Asia. For Turkey, the Transcaucasus is an important land route through which access could be secured to Central Asia via the Caspian while avoiding other overland routes through Russia or Iran. The Transcaucasus has been a troubled region in recent years. At the time of writing, a peace agreement between the disputing parties over Nagorno-Karabakh had still to be concluded. Within Georgia, the central authorities appear to have effectively relinquished control of Abkhazia which is in danger of becoming a Russian satellite. In Azerbaijan, President Haidar Aliyev has survived at least two coup attempts, although he himself had secured his position following the forced removal from power of the democratically elected president Ebulfez Elchibey by a bunch of renegade military officers. Historically, tsarist Russia, the Persian Empire, and the Ottoman Empire had struggled to secure control over the Transcaucasus. At present, it would appear that Russia, Iran, and Turkey, the eventual successor states to these three empires, are now engaged in a renewed competition to establish influence in the region.

The main priority of officials in Moscow is to ensure that problems in the Transcaucasus do not contribute to the destabilization of Russia. For example, the border between Azerbaijan and Chechnya was closed by Russian forces to prevent Chechen rebels from receiving assistance, including military aid, which, according to some Russian sources, originally came from Turkey. It would seem that the Russian authorities are concerned that a security vacuum should not emerge in the Transcaucasus that could be filled by Turkey or Iran (Trenin 1996: 97). This would account for the Russian military presence in Armenia and Georgia in bases and along the frontiers between Turkey and Georgia and Turkey and Armenia. It would also explain Russian pressure on Baku to secure similar rights in Azerbaijan. For economic, political, and geostrategic reasons it would seem that Moscow is concerned that oil and gas pipelines running across the region should pass through Russia rather than go southward to the Persian Gulf or the Turkish Mediterranean coast.

As in Central Asia, in the Transcaucasus it would seem that Iranian officials are pursuing a policy that is primarily based on pragmatism and economic self-interest. It does not appear that Tehran is seeking to destabilize the region by fomenting the spread of religious radicalism. That would run contrary to Iran's commercial interests. Certainly, Iranian officials were very annoyed when, because of American pressure, Baku forced Iran to surrender its stake in the Azerbaijan International Operating Consortium (AIOC), which is seeking to explore and develop three offshore oil fields in the Caspian Sea. In compensation, Iran was later given a 10% stake in a project to extract oil from another Azerbaijani Caspian oil field—the Shahdeniz oil field. Tehran's principal concern is that Baku and Ankara should not encourage the 20 million or so Azerbaijanis in northern Iran to rise up and seek union with Azerbaijan to form a Greater Azerbaijan. There is no firm evidence to indicate that the Turkish government has such ambitions. Competition between Turkey and Iran for influence in the region appeared to be evident when Tehran in February 1992 announced that a Caspian Sea Cooperation Organization would be formed composed of the Caspian Sea littoral states: Iran, Russia, Azerbaijan, Turkmenistan, and Kazakhstan. Significantly, this announcement was made at a time when it had become clear that a Turkish-sponsored Black Sea cooperation arrangement would soon be launched. In contrast to Turkey and BSEC, Iran has hitherto failed to establish a multilateral mechanism for the Caspian Sea. Rather, Moscow has attempted to hijack the Iranian initiative by seeking to create a body under Russian influence that would approve of, or block, energy-related projects concerning the Caspian Sea.

The Transcaucasus is a region of strategic importance for Turkey. Almost inevitably, therefore, in this area Turkish and Russian interests especially are bound to clash. For economic and political reasons Ankara is eager to pipe oil from Azerbaijan through Turkey rather than through Russia. In the longer term Kazakh oil could also be transported across Turkey via Azerbaijan. Because of common cultural, historical, ethnic, and linguistic ties and also on account of Baku's determination to toe a line independent from Moscow, the authorities in Ankara have been keen to maintain warm relations with Azerbaijan. There is pressure from within Turkey from various lobbies and Caucasian Solidarity groups (often composed of Turkish citizens of Caucasian descent) for Turkish governments to adopt a more active and anti-Russian policy in the Transcaucasus and northern Caucasus. Officially, though, no Turkish government has agreed to provide military aid to the Chechens. In retaliation, Moscow could always play the Kurdish card and lend more active support, for example, to Kurdish insurgents operating in Turkey. It would seem that Turkish policymakers have preferred to make use of various international organizations and agencies and have attempted, for instance, to take advantage of the Conventional Forces in Europe (CFE) Treaty to curb Russian activities in the Transcaucasus.

According to the terms of the original CFE Treaty, Russia had to limit the number of tanks, armored combat vehicles, and artillery pieces that could be stationed in the northern Caucasus—one of the two "flank areas" where restrictions were to be placed on Russian military equipment. Turkish officials were adamant that Russia should be compelled to adhere to these provisions, as this would help to allay Turkey's security concerns in the Transcaucasus. They were thus visibly annoyed when Moscow was allowed to violate the CFE Treaty when it came into effect in November 1995. The U.S. administration in particular was prepared to permit the Russians to maintain a larger military presence in the area because of the ongoing conflict in Chechnya. Turkey took the issue to the NATO Defense Planning Committee in late November 1995, where Western defense ministers in their communique criticized this flagrant transgression of the CFE Treaty. Nevertheless, the CFE Vienna Review Conference in May 1996 decided to modify the terms of the original CFE Treaty. Russia was allowed a further three years to meet its obligations in the flank areas. The flank areas were to be reduced in size, and a freeze was to be put on the level of Russian military equipment currently in these areas. By 31 May 1999 Russia would be obliged to lower its force levels in these areas, but even then Moscow could still deploy more equipment there than was envisaged by the original CFE Treaty (*The Economist* 8 June 1996). This so-called compromise was, in a sense, a victory for Moscow and a defeat for Turkey. International treaties in which Turkish officials may have placed confidence could be revised, and the modified treaty could then run counter to Turkey's perceived interests.

In the case of Nagorno-Karabakh, Ankara's efforts to further its policy objectives in the region through the use of various international bodies have met with only limited success. Initial attempts by the Turkish authorities to act as an impartial mediator between the factions warring over the disputed territory were doomed to failure because the Armenians accused Turkey of bias toward Azerbaijan. Turkey did succeed to secure its inclusion in the so-called Minsk Group of states which was mandated by the Conference on Security and Cooperation in Europe (CSCE) and then by its successor, the Organization for Security and Cooperation in Europe (OSCE), to search for a peaceful solution to the Nagorno-Karabakh issue. But a Russian initiative led to the announcement of a truce—but not a permanent cease-fire—in spring 1994. After Armenian forces seized Azerbaijani territory beyond the disputed enclave, Turkey was one of the co-sponsors of UN Security Council resolutions that demanded the immediate withdrawal of these forces and that emphasized the need to guarantee the territorial integrity of Azerbaijan. It seemed, though, that Turkish officials had been hoping that the UN would impose economic sanctions on Armenia. In spite of UN Security Council resolutions at the time of writing, large portions of Azerbaijani terriory beyond Nagorno-Karabakh remained under Armenian occupation.

Turkish officials have also endeavored to make use of the CSCE/OSCE to prevent Moscow from ensuring that only CIS peacekeeping forces (i.e., Russian-dominated forces) should be stationed in Russia's so-called near abroad— the former Soviet Union, in effect. With regard to the Transcaucasus, Turkey has had mixed success. Fierce lobbying in the CSCE by Turkish delegates failed to thwart Russia from deploying a CIS peacekeeping force to separate the warring Georgians and Abkhazians in July 1994. Ankara had to console itself by being allowed to send a small contingent as part of a UN observer mission that was established to monitor developments in Abkhazia. But further vigorous campaigning by Turkish representatives secured a pledge from the CSCE Budapest Summit in December 1994 that once a permanent cease-fire was secured in Nagorno-Karabakh, an OSCE peacekeeping force operating under a mandate of the UN Security Council would be deployed. Turkey has offered to dispatch 480 troops for this force and is ready to prepare a logistical support base for the OSCE in eastern Turkey. Armenia is opposed to the participation of Turkish forces in an OSCE peacekeeping operation.

Concerning Turkey's bilateral relations with states in the Transcaucasus, it seems that, initially, Ankara placed too much emphasis on its ties with Baku. Common Turkic bonds largely accounted for Turkey's interest in Azerbaijan, but economic factors were also important. In March 1993 the pro-Turkish president of Azerbaijan, Elchibey, signed a draft agreement that anticipated the transport per annum of 25 million metric tons of Azerbaijani oil and 15 million metric tons of Kazakh oil to the Turkish Mediterranean port of Ceyhan through the construction of a pipeline from Baku (Roberts 1996: 48). Immediately before this agreement was about to be finalized, Elchibey was deposed in what appears to have been a Russian-backed military coup. Moscow would prefer oil from Azerbaijan and Kazakhstan to be piped to the Russian Black Sea port of Novorossiisk rather than be transported across Turkey. Since Aliyev has been in power, Turkish-Azerbaijani relations have not progressed entirely smoothly. The pipeline deal negotiated by Elchibey was swiftly abrogated. Aliyev accused the Turkish intelligence services of involvement in an alleged coup attempt against him in March 1995. The Turkish prime minister at the time, Tansu Çiller, apologized to Aliyev for the work of "an uncontrollable Turkish right wing group" (*Turkish Daily News* 14 April 1995). Aliyev has also charged the Ankara-based Azerbaijan Cultural Association of being involved in criminal activities in Azerbaijan (*Cumhuriyet* 23 June 1996).

As of fall 1996 it was far from clear whether or not Azerbaijani oil from Caspian offshore oil fields would eventually be transported across Turkey by a new Baku-Ceyhan pipeline. It would seem that Russia still does not look favorably on this project. In October 1995 the AIOC, in effect, procrastinated and, instead of taking a final decision on the route or routes for the transport of the "main oil" from its Azerbaijani oil fields, rather agreed to carry only "early oil" from these oil fields to Novorossiisk and the Georgian Black sea port of Soupsa. The AIOC president, Terry Adams, has indicated that more than one route could be finally used for the transport of the main oil. Turkish officials also do not want to give the impression that this is a zero-sum game in which either Turkey or Russia must win or lose. Thus, Turkey obtained Russia's support to participate in a joint working group with Kazakh and Azerbaijani representatives to explore the possibility of constructing an oil pipeline from the Caspian to the Mediterranean. However, this group has achieved little hitherto (İskit 1996: 72). Although, in reality, it would seem that the two are major competitors in regional pipeline politics, it should also be remembered that Turkey and Russia are important trade partners and that Turkish companies have invested up to $6 billion in Russia. Russia is a vital supplier of energy for Turkey, particularly in the deliveries of natural gas. Turkey's consumption of some of the Azerbaijani and Kazakh oil that might be carried across Turkish territory would help to reduce Turkey's increasing energy dependence on Russia.

Pipeline politics has led to Turkey's focusing more attention on developing closer ties with Georgia. Given the difficulties in relations between Ankara and Yerevan, oil and gas pipelines running from the Caspian and Central Asia to the Turkish Mediterranean would most probably have to pass through Georgia. Turkish officials are thus eager to support Georgia's territorial integrity in the face of secessionist bids by the Abkhazians and South Ossetians and are anxious to check the increasing Russian influence in Georgia. The authorities in Ankara have even proposed the formation of a Benelux-type economic union for Turkey and the three states of the Transcaucasus. This could consist of a visa-free, preferential trading area (*Cumhuriyet* 4 August 1996). Speaking at a press conference in Turkey in April 1996, the Georgian leader Shevardnadze reiterated his support for such a union (*Cumhuriyet* 5 April 1996). In reality, such a scheme is unlikely for the foreseeable future on account of Russian opposition and probable Armenian suspicions. Significantly, in June 1996 Russia convened on its territory a summit meeting on the Caucasus attended by the representatives of Russia, the three Transcaucasian states, and the leaders of the north Caucasian republics within the Russian Federation. Turkey was not invited to participate, although several weeks earlier Shevardnadze had insisted that Turkey should be included in such talks (*Yeni Yüzyıl* 4 April 1996; *Monitor* [Jamestown Foundation] 1 March 1996). Immediately before the summit the Anatolian news agency questioned the rationale behind such a gathering without Turkey, while in what appeared to be a reference to Turkey, Yeltsin warned that no one should attempt to drive a wedge between Russia and the Caucasus (*Open Media Research Institute* June 1996).

Although Turkey did recognize Armenia as an independent state in December 1991, diplomatic relations between the two states have yet to be established. It is unlikely that there will be a normalization of relations until there is a permanent peace settlement for Nagorno-Karabakh. It would seem that Armenian claims of a genocide committed by the Ottomans in the First World War and Turkish concerns that some Armenian nationalists harbor claims on Turkey's eastern territories will not, in the long term, obstruct the development of ties between Armenia and Turkey. Certainly, the business communities in both states are pressing for a marked improvement in relations in order to promote trade. Heading a commercial delegation in Turkey in August 1996, Telman Ter Petrosian, the elder brother of the Armenian president, repeatedly appealed for the normalization of relations and the reopening of border gates. According to Ter Petrosian, within the space of a few years bilateral trade turnover between Turkey and Armenia could amount to $600–700 million (*Cumhuriyet* 2 August 1996; *Yeni Yüzyıl* 4 August 1996).

TURKEY AND CENTRAL ASIA

With regard to Central Asia, the post-Soviet world refers to the newly independent states of Kazakhstan, Kyrgyzstan, Tajikistan, Turkmenistan, and Uzbekistan. Post-Soviet Central Asia as a region is connected with the Caspian Sea and the Transcaucasus to the west, to Afghanistan, Mongolia, and China to the south and east, and also to the Middle East through the neighboring territory of Iran. With the exception of Tajikistan—also bearing in mind the large Russian-speaking minority in Kazakhstan—post-Soviet Central Asia is predominantly inhabited by peoples of Turkic ethnic stock. The former Soviet republics in this area are confronted with the problems of economic transition from planned to free market economies and are each engaged in the process of state and nation building. But each of these states is pursuing its own particular policies. Post-Soviet Central Asia should not be regarded as a monolithic unit.

With the disintegration of the Soviet Union, the Central Asians literally had independence thrust upon them. Many commentators referred to a new "great game" for influence in the region between especially Turkey, Iran, and a Russia concerned about the possible spread of radical Islam from the area and apprehensive about the fate of over 9 million Russians living in Central Asia. China, Pakistan, Saudi Arabia, Israel, the United States, the EU, and other states were also attracted to the region. In practice, references to a supposed great game are simplifications of a more complex reality. In addition to competition there are also elements of cooperation between Turkey, Russia, and Iran in the region. Another problem with the great game analogy is that it erroneously assumes that the Central Asians themselves are mere passive bystanders.

At the time of the breakup of the Soviet Union there were great expectations and high hopes in Turkey concerning the cultivation of close ties with the Central Asian Turkic republics. Turkish officials and the media whipped up popular enthusiasm in Turkey over the rediscovery of the long-forgotten "Turks" of Central Asia. Here was an opportunity to boost Turkey's prestige and increase the country's international stature in the eyes of the West. The U.S. administration in particular was eager to promote the importance and relevance of the "Turkish model" for the region as an alternative to the so-called Iranian model of "Islamic fundamentalism." The Central Asian leaderships themselves, desperate for international recognition and political and economic support, eagerly responded to overtures from Ankara. In late January 1992 an article in the magazine *Newsweek* was headlined "Turkey: Central Asia's Dominant Power." Certainly, by mid-1992 Turkey had made a "bold bid for leadership and influence in the region in the political, financial, cultural, military, and economic areas" (Aydın 1996: 163).

This euphoria was short-lived. The first Turkic Summit convened in Ankara in October 1992 and, attended by the leaders of Turkey, the Central Asian Turkic states, and Azerbaijan, proved to be a major disappointment for Turkish officials. The then president of Turkey, Turgut Özal, had declared that the twenty-first century would be the century of the Turks. Özal spoke of the creation of a "Turkic" Trade and Development Bank and a "Turkic" Common Market. However, the first Turkic Summit was concluded with only the formation of various working groups and the release of a vaguely worded declaration short on specific commitments. The more confident newly independent states, bearing in mind the shortcomings of the Turkish economy, were by this time aware of the limits of Turkish economic aid. The Central Asians and Azerbaijanis were eager to secure political and economic support from whatever quarter and were not prepared to bind themselves to exclusively "Turkic" bodies. Nevertheless, Turkey was destined to remain an important actor in post-Soviet Central Asia.

The "failure" of the Ankara Summit appears to have prompted Western commentators to reassess Turkey's role in Central Asia. According to one commonly expressed argument, Turkish officials assumed a more cautious and realistic attitude and were no longer motivated by sentiment but rather concerned with political and economic self-interest.[6] Certainly, most of the Kazakhs, Kyrgyz, Turkmens, and others were beginning to regard themselves as part of a Kazakh, Kyrgyz, or Turkmen nation. At most, they were prepared to consider themselves as part of a wider ethnic Turkic umbrella. They did not perceive themselves as being "Turkish" or "Turkish-speaking." But officials in Ankara continue to lay great emphasis on the importance of common ethnolinguistic criteria. They refer to the Central Asians as Turks who are part of the "Turkish" or "Turkish-speaking" world. Officially, in Ankara, the Turkic summits are referred to as "summits of the Turkish-speaking countries." The Ministries of Education and Culture, in particular in Turkey, appear to be attracted to what may be identified as cultural Pan-Turkism. The Pan-Turkist Alparslan Türkeş has organized in Turkey a series of Turkic States and Turkic Peoples' Friendship and Cooperation Summits attended by delegates from not only Azerbaijan and post-Soviet Central Asia but also by "Turks" from republics and regions within the Russian Federation, such as Tatarstan, Bashkortostan, Yakutia, and Tuva. Although nonofficial gatherings, various Turkish heads of state and government have addressed these meetings.

Russian officials, always ready to exaggerate the threat posed by the Pan-Turkic bogeyman, have expressed their alarm at the convening of the official Turkic Summits and the nonofficial Turkic States and Turkic Peoples' Friendship and Cooperation Summits. When the Second Turkic Summit was about to open in Istanbul in October 1994, the spokesman of the Russian Ministry of Foreign Affairs noted, "It is unthinkable that a summit based on the principle of nationality will not disturb Russia." He added that the Antalya gathering of the Turkic States and Turkic Peoples the previous year was an earlier example of aggressive nationalism (*Turkish Daily News* and *Hürriyet* 19 October 1994). Significantly, when visiting Moscow as Turkish prime minister in September 1993, Çiller reportedly criticized President Demirel's past use of slogans which referred to an enlarged Turkish world. Çiller noted that such provocative remarks undermined trust between Ankara and Moscow (*Hürriyet* 9 September 1993).

The Turkic Summits, another initiative of Turkey, have not resulted in the creation of an organization of Turkic states. Rather, the summits have become a regular forum for discussion. Institutionalization of ties between the Turkic states is limited. The summits—which are now meant to be held annually— have led to periodic meetings of the foreign ministers, education ministers, and culture ministers of the participating states. There is also a measure of inter-parliamentary cooperation. It is open to question, though, whether or not, initially, certain Turkish officials may have hoped that the Turkic Summits could have evolved into something more substantive. For example, on a tour of Central Asia as prime minister in spring 1992, Demirel had openly spoken of the possibilities of forming an "association of independent Turkish/Turkic states" (*Turkish Daily News* 4 May 1992).[7] Did Demirel have in mind the emergence of some sort of Turkic Commonwealth? Immediately before the Second Turkic Summit in October 1994, the then speaker of the Turkish Parliament, Cindoruk, in talks with President Nursultan Nazarbayev of Kazakhstan, proposed that the Turkic states could cooperate more closely by taking BSEC as a model (*Hürriyet* 18 October 1994). The Central Asians were not prepared to countenance such suggestions. However, the Turkic Summits continue. One analyst has questioned the value of these meetings and argued that it would be better for peace and stability in the area if Turkey were to assume the role of a "catalytic agent" in the establishment of "regional regimes" that should be functional in nature and possibly linked to other regional and extra-regional actors (Kramer 1996: 126–7). The Economic Cooperation Organization (ECO) is an example of such a regional regime.

The Turkic Summits are not under the tight control of Ankara. The Central Asians also have a say in setting the agenda of the meetings. Thus, the Bishkek Declaration issued in August 1995 at the conclusion of the Third Turkic Summit expressed support for the efforts of Kazakhstan, Kyrgyzstan, and Uzbekistan to set in motion and expand "integration processes" in Central Asia in which Turkey was not involved. This was a reference to the attempts of these three states to become more integrated economically and politically. The declaration also noted that all the participating states pledged to boost bilateral and multilateral economic ties "without undermining their current international obligations."[8] This appears to have been a reference to the ties of the Central Asians and Azerbaijan to the CIS and Turkey's commitments to the EU.

With regard to bilateral relations, Turkish policy-makers appear to be concentrating their attention specifically on Kazakhstan, Turkmenistan, and Uzbekistan. Each of these states is endowed with important raw materials and sources of energy such as oil and gas, and it seems that Kazakhstan and Uzbekistan in particular are competing to be regional hegemons. In May 1996 in Tashkent Presidents Demirel and Islam Kerimov signed an "Eternal" Friendship and Cooperation Treaty between Turkey and Uzbekistan. Turkey had not previously concluded a treaty of such nature (*Cumhuriyet* 9 May 1996). Traditionally, relations between Turkey and the Persian-speaking Tajikistan have been less close. Russia has maintained a dominant influence in strife-ridden Tajikistan. Turkish officials seem to be less concerned about developments in Kyrgyzstan, which is likely to come under the increasing economic (and possibly political) influence of China.

The relationship between Turkey and Iran in general and with regard to Central Asia specifically is a complex one. This became even more so with the emergence of a Welfare Party-dominated government in Ankara. Traditionally, ideologically secular Turkey and theocratic Iran were poles apart. The Turks also suspected that Iran was supporting Kurdish insurgents hostile to the Turkish state. But Ankara and Tehran are important trading partners. Central Asia is a region of less immediate strategic significance for Turkey. Consequently, in contrast to the Transcaucasus, relations between Ankara and Tehran and, indeed, between Ankara and Moscow are less fraught with tension. But Iran has considered Turkey as being, in effect, a vehicle for the United States to extend its influence in Central Asia.

Both Turkey and Iran are members of ECO, together with Pakistan, Afghanistan, and the post-Soviet Central Asian states. Iran sponsored the formation of ECO, and it was due to Tehran's prompting that the newly independent Central Asians were admitted to the organization in 1992. The Turkish authorities most probably would have preferred to work with the Central Asians through their own "Turkic" multilateral mechanism, but, as noted earlier, the post-Soviet republics were eager to diversify their ties. One commentator has shrewdly noted that ECO serves as a forum where Turkey and Iran may make public their interest in regional cooperation and where, perhaps more important, the two could keep a "watchful eye" over each other (Barkey 1995: 162). The two states have differed over the organization's economic objectives. Iran has lobbied for member states to scrap outright their tariffs in trade with one another. Because of its commitments to the EU, Turkey has favored only the establishment of a preferential trading arrangement to boost trade.

Concerning pipeline politics and the transportation of Central Asian oil and gas, Iran and Turkey are both potential rivals and partners. In theory, Kazakh oil and Turkmen gas could be carried to the Persian Gulf instead of to the Turkish Mediterranean. But although Kazakhstan and Iran have agreed to a swap deal that involves the delivery of a certain amount of Kazakh oil to northern Iran, it is extremely unlikely that oil from the Tengiz oil field in Kazakhstan will flow in the same direction, because of the active involvement of the U.S. oil company Chevron in the Tengiz deal. In August 1996 on a visit to Tehran, Prime Minister Erbakan signed a $20 billion natural gas deal. After the construction of a gas pipeline between Tabriz and Ankara, Turkey would eventually import up to 10 billion cubic metres of Iranian gas. An important point to note here is that this pipeline could complement a Turkmen-Iran natural gas project and could also form a section of a possible Turkmenistan-Iran-Turkey-Europe gas pipeline, which has been the subject of discussion since 1992 (Roberts 1996: 69).

The leaderships in Ankara, Moscow, and in the newly independent Central Asian states share a fear of the spread of political Islam in the region, which is more likely to originate from Afghanistan rather than from Iran, bearing in mind the largely pragmatic nature of Iranian policy toward Central Asia. The authorities in Ankara appear to be aware that the Central Asians wish to remain under a Russian security umbrella. However, in May 1996 Demirel and Kerimov expressed their "irritation" at the "moves" and "expressions" seemingly aimed at restoring the Soviet Union following the signing of an agreement on economic and cultural integration between Russia, Belarus, Kazakhstan, and Kyrgyzstan (*Yeni Yüzyıl* 9 May 1996).

As in the case of Turkey and Iran, Turkey and Russia could also cooperate as well as compete with regard to the passage of Turkmen gas and Kazakh oil. Turkmenistan has been dependent on exporting its gas to the West via the Russian network of pipelines. But, interestingly, Russia, along with Turkey, is represented on the steering committee set up to explore means by which Turkmen gas could be piped to Europe. Perhaps because of the costs involved—$7 billion, according to some estimates—the Russians may believe that a Turkmenistan-Iran-Turkey-Europe gas pipeline may never be completed. Moscow, though, is also prepared to transport Turkmen gas to Turkey via Russia and Georgia (*Pipeline News* 27 July–2 August 1996). Turkey would thereby remain dependent on Russian goodwill for the transport of Turkmen gas. Turkish officials have also lobbied for the transport of Kazakh oil from the Tengiz oil field to Turkey which would be in addition to the new oil pipeline that is being built by the Caspian Pipeline Consortium to connect Tengiz with Novorossiisk. In the eyes of Turkish officials at least a second route across the Caspian—possibly by tanker—and then through the Transcaucasus and Turkey, joining up at some point with a Baku-Ceyhan oil pipeline, could thus complement a new Tengiz-Novorossiisk connection. It would seem though that Moscow would wish to maintain a monpoly on the transport of oil from Tengiz to the West.

CONCLUSION

It is not clear how Turkish governments in the future will respond to developments in the Black Sea, the Transcaucasus, and Central Asia. This will be dependent, to some extent, on the nature of the government in Ankara. An administration under the Welfare Party's sole control, no longer constrained by coalition partners, could attempt to embark on a radical change of course in Turkish foreign policy. Or a change of regime in Moscow especially, but also in other states of the post-Soviet world, could force Turkish policy-makers to reassess their position.

Turkish officials have emphasized the importance of Turkey's geographical location and depicted their state as forming the center of "Eurasia." Eurasia in this context appears to consist of at least Europe and the territory of the former Soviet Union. When touring Tajikistan and Mongolia in September 1995, President Demirel remarked that these states and also Afghanistan formed part of Eurasia. The Turkish press wildly speculated at the time that Turkey had become interested in creating a "Eurasian Union" as opposed to a more territorially limited "Turkic Union" (*Turkish Daily News* and *Yeni Yüzyıl* 12 September 1995). Turkish officials may continue to promote what has, in effect, become a "Eurasian" line in their policy toward the post-Soviet world. Turkey is thus able to exploit both its European and Asian identities. Entry to the EU is pursued while simultaneously seeking to cultivate special ties with the "Turkic" world. But there may be other "Eurasian" lines that could, for instance, seek to place greater emphasis on the Turkic world at the expense of Europe. A future Welfare Party government could develop the latter course of action. The Welfare Party could attempt to combine such a policy with its traditional interest in furthering relations with Moslem states. But that could set Turkey on a collision course with Iran over leadership of the "Islamic world," with Russia over Moscow's fear of the spread of radical politicized Islam, and with the various regimes in Central Asia and the Transcaucasus that are determined to maintain a secular approach. However, in attempting to make predictions more concrete, realities, including, for example, pipeline politics, should also be taken into consideration. At present, though, Turkey's political role in the post-Soviet world is still evolving.

NOTES

1. For a debate on this topic see Snyder (1995) and Winrow (1995a).

2. With the prospects of a greatly expanded membership for BSEC in the future this cooperative scheme may be renamed, and the term "Black Sea" substituted.

3. For the texts of the Summit Declaration and the Bosphorus Statement, 25 June 1992, see BSEC (1994: 51–60).

4. Interview with a Turkish official in PABSEC, June 1995.

5. There are approximately 150,000 Orthodox Christian Gagauz Turks living in southern Moldova.

6. See, for example, Carley (1995).

7. Because of direct translation problems from Turkish to English it is not possible to distinguish between the terms "Turkic" and "Turkish" when used in Turkish.

8. The text of the Bishkek Declaration was provided by the Turkish Foreign Ministry.

7

The Black Sea Economic Cooperation Project
Serdar Sayan and Osman Zaim

INTRODUCTION

The late 1980s and the early 1990s witnessed profound changes in Europe, the Middle East and the world. Disintegration of the Soviet bloc was followed by the collapse of the Soviet Union itself. The outbreak of the Gulf War just before the formal dissolution of the USSR dramatically upset strategic balances. Somewhat baffled, the world community was forced to reconsider political and economic priorities in international relations. Due to its truly unique position as a country in the Balkans and in the Middle East, with a Black Sea as well as a Mediterranean coastline, and as a North Atlantic Treaty Organization (NATO) member sharing a common border with the former USSR in the Caucasus, this shuffling of the world order put special challenges before Turkey. This part of the world around the country was going through a rapid transformation, and Turkey had to adjust to this changing environment. The broader challenge facing Turkey in this new environment was the need to contribute to the restoration of peace and stability in its region while capitalizing on the opportunities presented by the developments. One initiative that Turkey took to meet this challenge was its active leadership in the formation of the Black Sea Economic Cooperation (BSEC) organization. The BSEC project was intended to serve regional peace and stability, as well as economic development through "the establishment of solid and effective mechanisms in order to achieve a higher degree of economic cooperation" among countries surrounding the Black Sea.[1]

The purpose of this chapter is to discuss the development of the BSEC project since its inception and to evaluate the economic implications for Turkey of BSEC membership. The chapter also investigates the effects of BSEC on the magnitude and the directions of Turkey's trade with other BSEC members and non-member countries in the region.

THE ESTABLISHMENT OF BSEC

As a party to NATO's containment policy under Cold War arrangements, Turkey had carefully distanced itself from its neighbors to the north. Likewise, its insistence on the maintenance of a secular, democratic regime, and a Western orientation with a predominantly Muslim population had set Turkey apart from the neighbors to the east and south. Despite their competing national ambitions and the differences in their regimes, views of the world, and cultures, Turkey managed to pursue mostly peaceful relations with its neighbors prior to the late 1980s and did not allow its relations with the West to become too binding a constraint on its relations with others elsewhere. In these surroundings, the cost of leaning too much toward a certain country or a group could range from isolation to war (Ergüvenç 1995). Turkey avoided serious conflicts and complete isolation largely by maintaining a low profile in its relations with neighbors.

The disintegration of the Soviet bloc relaxed the constraints upon Turkish foreign policy and cleared the way for Turkey's geo-strategic position to begin serving as a bridge and a major trade route in the area. This, in fact, represented the opening of new horizons for Turkey, as it offered the opportunity to mend long-damaged relations not only with the peoples living across the borders to the north but also with the newly independent Turkic republics of Central Asia and Azerbaijan—the peoples of which share the same racial and cultural background as Turks of Turkey. The challenge facing Turkey, in a broad sense, was to use this opportunity by contributing to the resolution of conflicts and without adding new animosities to the existing ones in the region.

Turkey had, and still has, an evident interest in peace and stability in the region, and the best way to maintain peace was to develop vested interests through economic cooperation. Such cooperation would put an end to animosities leading to welfare gains for all parties involved.[2]

Despite some ethnic grievances in the Balkans and the Caucasus, Turkey, with its experience in the development of a secular, democratic regime and a relatively well functioning free market economy, was the only role model for most of the newly independent states of the region. These states were also viewing Turkey as a likely source of technical and economic assistance in their own transition to a free market economy and a secular democracy. Turkey, therefore, stood as the only regional power capable of playing an active role in building confidence among countries of the region and the only candidate to lead regional cooperation efforts.

Actually assuming such a leadership role required Turkey to quit the low-profile foreign policy it had traditionally pursued, but the country was ready for this. Having strengthened its economy and significantly increased its international competitiveness through economic reforms of the 1980s, Turkey entered the 1990s as an emerging regional power and, with the associated self-confidence, willingly began to present itself as a role model to the transition states in the region.

President Turgut Özal himself was especially enthusiastic about this regional role that the country could play. Thus, when the formation of a regional organization for economic cooperation among countries around the Black Sea was suggested first in 1990 by Ambassador Şükrü Elekdağ, former head of the Turkish mission in Washington, D.C.,[3] Özal immediately reacted by starting a campaign to promote the idea (Garih 1995).

Taking the initiative on the formation of a regional organization for economic cooperation was consistent with the leadership role Turkey was ready to assume. Aside from purely economic concerns, President Özal perceived the BSEC project as a Turkish initiative that would not only contribute to the restoration of peace and stability in the region but also serve as a confirmation of the new status of Turkey as a regional power. The idea found support not only from the Turkish public but also from prospective members in the area.[4]

Although what was initially envisaged was the gradual formation of a free trade zone (with the possibility that it would evolve into a stronger form of integration) among countries with a Black Sea coastline, it was agreed later that the project would aim at the formation of a regional organization for economic cooperation in a broad sense, that is, an organization that would not require strong commitments from participating states.

The talks toward the formation of BSEC started with the Ankara meeting in December 1990 in Turkey. In addition to official representatives from Turkey, Bulgaria, and Romania, the meeting was attended by the vice-foreign ministers of Armenia, Azerbaijan, Georgia, and Moldova as well as by Russian officials. At the end of the Ankara meeting, the participants officially declared that they agreed to form a Black Sea Economic Cooperation Zone.

The Ankara meeting was followed by two technical meetings (Bucharest, Romania, in March 1991 and Sofia, Bulgaria, in April 1991), which convened to lay out the principles of the cooperation agreement. Finally, it was decided in a July 1991 meeting in Moscow that the agreement was ready for ratification. When the foreign ministers of Armenia, Azerbaijan, Bulgaria, Georgia, Moldova, Romania, the Russian Federation, Turkey, and the Ukraine got together in February 1992 in Istanbul, they reaffirmed their commitment to the project and decided to convene again in June 1992 to sign the declaration of the agreement. The ministers also agreed that Greece and Yugoslavia, attending the Moscow meeting with observer status, could be accepted as founding members provided that they apply to the Turkish Ministry of Foreign Affairs by the end of May 1992.

Following the application of Greece and, later, of Albania, the agreement (Black Sea Economic Cooperation Summit Declaration) was signed on 25 June 1992 in Istanbul by the presidents or prime ministers of 11 states—9 attending the February meeting in Istanbul plus Albania and Greece.[5]

BSEC PROJECT AS A MODEL FOR REGIONAL
ECONOMIC COOPERATION

Based on "the potential of the Participating States and the opportunities for enhancing the mutually advantageous economic cooperation arising from their geographic proximity and from the reform process and structural adjustments" (Article 3), the heads of state and government signing the Summit Declaration in Istanbul confirmed their "intention to develop economic cooperation as a contribution to the CSCE [Conference on Security and Cooperation in Europe] process, to the establishment of a Europe-wide economic area, as well as to the achievement of a higher degree of integration of the Participating States into the world economy" (Article 5).[6]

The Summit Declaration makes it clear that economic cooperation is viewed as a means to contribute, first and foremost, to the peace and security in the region. Various articles addressing peace and security issues reflect the security concerns of the summit participants. This is, in fact, evident also from the wording of the Bosphorus Statement issued after the summit.[7] This seems natural, once it is recognized that BSEC is an organization that was formed under special circumstances. There were unresolved problems among ex-Soviet republics, as well as varying degrees of bilateral conflicts and grievances, such as those between Armenia and Azerbaijan, Moldova, and Romania, and even Turkey and Greece. The existence of such tensions, coupled with the need to maintain stability in the region, assigned BSEC a political mission as a forum for dialogue and peaceful settlement of disputes, alongside economic considerations.

In view of the specific conditions of the participating states, the formation of BSEC was special also from an economic perspective. At the time of the formation of BSEC, all member economies except for Greece and Turkey were, for all practical purposes, centrally planned economies. Although they are considered transition economies trying to complete their integration into the world economy, BSEC might be viewed as the first (if not the only) economic cooperation organization formed between centrally planned economies and market economies. This point should not be overlooked in evaluating the performance or the structure of BSEC as a form of economic integration. The following discussion explains why.

The fundamental motivation behind any regional economic cooperation agreement among market economies is to improve welfare of the members through a reduction or elimination of barriers to trade in the region. The welfare gains that would accrue to members would, in the static sense, depend on the relative magnitudes of trade creation effects that tend to improve welfare and trade diversion effects that tend to decrease welfare.[8] Trade creation arises when domestic production in a certain sector of a member country is replaced, partly or entirely, by imports from another member that produces that output more efficiently, that is, at a lower cost. In this case, the more efficient producer is said to have a comparative advantage in that sector. Trade diversion, on the other hand, follows when a member quits importing from a third (non-member) party and starts importing the same commodities from another member, even though the cost of doing so is higher. Naturally, such a switch made on account of common membership decreases the welfare of the importing member. As long as the size of trade creation effect exceeds that of trade diversion, there will be net welfare gains.

Even leaving the non-economic considerations aside, several factors limit the usefulness of such a static welfare framework in explaining the rationale behind the formation of BSEC. One reason for this is that cooperation through BSEC does not require strong commitments on the part of members. It was agreed during the BSEC talks prior to the signing of the agreement that the integration would not be "an *a priori* commitment" for the participants.[9] Special conditions of the formerly communist members prevented them from committing to such an end. Article 10 of the BSEC Summit Declaration explicitly states that "the economic cooperation will be promoted gradually and, while determining the priorities in this process, they will take into account the specific economic conditions, interests and concerns of the countries involved, and particularly the problems of the countries in transition to market economy." Although the current BSEC structure does not exclude the possibility that consideration to such integration could be given later on, caution is required in taking the existing forms of regional integration arrangements as a reference for an evaluation of the performance or the structure of BSEC. A closer examination of the integration literature reveals that it would be very difficult indeed to classify BSEC as an example of any of the regional arrangements varying from preferential trade agreements to economic unions.[10] Judging from a trade policy perspective alone, the closest BSEC would get would be a preferential trade agreement requiring the parties to lower trade barriers among themselves. Under the circumstances, trade diversion effects in the sense described earlier are not likely to arise due solely to BSEC membership. Although there currently is some diverted trade going on between ex-Soviet bloc members of BSEC, this should be viewed as a continuation of a trend that started before the formation of BSEC. BSEC does have the potential to generate trade creation effects, as it aims to lower barriers to trade between its members. But even then, one should be careful about the nature of the barriers to be lowered. The barriers in this context are not of the type analyzed in the existing integration literature, and the trade creation effects resulting from their removal are not likely to lead to instantaneous welfare gains, limiting the usefulness of the static framework used in that literature.

By the BSEC Summit Declaration, the Participating States will promote their cooperation by "contributing," among others, "to the expansion of their mutual trade in goods and services and ensuring conditions favorable to such development by continuing their efforts to further reduce or progressively eliminate obstacles of all kinds, in a manner not contravening their obligations toward third parties." While this seems to represent a commitment to an across-the-board elimination of all barriers to trade among members, two warnings must be noted. First, the "obstacles" mentioned here refer mostly to *structural* barriers rather than tariff and non-tariff barriers in the conventional trade theory sense of the terms. Second, given that Greece is a member of, and Turkey is in a customs union with, the EU, there is little room for setting the levels of conventional barriers independently and without contravening commitments with third parties. As we describe in greater detail later, those structural barriers, in fact, determined the pre-BSEC trade patterns among current members.

These trade patterns could be characterized not so much by the lack of trade among members at large but rather by the lack of trade between Turkey and Greece, on one hand, and the remaining members on the other. In explaining trade flows between these two groups prior to the formation of BSEC, two types of structural factors that acted as trade barriers must be distinguished: factors referring to the socioeconomic structure of the countries as a whole and those referring to sector-specific structural problems in member countries. Factors of the first type cover ideological differences as well as the differences in trade regimes and in the nature of hard currency constraints facing members. Those of the second type, on the other hand, have to do with a lack of channels that would facilitate trade.

Within this framework, the lack, despite the proximity mentioned in Article 3, of sizable trade between former Soviet bloc members joining BSEC and the other two was not due to barriers such as high tariffs or quotas. It was due, instead, to the first type of structural factors resulting from differences in socioeconomic structures. So, as far as trade between NATO and Warsaw Pact members is concerned, no barriers could be removed for the purposes of welfare gains through increased trade. Once members of COMECON, the countries in the latter group had considerable trade among themselves even before the formation of BSEC.[11] But this was due, this time, to the similarities in trade regimes and ideologies and the possibility of barter trade, which enabled these countries to avoid their hard-currency constraints. Another equally important reason was the high degree of interdependence (or complementarity) among the economies of these countries, especially of ex-Soviet republic members. This existence of strong input-output linkages between industries located across national borders within the bloc effectively developed this interdependence and largely explains the diverted nature and the size of intra-bloc trade.[12]

Distinct from conventional tariff and non-tariff barriers that may be removed almost instantly, the elimination of barriers resulting from socioeconomic differences requires a structural transformation, which takes time. This points to another reason that a static, conventional trade theory framework is not totally appropriate to an analysis of welfare gains through increased trade among BSEC members. The gains here are rather dynamic, and the speed at which they will accrue to members, and their magnitude depend on the success of structural transformation that formerly communist members of BSEC undertake. In fact, the members have already started enjoying these gains, which are expected to continue as the formerly communist members proceed with their structural transformation and transition to a market economy. During the process, the market price signals become more and more relevant for their resource allocation decisions. However long it may take, the inefficient industries created under the interdependence schemes of Soviet planning will eventually be reformed or scrapped in favor of efficient industries. This is expected to lead to a change in the trade patterns of ex-Soviet bloc members by allowing them to specialize according to their natural comparative advantages. Once this transformation is complete, these economies will become enabled to generate the hard-currency receipts they need to finance their imports from whatever source they deem cost-effective. BSEC aims to act as a catalyst in this process by facilitating the integration of these countries into the world economy. In addition to Article 5, highlighting the role of BSEC as a channel for the integration of its members into the world economy, Article 7 made it absolutely clear that BSEC would not prevent members from participating in, and developing relations with, "third parties, including international organizations as well as the EC," nor would it prevent cooperation of members within other regional initiatives. Taken together, Articles 3, 5, and 7 may be argued to have been included to promote regionalism without violating the spirit of globalism.[13]

The magnitude of dynamic gains is expected to grow as the structural barriers are also removed over time. The removal of these barriers having to do with the inefficiency of channels for trade requires major restructuring and reorganization in many sectors and areas. Given the meager state of transportation and communications infrastructure in many of the member countries, for example, increasing the volume of trade flows would require more than a trade liberalization agreement to eliminate tariff and non-tariff barriers. Even in the complete absence of such barriers, the poor infrastructure for transportation and a lack of dependable communications facilities would impose structural barriers physically preventing larger volumes of trade among the members (Sayan 1996). BSEC aims to help this process through cooperation. Considering the importance of the issue, a Working Group [WG] on Transport and Communications was set up at the beginning. Later in December 1993, this WG was divided into two: the Working Group on Transport and the Working Group on Communications. Some of the projects carried out as recommended by the latter WG have already been completed. The projects include establishment of fiber-optic communications networks and radio link systems to connect Turkey (1) to Bulgaria, Romania, and Moldova (KAFOS); (2) to Italy, Ukraine, and Russia (ITUR); and (3) to Azerbaijan and Georgia (DOKAP). The work on other projects aimed at the improvement of the efficiency of the transportation network among members by integrating highways, railways, and maritime lines is currently under way (Sayan 1996).

In addition to tackling infrastructure problems, BSEC initiated cooperation in such fields as the standardization of products to be traded, harmonization of customs regulations and speeding up of customs formalities, and easing national visa regulations and the like so as to facilitate travel in the BSEC area by businessmen of member countries. While these may not be typical priority areas for other regional organizations trying to promote cooperation among members, they may play a significant role in preventing larger volumes of trade among BSEC members that are structurally different from each other. The incompatibility (or their lack, in some members) of banking regulations concerning financing of international trade, for example, posed serious difficulties for Turkish exporters, leading them to give up potential markets. An awareness of such structural problems was reflected by BSEC members at the very beginning when the Summit Declaration was signed: By Article 13 of the declaration, the establishment of the BSEC economic area was meant to encourage, first, the development of cooperation "in the fields of economics, including trade and industrial cooperation" but would also cover the fields of science and technology and the environment. Also, members decided to take concrete steps toward cooperation in quite a comprehensive list of areas: transport and communications, including their infrastructure; informatics; exchange of economic/commercial information, including statistics; standardization and certification of products; energy; mining and processing of mineral raw materials; tourism; agriculture and agro-industries; veterinary and sanitary protection; and health care and pharmaceutics.

As a closer look at this list of fields of cooperation would indicate, the task before BSEC as a regional economic cooperation organization is a more difficult one in comparison to similar organizations formed by market economies. Among others, the lack of private capital accumulation in ex-communist members poses special difficulties, as it implies the absence of a private sector. Despite an almost total lack of private property in these countries as recently as shortly before the formation of BSEC,[14] it was noted in Article 13 that the cooperation in all fields would be achieved by identifying, developing, and carrying out projects of common interest through an active participation of private enterprises and firms. This reflects BSEC's determination to help the structural transformation of these members by contributing to the creation of a market economy led by private enterprise. In order to maintain open channels for regular interaction between national business communities of the members and intergovernmental bodies of the BSEC, the BSEC Council (BSECC) was founded in 1992. The BSECC develops and maintains a network of useful contacts through bilateral business councils and chambers of commerce and similar national organizations.[15] The council is run by the board of directors headed by a chairman and is currently active in identifying private and public investment projects that are of common interest to members.[16]

The BSECC is only the inter-business component of an impressive organizational structure created within BSEC in just two years following the signing of Summit Declaration. This organizational structure, made up of intergovernmental, inter-parliamentary, inter-business, and financial bodies, was meant to be effective, operational, and non-bureaucratic. The intergovernmental component consists of the decision-making body, that is, the Meeting of the Ministers of Foreign Affairs (MMFA), the Sessional Officials Meeting, and the Working Groups of Experts as the subsidiary bodies established by the MMFA to deal with concrete issues. A Permanent International Secretariat was established and headquartered in Istanbul, Turkey. The Secretariat, working under the authority of the BSEC Sessional chairman, fully assumed its responsibilities as of March 1994.[17] The inter-parliamentary component was created in 1993, when the representatives of member countries (except Bulgaria and Greece) decided to establish the Parliamentary Assembly of the BSEC (PABSEC).

PABSEC aims, among others, include strengthening the pluralistic democratic structure and political stability in the BSEC area. The financial component of the BSEC structure is represented by the Black Sea Trade and Development Bank, which will have its headquarters in Thessaloniki, Greece. The bank is to become the principal source of financing within BSEC for implementation of joint regional projects. By a decision taken by the MMFA, the European Bank for Reconstruction and Development (EBRD) will be entrusted as the depository of the capital payments for the establishment of the Black Sea Bank until a different depository is picked by the bank itself (BSEC 1994).[18]

TURKEY-BSEC TRADE

An Overview

The BSEC area represents a vast territory, geographically diversified and well endowed with rich natural resources (such as gas, oil, coal, wood, and ore deposits, to mention a few) and populated by more than 300 million people. This rich natural resource base is coupled with human resource endowments made up of an often competitive and well-educated labor force.[19]

In terms of purchasing power parity (PPP) values of their per capita gross domestic products (GDPs), Albania is the poorest member, and Greece is the richest. With the exception of Albania and possibly Georgia, all members are middle- or upper-middle-income economies. It must be noted, however, that some members experienced wild fluctuations in their GDPs after their transition to a market economy began. Table 7.1 presents data on various indicators for member economies for the 1992–1994 period.

Member economies usually complement each other not only because of artificially developed linkages as in the case of former Soviet republics, but also naturally (Gültekin and Mumcu 1996: 196). In light of this complementarity, there appears to be room for mutually beneficial trade among members of BSEC, but the previously discussed structural differences have so far kept Turkey from developing even stronger trade ties to BSEC members.[20]

Past trade flows between Turkey and other members are presented in Tables 7.2 and 7.3. For comparison, figures for pre-BSEC years have also been included in the tables.

Trade share figures reported in Tables 7.2 and 7.3 indicate that Turkey has so far been a more important trade partner to some of the BSEC members than these members are to Turkey. When export shares are considered, the share of exports to Turkey in total exports of countries like Albania, Azerbaijan, and Georgia is typically much higher than the share in total Turkish exports of these countries. In the case of imports, the same observation can be made for countries like Azerbaijan and Georgia, but especially for Bulgaria and Ukraine. The situation is reversed for the Russian Federation in the case of both exports and imports, but the differences in shares are relatively smaller.

Table 7.1
Various Indicators of BSEC Members (1992–1994 Averages)

Country	GDP[a]	GDP per Capita[b]	GDP/Cap. Growth[c]	Population[d]	Pop. Growth[c]	Distance[e]
Albania	3.20	958	22	3.36	1.0	692
Armenia	7.87	2147	- 6	3.73	1.3	614
Azerbaijan	17.77	2446	-15	7.33	0.7	920
Bulgaria	33.90	3973	0	8.48	-0.6	530
Georgia	8.53	1578	-36	5.38	-0.5	634
Greece	89.93	8732	6	133	0.5	512
Moldova	14.87	3412	- 6	4.35	0.0	523
Romania	63.93	2791	2	22.76	-0.1	458
Russian Fed.	775.03	5218	-11	148.47	-0.1	1107
Turkey	278.87	4752	16	59.83	2.1	-
Ukraine	194.27	3731	-17	52.08	-0.2	733

Notes: [a] Purchasing Power Parity value in billions of dollars; [b] Purchasing Power Parity value in dollars; [c] Percent; [d] In millions; [e] Distance of the capital to Ankara, Turkey.

Sources: Data for columns 1 and 4 are from various issues of Central Intelligence Agency (CIA), *World Factbook* (on-line versions) and Economist Intelligence Unit (EIU), *Country Reports*. Distances in the last column were obtained from the on-line distance calculator at http://www.indo.com/distance. Per capita GDP figures as well as growth rates reported are the authors' calculations.

Also notable about the data in Tables 7.2 and 7.3 is the tendency toward increased trade between Turkey and BSEC members after the formation of BSEC. Especially in the case of exports, there is a nearly unbroken increase. But checking the validity of this argument requires further investigation, and such an investigation is formally carried out in the next section.

An Analysis of Trade Flows

To investigate the effects of BSEC membership on trade volume and patterns, different versions of a simple gravity model are employed. Inspired by Newtonian laws of gravity, the model is based on the argument that trade flows between two countries must be positively related to their economic "masses," i.e., GDPs, and inversely related to the distance between them.[21] The economic rationale behind this argument is that the potential of a country to supply products demanded by others depends on its own size, whereas the demand for these products is created (depends), to large extent, by (on) the income (size) of the demanding country. Thus, demand and supply potentials of trading partners can be measured by their respective GDPs. Yet, even when each of the two countries appears to be of the appropriate size to trade with the other, their trade potential will be inversely affected by the geographical distance between them, since this will increase transportation costs in terms of both freight charges and transportation time.

Table 7.2
Turkish Exports to BSEC Countries (millions of $)

	1990 TR Exp.	1990 Share 1	1990 Share 2	1991 TR Exp.	1991 Share 1	1991 Share 2	1992 TR Exp.	1992 Share 1	1992 Share 2	1993 TR Exp.	1993 Share 1	1993 Share 2	1994 TR Exp.	1994 Share 1	1994 Share 2	1995 TR Exp.	1995 Share 1	1995 Share 2
Albania	5.7	0.0	2.2	21.4	0.2	6.8	20.7	0.1	3.8	37.8	0.2	6.3	59.3	0.3	11.4	56.9	0.3	9.4
Armenia	–	–	–	–	–	–	3.4	0.0	n/a	–	–	–	–	–	–	–	–	–
Azerbaijan	–	–	–	–	–	–	102.3	0.7	13.0	68.2	0.4	9.5	132.1	0.7	16.7	161.3	0.7	18.3
Bulgaria	10.4	0.1	0.3	76.1	0.5	2.0	72.2	0.5	1.7	86.2	0.6	1.9	133.7	0.7	3.3	183.2	0.8	3.8
Georgia	–	–	–	–	–	–	11.6	0.1	1.8	34.5	0.2	4.8	67.1	0.4	8.4	68.1	0.3	6.8
Greece	139.4	1.1	0.8	143.7	1.0	0.9	145.7	1.0	0.7	118.1	0.8	0.7	168.9	0.9	0.9	210.0	1.0	0.9
Moldova	–	–	–	–	–	–	0.0	0.0	0.0	0.4	0.0	0.1	3.6	0.0	0.5	7.3	0.0	0.9
Romania	83.2	0.6	0.5	105.1	0.8	0.6	173.1	1.2	1.0	151.7	1.0	2.5	175.3	1.0	2.7	302.0	1.4	3.4
Russian F.	–	–	–	–	–	–	441.9	3.0	1.3	504.7	3.2	1.4	820.3	4.5	2.2	1238.2	5.6	3.0
Ukraine	–	–	–	–	–	–	35.9	0.2	0.7	39.5	0.3	1.4	76.3	0.4	2.2	198.5	0.9	5.7
USSR	531.1	4.1	n/a	610.6	4.5	n/a	–	–	–	–	–	–	–	–	–	–	–	–

Notes: TR Exp.: Turkish exports in millions of dollars.
Share 1 : Share of Exports to respective BSEC member in total Turkish exports.
Share 2 : Share of Exports to Turkey in total exports by the respective BSEC member.
n/a: Not available.

A Turkish embargo was imposed on Armenia in 1992 because of the failure by this country to cooperate in resolving the conflict over Nagarno-Karabakh, the Armenian enclave within Azerbaijan. Thus, officially there are no exports to (nor imports from) this country under the embargo, but Armenian sources report non-zero imports from Turkey indicating that some border trade is going on.

Sources: State Institute of Statistics (SIS) of Turkey, *Foreign Trade Statistics*, Ankara: SIS, 1994; SIS Web (http:// www.die.gov.tr/BSEC/bsec.html), and EIU, *Country Reports*, various issues.

Table 7.3
Turkish Imports from BSEC Countries (millions of $)

	1990			1991			1992			1993			1994			1995		
	TR Imp.	Share 1	Share 2	TR Imp.	Share 1	Share 2	TR Imp.	Share 1	Share 2	TR Imp.	Share 1	Share 2	TR Imp.	Share 1	Share 2	TR Imp.	Share 1	Share 2
Albania	1.5	0.0	0.6	0.6	0.0	0.2	0.9	0.0	1.3	1.8	0.0	1.3	1.5	0.0	1.1	1.3	0.0	0.7
Armenia	–	–	–	–	–	–	0.1	0.0	n/a	–	–	–	–	–	–	–	–	–
Azerbaijan	–	–	–	–	–	–	35.1	0.2	2.8	33.9	0.1	4.7	8.9	0.0	1.4	21.8	0.1	4.0
Bulgaria	31.9	0.1	1.0	139.9	0.7	3.7	224.5	1.0	5.6	243.2	0.8	6.6	195.5	0.9	5.0	402.0	1.1	7.9
Georgia	–	–	–	–	–	–	6.3	0.0	2.4	21.9	0.1	6.1	25.6	0.1	5.1	50.2	0.1	16.7
Greece	129.0	0.6	0.8	77.0	0.3	0.5	88.2	0.4	1.5	120.5	0.4	2.4	105.1	0.5	2.0	200.7	0.6	3.5
Moldova	–	–	–	–	–	–	1.7	0.0	0.4	28.9	0.1	6.0	20.5	0.1	3.2	15.6	0.0	2.1
Romania	202.5	0.9	2.2	198.6	0.9	3.7	256.1	1.1	5.8	300.8	1.0	6.1	228.9	1.0	3.7	367.9	1.0	4.9
Russian F.	–	–	–	–	–	–	1040.8	4.5	2.5	1542.3	5.2	3.4	1045.4	4.6	2.0	2082.4	5.9	3.2
Ukraine	–	–	–	–	–	–	90.0	0.4	1.5	472.7	1.6	11.3	535.1	2.4	11.6	856.3	2.4	16.5
USSR	1247.4	5.6	n/a	1096.6	5.2	n/a	–	–	n/a	–	–	–	–	–	–	–	–	–

Notes: TR Imp.: Turkish imports in millions of dollars.
Share 1 : Share of Imports to respective BSEC member in total Turkish imports.
Share 2 : Share of Imports to Turkey in total imports by the respective BSEC member.
n/a: Not available.

Sources: State Institute of Statistics (SIS) of Turkey, *Foreign Trade Statistics*, Ankara: SIS, 1994; SIS Web (http://www.die.gov.tr/BSEC/bsec.html), and EIU, *Country Reports*, various issues.

So, in its simplest form, the model can be represented by the following equation:

$$E_{i,j} = A \cdot Y_i^{\beta} \cdot Y_j^{\theta} \cdot DIST_{ij}^{\delta} \qquad (1)$$

where $E_{i,j}$ is the value of exports from country i to country j (and i, j = 1,...n); $Y_i(j)$ is GDP of country i (j); $DIST_{ij}$ is the distance between the countries (usually between major ports of each country), and A, β, θ and δ represent parameters. Given cross-section data on exports, respective GDPs, and the distances between major ports of the countries, parameters of the equation can be estimated. The estimated parameters are expected to be positive for A, β, and θ and negative for δ.

Despite a lack of solid theoretical foundations, the gravity model has performed well empirically and has been a popular tool in a variety of circumstances. The gravity model proves especially useful when trade flows among a large number of countries need to be considered. It also provides a convenient way of investigating export potentials of countries when data on other variables that are thought to have a significant effect on exports are not available or not reliable.[22] It is especially appropriate for an analysis of export potentials of transition economies. Until their suspension recently, the central planning practices in these countries made relative price signals and market-determined exchange rates irrelevant to resource allocation decisions, thereby rendering conventional trade theory inapplicable. In light of this unreliability of exchange rate and price information for these countries, there is almost no other choice of empirical models that can be used in explaining the determinants of trade flows between these countries, besides the versions of the gravity model. This is exactly why the gravity model was chosen for the empirical analysis here, but the simple gravity framework was extended in two directions. First, the significance of BSEC membership and other characteristics to Turkey's selection of trade partners was investigated by using different dummy variables. Second, to be able to take the effects of changes in GDPs of member economies into account, the estimation was carried out by pooling cross-section and time series data. This enables the model to capture the possible trade effects resulting from the dynamic nature of structural transformation that ex-communist members of BSEC have undertaken. The general forms of equations used for parameter estimation are given as follows for the cases of Turkish exports and Turkish imports, respectively:

$$X_{i,t} = E \cdot Y_{i,t}^{\beta} \cdot TRY_t^{\theta} \cdot DIST_i^{\delta} \cdot \Pi_k (DMY_k)_i^{\mu(k)} \qquad (2)$$

$$M_{i,t} = Z \cdot Y_{i,t}^{\alpha} \cdot TRY_t^{\lambda} \cdot DIST_i^{\varphi} \cdot \Pi_k (DMY_k)_i^{\phi(k)} \qquad (3)$$

where $X_{i,t}$ is Turkish exports to country i in year t $\in \{1992, 1993, 1994\}$ (in millions of dollars); $M_{i,t}$ is Turkish imports from country i in year t (in mil-

lions of dollars); $Y_{i,t}$ is GDP of country i in year t (in billions of dollars); TRY_t
is Turkish GDP in year t (in billions of dollars); $DIST_i$ is the distance from
Turkey to country i (in hundreds of miles); $(DMY_k)_I$ is k^{th} dummy variable
distinguishing country i from others by some criterion; and Π_k is product sign
indexed over $k \in \{0,1,2,3\}$. E, Z and other superscripts represent parameters to
be estimated.

The peculiarities of some of the BSEC economies made the gravity framework
requiring relatively few variables the best alternative available. Yet, even with the
gravity model, the introduction of the time element posed special challenges with
respect to data requirements: during the relatively short period of time since they
quit central planning practices, transition economies in BSEC have experienced a
sharp decline in the value of their domestic currencies and GDPs. In addition, 6 of
the 11 members of BSEC are brand-new economies that used to be regions within
another country (i.e., Soviet Union) until recently, and some of them issued their
own currencies to replace the ruble. Reliable GDP data in dollars were not available
for these economies, and it was impossible to convert GDP data measured in domestic currency terms into common dollar terms by using exchange rates. To overcome this problem, PPP values of GDP were used (the 1992–1994 averages of which
are given in Table 7.1) in estimation. [23]

Linearizing equations (2) and (3) and adding the stochastic disturbance terms,
$e_{i,t}$ and $e'_{i,t}$, yield estimable forms of these equations:[24]

$$\ln X_{i,t} = \ln E + \beta \ln Y_{i,t} + \theta \ln TRY_i + \delta \ln DIST_i + \qquad (2a)$$
$$\Sigma_k \mu(k)\ln (DMY_k)_i + e_{i,t}$$
$$\ln M_{i,t} = \ln Z + \alpha \ln Y_{i,t} + \lambda \ln TRY_t + \varphi \ln DIST_i + \qquad (3a)$$
$$\Sigma_k \Phi(k)\ln (DMY_k)_i + e'_{i,t}$$

The first version of the model was estimated without any dummy variables
(i.e., with k=0) so as to seek an answer first to whether or not Turkey's exports
to (imports from) BSEC members can be evaluated within the framework of the
gravity model. The same exercise was repeated by adding to the sample four
other trade partners that are about as close geographically to Turkey as BSEC
members.[25] Then, the introduction of a dummy variable distinguishing BSEC
members from these trade partners enabled a second version of the model to
produce an answer to whether or not BSEC membership plays a significant role
in determination of Turkey's trade patterns. This is essentially a way of investigating whether or not the establishment of BSEC has contributed to a diversion
of Turkish exports or imports toward BSEC members and away from non-
BSEC members. Two other dummy variables were introduced to address other
questions such as whether or not Turkey's current trade with countries that are
not former COMECON members was just a continuation of historical trends,
and whether the existence of a common border would have a significant role in
explaining Turkey's trade patterns regardless of BSEC membership. Results

from estimation of different variants for each of exports and imports equations are discussed in greater detail below.

The first step in the investigation was the estimation of the gravity equation for Turkish exports to BSEC countries only. This was followed by the estimation of the gravity equation for a larger sample that also includes Turkey's trade partners to the south: Egypt, Iran, Jordan, and Syria, that is, countries that are of comparable distance from Turkey as its BSEC partners. To evaluate the effect of BSEC membership on the destination of exports, a dummy variable was included that assumes the value of *e* (the base to the natural logarithm) if country i is a BSEC member and a value of one if not. Given the lack, due to structural differences, of inter-bloc trade before the formation of BSEC, the habit-forming demand for Turkey's exports by its trade partners that are not former COMECON members (Greece, Egypt, Iran, Jordan, and Syria) might have persisted dominating over the newly emerging demand from BSEC countries other than Greece. To take this possibility into consideration, a second dummy variable was allowed to take the value of *e* for the countries that are not former COMECON members, and 1 for others. Finally, a third dummy was introduced to assume the value of *e* if the trade partner shares a common border with Turkey, and 1 otherwise, so as to capture the sensitivity of Turkish exports to border trade.

The parameters of the basic gravity equation and its variants for Turkey's exports were estimated by the generalized least squares estimation technique and are reported in Table 7.4. The results in the first column of the table show that neither the distance between Turkey and BSEC countries nor Turkish GDP is a significant variables in explaining Turkey's exports to BSEC member countries. This result continues to hold even when the sample size is increased so as to include Turkey's southern trade partners (column 1 on the right). The resulting parameter estimates indicate that increases in GDPs of (importing) partners will tend to increase Turkish exports, whereas the distances between partners and Turkey and the growth in Turkish GDP (thought to represent increased export supply potential of the country) play no significant role. Column 2 presents parameter estimates from the extended version of the model, where three dummy variables were introduced. Given that none of the dummy variables are statistically significant, the results from this version imply that BSEC membership does not play an important role in determining the destinations for Turkish exports.

Coupled with low BUSE-R^2 values, the results point to a rather poor empirical performance by the gravity model as a tool for estimating Turkish exports to BSEC members and the other countries to the south. The most likely explanation for the failure of the gravity model is the increase in Turkish exports to BSEC members, even though many of these countries (including Azerbaijan, Georgia, Russia, and Ukraine) have experienced sharp declines in their GDPs as measured in PPP terms (Tables 7.1 and 7.2). Then, it is perhaps ironic that the failure of the gravity model is due, in a sense, to the success of BSEC for

Turkey, which managed to secularly increase its exports even to a country like
Georgia, whose per capita GDP has been substantially lowered over the 1992–
1995 period. Despite its poor performance, the gravity model presents results
that support this explanation. It must be noted, within this context, that the
coefficient for GDP of trade partners and the constant term representing the
effects of variables not explicitly accounted for are statistically significant for
all three versions and for any conceivable level of significance.

The Turkish Exim Bank credits that Turkey generously extended to BSEC
members (especially Azerbaijan and the Russian Federation) may be considered
among the latter type of variables (Togan 1994: 5). Then, it can be argued that
Turkish exports to BSEC are likely to increase as the incomes of the members
and export credits and other incentives offered by Turkey increase, but increases in Turkish GDP must not be expected to lead to a similar outcome.
Moreover, even though it was cited in the Summit Declaration as one of the
important factors to facilitate mutual welfare gains through increased cooperation, the significance of distance as a factor affecting the volume of Turkish
exports is dubious—at least until cooperation through BSEC leads to notable
improvements in the quality and capacity of transportation and communications infrastructure and to an elimination of other obstacles to trade, as previously discussed.

Table 7.4
Turkish Exports to BSEC Countries: Estimation Results

Coefficients	Turkish Exports to BSEC	Turkish Exports to BSEC & Others	
		(1)	(2)
Constant	11.6340	15.7990	16.7690
	(3.0660)	(8.6170)	(9.2950)
θ for Turkish GDP (TRY)	0.8203	0.2168	0.1541
	(1.2680)	(0.6777)	(0.4950)
β for Others' GDP (Y)	0.4841	0.4638	0.2827
	(4.2700)	(5.9590)	(2.6590)
δ for Distance (DIST)	0.2376	-0.1235	-0.0960
	(0.5225)	(-.5234)	(-0.4235)
Dummy variables (DMY): $\mu(1)$ for BSEC Member Dummy (e: if member; 1: otherwise)			-0.3958
			(-1.0420)
$\mu(2)$ for Former COMECON Dummy (e: if not; 1: if so)			0.2296
			(0.5770)
$\mu(3)$ for Border Dummy (e: if there is a border; 1: if not)			0.2106
			(0.7386)
BUSE R-square	0.4592	0.5098	0.4165
SSE	18.4310	22.8620	22.8640

Note: Numbers in parentheses are t-statistics.

As for Turkish imports from BSEC members and others, the results reported in Table 7.5 present evidence that is more conclusive. The first two columns in the table show parameter estimates obtained from two different versions of the gravity equation over a sample that includes only the BSEC member countries, whereas those in the last two columns were obtained from the larger sample of countries, including Egypt, Iran, Jordan, and Syria.

Table 7.5
Turkish Imports from BSEC Countries: Estimation Results

Coefficients	Turkish Imports from BSEC		Turkish Imports from BSEC & Others	
	(1)	(2)	(1)	(2)
Constant	5.6722	6.2264	6.9110	7.6162
	(1.6530)	(1.7720)	(3.8210)	(4.2930)
λ for Turkish GDP (TRY)	1.6303	1.4448	1.1419	1.1064
	(2.7640)	(2.3690)	(3.6480)	(3.7260)
α for Others' GDP (Y)	1.0597	1.2068	1.0649	1.1088
	(11.7600)	(16.8600)	(15.7900)	(16.9900)
φ for Distance (DIST)	-0.5696	-0.8210	0.2933	0.0523
	(-1.1720)	(-1.9840)	(1.2780)	(0.2224)
Dummy variables (DMY): $\phi(1)$ for BSEC Member Dummy (e: if member; 1: otherwise)				-0.3740
				(-1.2580)
ϕ (2) for Former COMECON Dummy (e: if not; 1: if so)		-1.8010		-1.0279
		(-4.8780)		(-3.0360)
ϕ (3) for Border Dummy (e: if there is a border; 1: if not)		1.5185		0.9800
		(4.5360)		(4.6810)
BUSE R-square	0.8625	0.9342	0.8935	0.9253
SSE	24.4130	22.4840	32.9780	30.5170

Note: Numbers in parentheses are t-statistics.

All parameters in column 2 on the left are statistically significant at the 90% level. These results suggest that Turkey's demand for imports from BSEC members have an income elasticity of about 1.4. Furthermore, this demand is significantly determined by the ability of these countries to deliver the demanded goods. Combined with the elasticity result, this implies positive growth rates to be enjoyed by the members in the BSEC area as a whole are likely to enhance Turkey's demand for imports from these countries. The negative sign for the coefficient of the distance variable, however, implies that a greater share of the increases in Turkish import demand is expected to be met by BSEC members that are relatively closer to Turkey. The positive sign for the border dummy also supports this conclusion. Despite its common border with Turkey, Greece is not likely to face a higher import demand from Turkey, as indicated by the negative sign of the other dummy variable. Given that all member economies have positive outlooks concerning real GDP growth starting from

1997,[26] former COMECON members in BSEC can expect a sizeable increase in
the Turkish demand for their products.

SUMMARY AND CONCLUSIONS

At the beginning of the 1990s, the challenge before Turkey was to use the
opportunities presented by the disintegration of the Soviet bloc, but without
adding new animosities to the existing ones in its region. Turkey viewed playing an active role in formation of a regional organization for economic cooperation as one of the means of facing this challenge and assumed the leadership that
such a project would require. In taking the initiative for the formation of an economic cooperation organization among the countries around the Black Sea, Turkey
calculated that such a project would not only contribute to the restoration of peace
and stability in the region but also serve as a confirmation of its new status as a regional power. But as it was argued in the foregoing discussion, special difficulties
needed to be resolved. The major difficulty was the historical lack of a market orientation in most of the members, even though the idea was to emulate existing regional organizations formed by market economies. At the time of its formation, all
BSEC members but two were centrally planned economies for all practical purposes.
In this sense, BSEC was perhaps the first economic integration attempt between
economies that once belonged to two different blocs in the "Cold War era" sense of
the term.

This chapter aimed to evaluate BSEC as a regional economic cooperation organization against this historical background and with special reference to its effects on
trade patterns of Turkey. While there is a wide theoretical and empirical literature
on the analysis of welfare gains from regional trade liberalization brought about by
varying degrees of regional economic integrations among market economies, this
literature was noted to be a not entirely suitable framework for the purposes at hand.
The special conditions underlying the formation of BSEC were argued to give rise to
certain structural problems, the solution of which could not be as easy as the removal
of conventional (tariff or non-tariff) trade barriers through an economic integration
agreement signed by market economies.

In light of these structural problems, the choice of explanatory variables for investigating Turkey's trade with BSEC members was restricted. To overcome this
problem, the volume of trade between Turkey and BSEC members was estimated
using different versions of a gravity model. The estimation was carried out by pooling cross-section and time series data. The selection of this estimation technique was
based on the argument that the trade volume should change over time as transition
economies in BSEC continue with their structural transformations. Both the simple
gravity model and its extended versions performed poorly in precisely identifying the
determinants of Turkish exports to BSEC members, but Turkish imports from these
countries were shown to be affected by the respective GDPs of Turkey and its partners and the geographic distance between them. In the case of imports, the best results were obtained from a version of the gravity model that was extended to include

two dummy variables. The analysis successfully identified the relative contributions of growth in the Turkish GDP and the GDPs of the other members. Despite its poor performance in the case of exports, the gravity equation also yielded estimation results that proved useful: the results indicated that factors not directly related to the export supply conditions of Turkey have been instrumental in the maintenance of the continuous growth in these exports. While this is a low precision finding, it is not incompatible with the previously cited role of Turkish Exim Bank credits extended to formerly communist members of BSEC. Special barter deals that Turkish exporters arranged to overcome hard currency constraints of their trade partners in these countries may also be cited as reasonable explanations for this growth.

Various estimation exercises were repeated by increasing the sample size also to cover four other countries that are not BSEC members but are of comparable distance to Turkey as are these countries. When carried out by including a BSEC membership dummy, the estimation over this larger sample yielded results that attribute no significant role to BSEC membership in the determination of Turkey trade patterns. This implies, at least as far as Turkey's trade with formerly communist members of BSEC is concerned, that the formation of BSEC does not divert members' trade away from non-members. This, in turn, leads to the conclusion that observed increases in trade volumes between Turkey and BSEC members must be due to trade creation in a dynamic sense.

It may be argued, therefore, that there are dynamic gains from trade within the BSEC area. These gains have already started to accrue to members and may be expected to continue as the formerly communist members proceed with their structural transformations. Their transition to market economies will make the relative price signals increasingly more relevant for their resource allocation decisions. However long it may take, the inefficient industries, created under the interdependence schemes of Soviet planning, will eventually be reformed or scrapped in favor of efficient industries. This is expected to lead to a change in the trade patterns of ex-Soviet bloc members by allowing them to specialize according to their natural comparative advantages. Once this transformation is complete, these economies will become enabled to generate the hard currency receipts they need to finance their imports from whatever source they deem cost-effective. Even now, *all* member economies have a positive outlook concerning real GDP growth starting from 1997, which will be the first overall growth year for BSEC since 1992. Coupled with the geographic proximity of member economies to Turkey, these positive growth prospects make larger trade volumes between Turkey and other members more likely in the future. Their continuing cooperation within BSEC to eliminate obstacles to trade increases this likelihood even further.

Even though it has not been that effective in preventing the rise of serious conflicts between its members at times (witness Armenian-Azeri conflict over Nagorno-Karabakh), the BSEC has so far contributed positively to the maintenance of peace and security in the region. The development over time of stronger ties through economic cooperation, in general, and increased volumes of trade and joint investments, in particular, is likely to increase the importance of BSEC as a forum for dialogue on economic as well as political issues. As for Turkey itself, the active role it played in the formation of BSEC has already proved to be a step in the right direction: Turkey has lost nothing so far and is likely to enjoy gains that will be easier to measure in medium to long runs.

NOTES

1. A copy of the statement in English can be found on-line through the Web sites of the Turkish Ministry of Foreign Affairs or the Turkish Embassy in Washington, D.C., at: *http://www.mfa.gov.tr/grupf/bsec8.htm* or *http://turkey.org/turkey/bsec8.htm.*

2. This was, in fact, the key idea that the late president Turgut Özal picked as the central theme of Turkish foreign policy during his career as the prime minister first and, later, as the president. For a more detailed discussion on this point, see Gürbey (1995).

3. See Togan (1994). For a list of articles on BSEC written by Ambassador Elekdağ himself, see Kut (1995: 94).

4. Part of the public, including most of the policy-makers and the Turkish elite, hoped that the project would give Turkey a dominating influence over the transition states of the region, possibly increasing chances of Turkey for full membership in the European Union (EU)—traditionally, the fundamental objective of Turkish foreign policy. Others (who were frustrated enough by the continuing reluctance of the EU to admit Turkey as a full member) viewed it as an alternative to seeking EU membership, but Turkey has never taken this position officially. For a general discussion on why BSEC might be viewed as an alternative to EU, see Gençkaya (1993).

5. See Balkır (1993b: 21) and Ad-Hoc Commission on Turkey—BSEC Relations (1995: 3).

6. The full text of the BSEC Summit Declaration can be found in Permanent International Secretariat of BSEC (1995: 3–6). On-line versions can be accessed through the Turkish Ministry of Foreign Affairs web site at *http://www.mfa.gov.tr/grupf/bsec7.htm*, or at *http://turkey.org/turkey/bsec7.htm*, the Web site of the Turkish Embassy in Washington, D.C.

7. The Bosphorus Statement issued after the summit read:

The Heads of State and Government acknowledged that the region is already faced by serious conflicts and that there is the danger of new tensions arising. They therefore emphasized the need for the peaceful settlement of all disputes by the means and in accordance with the principles set out in the CSCE documents to which they all subscribe. They further reaffirmed their determination in resisting aggression, violence, terrorism and lawlessness and their resolve to help establish and restore peace and justice.

(A copy of the statement in English can be found on-line through the Web sites of the Turkish Ministry of Foreign Affairs or the Turkish Embassy in Washington, D.C. at: *http://www.mfa.gov.tr/grupf/bsec8.htm* or *http://turkey.org/turkey/bsec8.htm*).

8. The concepts were developed in the 1950s by Jacob Viner, who used them as main tools of analysis for investigating the welfare effects of customs unions. See Viner (1953). For a more contemporary discussion of the conceptual framework, see Asheghian (1995).

9. The Turkish side initially envisaged the development of a stronger form of cooperation that, however gradually, would lead to the formation of an economic integration among member countries eventually. President Özal, for example, had European Union as a model for BSEC in mind. See Gürbey (1995: 54). But in the light of the special conditions of other members, Turkey did not insist on this position. See Garih (1995).

10. Previously, two studies attempting to evaluate the BSEC agreement against the known forms of regional integration arrangements in the literature have shown this. See Balkır (1993b), Gültekin and Mumcu (1996); Mastny and Nation (1996: 179–201). For this reason, BSEC is often referred to as a "unique" model of regional economic cooperation (see Yeşilyaprak on-line document at *http://turkey.org/turkey/bsec6.htm*).

11. Albania stayed as a member between 1949 and 1962. After its withdrawal from COMECON, it pursued isolationist policies and remained rather closed to international trade.

12. This interdependence still makes specialization of these countries in the sectors in which they have a comparative advantage difficult, thereby limiting their potentials for mutually beneficial trade with others. See Balkır (1993b) for a general discussion and an example. The same issue is discussed also by Togan (1994) and Gültekin and Mumcu (1996).

13. Gençkaya (1993: 556) also makes a similar point, but perhaps an equally important reason for the inclusion of Article 7 was the uncertainty over the feasibility of a successful exploitation of "the potential for mutually advantageous economic cooperation" mentioned in Article 3.

14. This was the major concern of President Özal about the chances of success of BSEC. See Gürbey (1995: 54).

15. National and bilateral organizations with which the BSECC maintains contact are as follows: Albania—Chamber of Commerce and Industry; Azerbaijan—State Committee of Foreign Economic Relations; Bulgaria—Bulgarian-Turkish Business Council; Georgia—State Committee of Foreign Economic Relations; Greece—Council for Greek-Turkish Economic Cooperation; Moldova—Ministry of Trade and Material Resources; Romania—Romanian Electricity Authority; Russian Federation—Ministry of Foreign Economic Relations; Turkey—Foreign Economic Relations Board (DEİK); and Ukraine—Chamber of Commerce and Industry.

16. For example, the council reviewed project proposals for the modernization of small and medium-sized enterprises in Bulgaria so as to recruit international partners to carry out the promising ones. Another proposal considered by the BSECC was construction of a viaduct to connect Romania and Bulgaria over the Danube.

17. The BSEC Council also operates through the Permanent Secretariat based in Istanbul.

18. For information in English on the structure of BSEC, see the on-line document entitled "The BSEC Structure" at either: *http://www.mfa.gov.tr/grupf/bsec3.htm* or *http://turkey.org/turkey/bsec3.htm*.

19. See the on-line document *bsec2.htm*, entitled "Common Interests and Priorities" at either of the Web sites cited in note 18.

20. The development of stronger trade ties between Turkey and Greece has been prevented mainly by political problems and historical friction between these two countries even though they both have been parts of the Western alliance as members of NATO, the Organization for Economic Cooperation and Development (OECD), and so on. Less important, similarity of exports has kept these countries from having a larger bilateral trade volume.

21. The gravity model as a tool for the analysis of trade flows between countries was first introduced by Tinbergen (1962).

22. See Deardorff (1984) for a brief survey of gravity literature. For a general discussion and examples of more recent applications of the gravity model on the effects of German unification on world trade flows, see van Bergeijk and Oldersma (1990). An

application of the gravity framework to trade flows within BSEC area where the estimation was based on cross-section observations alone can be found in Togan (1994).

23. Wildly fluctuating exchange rates for some countries implied a depreciation against the dollar of their domestic currencies by hundreds of times a year.

24. The estimation of (2a) and (3a) would require a pooling technique that would employ a set of assumptions on the disturbance covariance matrix. Under relatively less restrictive assumptions, the model would typically be cross-sectionally heteroskedastic and time-wise auto-regressive. That is,

$E(e_{it}^2) = S_i^2$ (Heteroskedasticity)
$E(e_{it} e_{jt}) = 0$ for i'j   (Cross-sectional independence)
$e_{it} = R_i.e_{it-1} + u_{it}$ (Auto-regression)

While this specification allows the value of the parameter R to vary from one cross-sectional unit to another, the unavailability of time series BSEC data for a longer period of time forced the estimation to be carried out by assuming a common R for all cross-sectional units.

25. In estimating the parameters for the distance variable, the observations used were different from the ones reported in Table 7.1. In calculating distances, Istanbul was taken as the relevant port in Turkey. For landlocked countries, the distance from Istanbul to the capital and, for other countries, to the Black Sea or Mediterranean ports were considered (e.g. Novorossiisk in Russia and Alexandria in Egypt).

26. Economist Intelligence Unit, *Country Reports*, various issues.

8

The Political Economy of Relations between Turkey and Russia

Gülten Kazgan

INTRODUCTION

It is not possible to understand or to analyze the nature and progression of economic relations between Russia and Turkey without probing their political relations. This stems primarily from the priority assigned by both countries to a number of sociopolitical factors that are partly associated with their political integrity and partly with their desire to create spheres of influence in neighboring countries. Historical legacy, geographic location, and non-democratic state traditions deeply engrained in their sociopolitical cultures have all been conducive to ascribing a secondary role to economic benefits. The pressure as well as the opportunity to reverse this trend, on the advent to power of Mikhail Gorbachev and his ideology in the mid-1980s, seemingly did achieve the aim of improving economic relations for some time. Improvement in economic relations conferred benefits on both parties accompanied by the amelioration of sociopolitical tensions at all levels.

The disintegration of the USSR, however, seems to have revived the historical specters that may overshadow the prospective benefits to be derived from more amicable relations. Not surprisingly, this revival has followed the resurgence of alarming economic problems in both countries in the 1990s. Radical political movements, which flourish in the prevalence of socioeconomic ills, threaten the survival of all that has been built on the way to ameliorate overall relations through strengthening economic interdependence.

However, despite the souring of governmental rhetoric on both sides after 1993, economic relations at the level of private agents have continued their upward trend. For Turkey, Russia has proved to be an irreplaceable trading partner. The economic crisis that Turkey has been living through since 1988 would definitely have been aggravated had the Russian market remained closed.

This chapter studies Turkish-Russian relations in this light. This first section presents an overview of economic relations between 1980 and 1991. The second section is devoted to the study of the political economy of relations between 1992 and the first half of 1996, when political frictions came to be intertwined with economic relations that boomed at the private level. The third section gives a synopsis of the complementarity in the current economic structures of the two countries. The fourth section studies merchandise and service trade as well as capital flows plus scientific and technical cooperation. Prospects for the near future are discussed in the fifth section.

An Overview of Economic Relations: 1980-1991

Throughout the Cold War period until the 1980s, economic relations between Turkey and the USSR remained captive to the ideology and policies of their opposing camps. Relations in all lines of activity were sustained at levels considered extraordinarily low for two contiguous countries. The volume of yearly total trade between them hardly reached $300 million in the 1970s; economic cooperation was confined to Turkey's resorting to the USSR, on the refusal of the West to do so, for technology transfer and credits for investments by state economic enterprises in heavy industry. The small volume of trade was carried out on the basis of a clearing agreement, since both countries suffered from shortages of hard currencies.

This dim picture, however, came to be gradually altered in the 1980s with the emergence of economic pressures in Turkey as well as new opportunities to be explored in the USSR.

New pressures and new opportunities. Beginning with 1980, Turkey had to embark upon a liberalization program, the so-called structural adjustment program, under the International Monetary Fund (IMF) and World Bank surveillance. This program precluded the implementation of a controlled foreign payments regime and rather demanded a strong and steady export expansion to bring down the external deficit. In effect, Turkey did abolish its clearing agreement with Russia in 1982, and from 1983 onward the payments regime was liberalized. Its immediate result was a more than halving of Turkey's exports to the USSR (from $193.7 million in 1981 to $88.7 million in 1983), whereas imports therefrom jumped (from $151.1 million to $219.9 million, respectively). The trade deficit with the USSR was thus on the rise in a period when Turkey was under great pressure to bring down its overall external deficit to a manageable level. Moreover, the jump in oil prices in 1979 and 1980 had inflated Turkey's import bill, exerting a new upward pressure on the overall external deficit (Kazgan 1993: 73-76).

The early 1980s witnessed attempts on Turkey's part to enhance economic cooperation with the USSR for reasons other than external deficit reduction. The European Community (EC), as it was then called, had suspended the operation of its customs union agreement with Turkey in the wake of the military takeover of 12 September 1980; in addition, most Western European countries had introduced visa controls for carriers of Turkish passports. This was an omen of Turkey's marginalization by Europe in general. To lift the freeze on economic relations with Europe, Turkey applied for full membership in the EC as of April 1987 but was hastily refused on economic as well as non-economic grounds. It became evident that Turkey's perennial dream of becoming a member of the Community could not be realized, at least in the foreseeable future.

Similarly, discouraging events in the Middle East followed. Turkey did benefit, to a large extent, from the expansion in the Middle East market in the first and second oil boom years in several ways: exports of manufactured and agricultural products recorded significant increases; contracting activity boomed; workers went to work in the Gulf sheikdoms; and tourists therefrom came to Turkey in large numbers. In the late 1980s, however, the boom ceded its place to stagnation, as oil prices dropped, as the Gulf War between Iran and Iraq ended, and as the United Nations (UN) embargo on Iraq replaced it (Kazgan 1995: 21).

The advent to power of Gorbachev and his announcement of the glasnost and perestroika programs, on the other hand, created new opportunities for enhancing economic relations with the USSR. Note, however, that many steps had already been taken for this purpose prior to his coming to office. The period 1980–91 turned out to be one of persistent improvement in relations on all fronts. In effect, confidence attained a level where even the formation of a regional trading block between countries located around the Black Sea came to be discussed by 1990. Thus, on the eve of the disintegration of the USSR but in the wake of the pulling down of the Berlin Wall, economic integration between Turkey and the Soviet Union, as well as a number of other Black Sea countries, was put on the agenda.

The distinguishing characteristic of this period is that "trade followed the flag" in the sense that economic cooperation came to be enhanced through governmental efforts initially, and then private enterprise followed suit. This sequence was reversed, however, in the post-Cold War era.

Governmental efforts to enhance economic cooperation. The goodwill to enhance economic cooperation between the two countries is well evidenced by the signing of several agreements between them for this purpose.

The agreements signed in the first half of the 1980s seem to have paved the way both for those signed in the latter half of the decade and for the boom in economic relations on all fronts. The most notable agreements were the expansion of the Alumina Plant, set up in cooperation with the USSR in the 1970s (1981); the abolition of the clearing agreement and liberalization of the payments regime (1982); the coming into effect, through the drawing up of a protocol, of the 1977 agreement on scientific and technological cooperation (1982); an intergovernmental economic cooperation protocol (1983); the sale of natural gas by the USSR to Turkey and the related offset agreement (1984); a long-term cooperation program in economic and commercial as well as scientific and technical fields (1984); an economic cooperation protocol (1986); the protocol for merchandise trade over the 1986–90 period (1986); the inclusion of contracting services, to be rendered by Turkish firms, in the offset agreement related to Turkey's natural gas purchases (1986); the opening of Turkey's northeastern border gate at Sarp and the liberalization of cross-border trade (1989); the extension of Turkish Exim Bank credits by Turkey to the USSR over the 1989–91 period (1989); initiation of negotiations for the formation of the Black Sea Economic Cooperation Area; and assurance of friendly and good-neighborly relations between the Turkish Republic and the USSR for enhancing cooperation, signed between President Turgut Özal and President Gorbachev in March 1991 on the eve of the disintegration of the USSR.

These governmental efforts to enhance economic cooperation yielded their results beginning in the second half of the 1980s, when private initiatives gained momentum. Not only did the trade volume rise exponentially, but also joint efforts were initiated to enhance cooperation in all lines of activity.

THE POLITICAL ECONOMY OF RELATIONS IN THE POST-COLD WAR ERA: 1992–1996

On the eve of the disintegration of the USSR, economic relations between the two countries had gone beyond the signing of agreements. The ending of the Cold War was, therefore, heralded by Turkish officials as the commencement of a new and more promising era. The already improving relations at the governmental level and the incipient boom at the level of private agents could be sustained, this time, with the Russian Federation, on the one hand, and the remaining ex-Soviet republics, on the other hand. The independence of the republics located in the Caucasus and in Central Asia was considered to be an unexpected boon; Turkey had deep interests in these regions for economic, political, and national defense reasons (MacFarlane 1995).

In the course of the first two years following the dismemberment of the Soviet Union, these expectations were, by and large, realized, notwithstanding the emergence of extreme hardships all over the ex-Soviet territory and increased macroeconomic instability in Turkey. From mid-1993 onward, however, the political rhetoric came to be filled with sourness, and indictments were voiced reciprocally. Local armed strife and emergence of radical political movements in each, plus competition over the exploitation and pipeline routes of oil and natural gas, turned out to be inimical to enhancing friendly relations at the governmental level. However, Turkish private enterprise had acquired such vested interests in Russia and the other ex-Soviet republics that souring political rhetoric hardly exerted any adverse effects on the boom in economic relations at the private level (Fuller 1994: 7–10).

Economic Conditions and Their Consequences

Socioeconomic disruption in Russia's economy in transition. What the people living in the former USSR territory in general and in the Russian Federation in particular have been experiencing is the total collapse of the communist system; but the building of a totally new system, including political democracy and market institutions, seems to be no easy task and is unlikely to be achieved soon. In the case of Russia, there is an additional political issue that should not be overlooked: the marginalization and increased dependency on the West of the onetime global superpower and the reduction to the ranks of a semi-industrialized developing country of this superpower crushed under political turmoil and economic impoverishment. Russia's problems boil down to causes and create outcomes that are basically not too dissimilar to those experienced by Turkey in the 1990s, though, of course, on a much smaller scale. This surprising similarity, at least partly, lies at the source of the souring of governmental relations.

Russia's real economic output in agriculture and industry shrank to half its Cold War size between 1991 and 1996; according to IMF estimates, there was already an approximately 15% drop in the Gross National Product (GNP) of the USSR on the eve of its disintegration (1989–1991). This drastic impoverishment has been accompanied by the emergence of an extremely rich social class thanks to "asset grabs" as the government privatized state economic enterprises and/or through sheer black marketeering and other sorts of Mafia-like activity, such as money laundering, as the unrecorded economy expanded. It is estimated that about a quarter of the population live on less than $68 per month, the estimated subsistence level. Notwithstanding the disastrous collapse of its economy, accompanied by the outbreak of hyperinflation for a few years, Russia could contain its inflation rate in the following two years, from 214% in 1994 to 131% in 1995 (Barings 1996: 16). The inflation rate dropped to two-digit levels in 1996, thanks to the decreasing fiscal imbalance. The government covers the deficit through non-monetary financing, mainly by floating bonds in international markets.

This latter policy, an outcome of the liberalization of short-term capital flows under the convertibility of the Russian ruble, has led to a significant overvaluation of the currency beginning with 1995. Although, by the beginning of 1996, the inflation-adjusted theoretical level of the ruble was estimated to approximate 10,000 rubles to one dollar, its actual level was somewhat less than half this amount (Barings 1996: 27–28). In all probability, on account of low domestic demand, notwithstanding the currency overvaluation, the current account has been yielding surpluses on the order of 2–2.5% of the gross domestic product (GDP). But, obviously, this overvaluation creates tendencies to impose import restrictions so as to stem the unfair competition posed by imported goods—hence, the protective policies implemented in 1996.

The dismal state of the Russian economy, and its marginalization, in a sense, after having assumed a "global power" status for about half a century have left strong imprints on Russian social psychology and the policies to be pursued by decision makers. First, Russia wants to hold together the onetime Soviet republics under the Commonwealth of Independent States (CIS) banner, no matter what the cost. "Creeping expansionism has been the recurring theme of Russian history . . . Russia has subordinated the well-being of its population to this relentless outward thrust and threatened all its neighbors with it" (Kissinger 1996: 20). This tendency brings Russia into conflict with Turkey, in particular in the Caucasus and Central Asia (Bilge 1995).

Second, Russia is now much more sensitive than ever about the exploitation or the marketing of the natural resources located in the Russian or the CIS territory at large, since its agricultural and industrial output have fallen so drastically. Azerbaijan, located in the Caucasus, and the Central Asian republics are extremely rich in oil and/or natural gas reserves. Referred to as Turkic republics, their peoples display fairly close cultural affinity to the people of Turkey. Turkey expected, in the wake of the disintegration of the USSR, to establish close cooperation with these republics, in particular in this line of activity. The purpose was partly to obtain economic benefits and partly to tilt the power balance in the region in its favor. But Russia vehemently opposed encroachments upon its sphere of influence by what it considered to be a competitive regional party. Natural resources, hence, turned out to be the major underlying economic cause of the conflict.

Third, the extreme socioeconomic hardships suffered by most of the Russian people have reinforced radical nationalistic tendencies. One must add to this the ethnocentric nationalism of the post-modern era and its role in the civil armed strife in Russia as well as in Turkey. Secessionist tendencies of ethnic groups that are divided between Turkey and Russia, then, can easily become the topic of dissent; each party can indict the other for creating social turmoil on its territory. Lately, such indictments have tended to replace governmental efforts to enhance economic cooperation as each party struggles to acquire monopoly power over the exploitation and/or distribution routes of oil and natural gas.[1]

Increased Macroeconomic Instability and Socioeconomic Disruption in Turkey

Turkey entered the last phase of its liberalization program as the Berlin Wall was being pulled down. In the post-Cold War era, Turkey has been suffering from extreme macroeconomic instability: the coming into effect of the convertibility of the Turkish lira (TL) and the liberalization of financial markets have been conducive to reinforcing the fiscal and social imbalances, given their already high levels at the start. The annual inflation rate has reached global highs

(80%). An economic crisis, accompanying a financial crisis, is now becoming a biannual occurrence, with GNP growth and the inflation rate alternating between sudden jumps and sudden falls. In fact, macroeconomic instability has become a dizzying phenomenon. Additionally, Turkey's annual real GNP growth between 1988 and 95 (3.5%) has been only about half its long-run trend rate (about 5.5–6% per year); that is, it leaves a narrow margin of per capita income growth above the population growth rate (2.2%). Quite similar to the case of Russia, agriculture and manufacturing industry have been the sectors most adversely affected on account of the ongoing instability. Growth in agricultural output has barely exceeded 1% per year and in manufacturing has barely reached half its long-term trend rate.

The unrecorded economy has strongly expanded throughout this period; in Russia it is estimated to have attained 50% of the recorded economy, whereas in Turkey, the available estimates vary in the 20% to 40% range. This is accompanied by highly strengthened organized crime, which is by now intertwined with a large number of economic activities as well as political organizations.

This adverse evolutionary process has deepened Turkey's existing social imbalances and is, seemingly, one of the factors that underlie the armed strife along Turkey's eastern and southeastern borders as well as on its own territory. The Gulf War and the embargo on Iraq have been conducive to economic and social disruption in Turkey's southeast region; the Kurdish terrorist organization (PKK), activity has been fueled by the collapse in the economy of the already poor southeastern provinces. Additionally, it has resulted in a serious contraction of trade and other relations with the neighboring countries, as well as given rise to political frictions with them on this count (Kazgan 1994: 21–23).

High military expenditures to contain the armed strife explain, at least partly, the high fiscal deficits and, hence, soaring real interest rates. These two, in turn, explain the significant drop in fixed investment and GNP growth, on one hand, and the induced short-term capital inflows and real appreciation in the value of the TL, on the other. As different from the Russian case, Turkey, leaving aside the intermittent surpluses in years of financial crisis, suffers from persistent current account deficits. This dim picture has lately been completed, after a period of extreme political instability, by the ascension to power in the coalition government in mid-1996, with the radical Islamist party, Refah or Welfare Party, as the major partner. The coalition ended in mid-1997.

Russia was not alone in its experience of the emergence or the reinforcement of radical political movements, under the pressure of socioeconomic disruption. Turkey has been living through a similar experience. Its seemingly insurmountable economic problems, the ethnocentric warfare and the human rights issues this involves, and the enhancement in the political power of the Islamist movement and its recent ascension to power have gradually distanced Turkey from Western Europe. One should also add, at this juncture, deliberate actions on the part of Greece to preclude Turkey from establishing closer relations with the European Union (EU). Despite the finalization of the customs union agreement with the EU as of 6 March, 1995[2] Turkey is still faced with the "Fortress Europe" and has not yet been extended any of the financial aid packages pledged to support its economy.

Given the not-too-promising relations with the EU, its loss of the Iraqi market on account of the UN embargo, and the contraction of economic relations with the neighboring Arab countries, Turkey looks to Russia as well as the other CIS countries for market expansion as well as other economic benefits.

Private agents seem to be suffering from claustrophobia in the domestic market; this is primarily because of the soaring imports, while export expansion lags behind. Contraction in the domestic market on account of the impoverishment of the population at large while "the rich get richer" (plus the invasion of the market by imported products, partly due to the overvaluation in Turkish lira and partly to the complete import liberalization vis-á-vis the EU under the customs union agreement) constitutes one of the legs of the claustrophobia; the other leg is contributed by the closed export markets in Turkey's traditional trading partners, mainly Western Europe, the United States, and the Middle East, for its major exportables.

In the post-Cold War years, hence, the Turkish economy has come to display greater dependence on the Russian market, or the CIS at large, than previously. Support for this statement lies in the reaction of some businessmen, mainly retailers and producers of goods demanded by "suitcase tourists" from Russia (and other CIS countries), to the Russian presidential elections held in 1996. They were deeply involved in the election campaigns of Boris Yeltsin and Gennady Zyuganov; the former was viewed as the guarantor of the free market economy, whereas the latter was expected to install protective policies to stave off the increase in imports. They, therefore, collected money among themselves, of which estimates vary between $5 million and $100 million, according to newspaper reports (*Milliyet* 16 June 1996), to support Yeltsin's presidential campaign, and thousands of T-shirts, carrying his portrait and his campaign slogans, were produced and forwarded to his campaign team.

Such a political involvement by Turkish businessmen in the prospective economic policies of a foreign country is a unique event in Turkey's social history. But it is a succinct indicator of this dependence, at least in the case of some specific sectors.

Similarly, region-wise, the economy of northeast Anatolia, which remained dormant at the time of the USSR, has been revived, thanks to the expansion of trade relations and the establishment of transport links with the republics in the Caucasus as well as with the Russian Federation. Businessmen of this region also have come to enjoy a strong vested interest in the Russian market for their exportables. As the Turkish government failed to duly open up a consulate in Sochi (Georgia), the stepping-stone to the Russian market, they did so themselves and nominated a Bulgarian Turk who speaks Russian fluently as the commercial attaché. Though he is unofficial, Russia has recognized him and has nominated a Russian commercial attaché to cooperate with him (*Milliyet* 15 June 1996). This also is a unique event, indicating the crucial importance of the Russian market for the region.

Cooperation and Conflict between Governments

Governmental efforts to enhance economic cooperation. Turkey's economic as well as overall relations with the Russian Federation went on improving at the governmental level in the wake of the disintegration of the USSR. The pinnacle seems to have been attained with the signing of the Black Sea Economic Cooperation Agreement, for, from the end of 1992 onward, tensions and frictions arose between the two governments as their interests conflicted on some economic and political issues. Nonetheless, the following agreements were signed, which effectively helped enhance economic cooperation.

Turkey signed the Black Sea Economic Cooperation Agreement with the Russian Federation and nine other countries located in the Balkans and the Caucasus in June 1992. This agreement enabled Turkey to sign, in turn, some bilateral agreements with some of the individual members. As the signatories were ex-Soviet republics, this process evoked Russia's reaction as an encroachment on its sphere of influence (Aydın and Bekar 1995: 31).

This agreement was preceded by the signing of the agreement on the "Basic Principles of Relations between the Turkish Republic and the Russian Federation" in May 1992. Thereby, each signatory pledged to honor the territorial integrity of the other, to enhance cooperation in economic and cultural fields, and to take common action against terrorist activities. Similar to the March 1991 agreement, this one also gave support to Turkey's moving to closer cultural and economic cooperation with the Turkic republics.

The Agreements on "Cooperation in the Field of National Security" (1993), on "Turkey's Purchases of Military Equipment from the Russian Federation" (1993), and on "Cooperation in Military Technology and Military Industry" (1994) were of utmost significance from Turkey's standpoint, since some Western countries and major arms and military equipment producers and exporters refused to sell such to Turkey, with the pretext that in the course of the ongoing armed strife in its southeast, Turkish armed forces were violating human rights. Turkey can produce only 7–10% of its required military equipment. These agreements, therefore, helped Turkey overcome the bottlenecks it was likely to be faced with.

In addition to the signing of agreements and protocols of a general nature, Turkey cooperates with Russia on a project basis in the undertaking of infrastructure investments in the context of the Black Sea Economic Cooperation Agreement. The trans-Asia railway project, which will help open up to world markets the landlocked republics of Central Asia and the Caucasus, as well as linking Turkey with Russia; the energy project between Turkey, Russia, and the three republics located in the Caucasus (Georgia, Armenia, Azerbaijan); and the highway project around the Black Sea linking a number of countries, inclusive of Russia and Turkey, are three of the most noteworthy of such projects.

Between 1992 and 95, the number of agreements and protocols signed between Russia and Turkey exceeded 20 and covered fields ranging from the economy to technology, science, culture, tourism, and public health.

Governmental conflicts that hamper the enhancement of economic cooperation. While the Turkish and Russian governments went on to sign one cooperation agreement after another with each other, an upsurge in conflicts between them accompanied this process, beginning in 1993. The agreement on the sale of natural gas by the USSR from 1985 and by the Russian Federation from 1992 onward had served as the major basis on which economic relations expanded. But, ironically, Turkey's attempts to play a role in the exploitation and distribution projects of oil and natural gas proved to be the major source of conflict between them, given the ethnic turmoil and the deterioration of economic conditions in both (Kazgan 1995: 20).

The ex-USSR's vast territory extended over a number of republics and autonomous regions where the population majority was non-Slavic. Those political formations located in the Caucasus and Central Asia house population groups that, ethnically and/or linguistically, display close affinity to those currently living in Turkey, for example, Georgians, Armenians, Azerbaijanis, Abkhazis, Chechens, Kurds, and others. On the disintegration of the Soviet Union, a number of such groups initiated political movements and often armed strife to gain complete independence of the Russian Federation, refusing to become a part of the CIS. The ethnic turmoil that followed in the Caucasus became intertwined with the "great game" played over the exploration of oil and natural gas reserves located in the Caspian Sea region and the pipeline routes for the products. This has given rise to serious tensions between the Russian and Turkish governments, disrupting, somewhat, prospects of further enhancing economic cooperation.

The Russian government has voiced strong indictments against the Turkish government for involvement in the Chechen uprising. The argument is that Turkey wants to create ethnic turmoil on the prospective pipeline route from Baku to Novorossiisk so as to downplay the project, since this route will have to traverse Chechen territory. The Turkish government voices a similar indictment against Russia, since Turkey proposed an alternative pipeline route for oil and natural gas distribution. The pipeline from Baku, in this case, would have to traverse eastern and southeastern Turkey to reach the terminal at Ceyhan on the Mediterranean coast. Some of Turkey's ethnic Kurds reside in this region; also, PKK terrorists infiltrating the country along these borders from the neighboring countries launch attacks on the local population and security forces. Turkey indicts Russia for inciting to activism against Turkey its ethnic Kurds, as well as those living elsewhere in the Caucasus.[3] The purpose is, allegedly, to thwart Turkey's pipeline project proposal by creating political turmoil on the pipeline route (Fuller 1994: 7–10).

But the Russian pipeline project, when accepted, will lead to an enormous increase in the number of oil tankers navigating through the straits that connect the Black Sea with the Aegean Sea. Environmental and security threats of increased tanker passage are particularly strong in the case of the Bosphorus. The Turkish government has resorted recently to taking safety measures to reduce the risk exposure of the country's largest city, Istanbul, on this count. Regulating and controlling tanker passage are considered the best way to reduce the city's risk exposure.

But this has turned out to be another source of political friction between governments. The Russian government alleges that regulated tanker traffic will result in an increase in transport costs. This issue, yet unresolved, represents clashes of economic interest intertwined with power conflicts. The Russian government's claim is that the Montreux agreement, signed in 1936, allows free, unimpeded navigation through the straits; the Turkish government, in turn, alleges that the more than half-a-century-old agreement could not have foreseen the dangers posed by the heavy traffic of huge oil tankers running in and out of the straits day and night and that it has a right to take safety measures (*Milliyet* 6 July 1996).

Hegemonic conflicts have also been taking place in Central Asian republics as well as in Azerbaijan, where the population majority is of Turkic origin. Turkish governments, quite erroneously, assumed that the dissolution of the Soviet Union would put an end to Russian domination in these republics (Halefoğlu 1996: 6). Attempts have been made, both at the governmental and at the non-governmental organization (NGO) levels, to strengthen cultural, political, and economic ties with these people; direct investments by Turkish entrepreneurs in these republics in lines of activity ranging from education to retail trade to manufacturing have soared (Kazgan 1995).

However, the availability of rich natural resources, headed by oil and natural gas, in these republics and Turkey's concerted efforts to take part in their exploration and/or distribution systems hit against Russian sensitivity. The Russian government interpreted these efforts as an encroachment upon its sphere of influence.[4] On the emergence of frictions, the Turkish government had to tone down its rhetoric about the integration of Turkic peoples (Bilge 1995: 90).

This brief account shows that in cases where competition between governments involves a zero-sum game over the grabbing of a monopolistic position or where spheres of influence clash in particular over areas harboring rich natural resources or where governments try to display hegemonic power reciprocally, the ensuing political frictions or conflicts are likely to overshadow the economic benefits from enhanced cooperation; but if, at the same time, each partner has great stakes involved in the other, notwithstanding frictions and tensions, a modus vivendi in peaceful relations can be created.

A COMPARATIVE ANALYSIS OF ECONOMIC STRUCTURES

A comparison between the present Russian and Turkish economies can be made only with certain reservations, for mainly two reasons. First, Russia's economy in transition in the post-Cold War years has been disrupted to such an extent that its current state can hardly indicate its capacity or its potentials. Moreover, the large size of its unrecorded sector, the overvaluation of the ruble, and the scantiness of available comparable data, as well as the differences in data published by different sources, hamper the reliance of comparisons. Add to this the dismal state of the Turkish economy and the uncertainties surrounding it, and the picture for both economies becomes pretty blurred.

Given the preceding observation, Table 8.1 helps give an idea about the comparative development levels and the economic structures of the two countries: per capita income level, as of 1992, is about 27% higher in Russia than in Turkey, but both may be classified as semi-industrialized economies. The structure of the two economies, however, is vastly different.

Table 8.1
Some Economic Indicators of Russia and Turkey (1992)

	Russia	Turkey
GDP per capita (billions of $)	2510	1980
Share of sectors in GDP (%)		
Agriculture	13	15
Industry	49	30
Services	39	55
Distribution of GDP (%)		
General government consumption	23	18
Private consumption	40	63
Gross domestic investment	32	23
Gross domestic savings	37	20
Exports of goods and non-factor services	-	21
Resource balance	5	-3
Merchandise Trade (billions of $)		
Exports	40.0	14.72
Imports	36.9	22.9
Energy use per capita (kg)	5665	948

Source: World Bank, *World Development Report* 1994.

The contribution of services to Russia's GDP is relatively small (39%), although the mushrooming private enterprise is concentrated in this sector. In contrast, service industries contribute more than half (55%) of Turkey's GDP, and it is a major exporter of services ranging from transport to tourism and contracting. In effect, trade and direct investments in services have been contributing a non-negligible proportion of the expansion in overall relations.

Russia is a huge producer of crude oil (300–350 million metric tons annually), natural gas (600–650 billion cubic meters annually), and coal (about 250 million metric tons). In contrast, Turkey displays significant deficits in all the fuel materials. Its annual domestic production of oil hardly meets 15% of domestic consumption, and the percentage rate is even smaller in the case of natural gas. Turkey has been importing crude oil mainly from the Middle East; in the "cold" Cold War years there were almost no imports from the USSR, but following Gorbachev's advent to power and the thaw in overall relations, imports of crude oil appeared on the list. By the 1990s, Turkey came to meet about 5% of total imports in this fuel material from Russia. Natural gas imports, in contrast, draw a completely different picture. The agreement signed in 1984 turned, first, the USSR and, from 1992 onward, the Russian Federation into Turkey's major suppliers. Turkey came to meet 50–60% of natural gas imports from this source, beginning in 1987. In Turkey's overall imports of energy materials, Russia has come to contribute 17.4% of the total, whereas the share of the USSR, as of 1986, stood at only 3.6% (Aydın and Bekar 1995: 160–61).

Table 8.1 also shows that the share of industry in Russia's GDP approximates half of the total, whereas its contribution in Turkey is less than one-third. Not only is Russia much more industrialized, but also its production is concentrated on heavy industry, rather than light industries that mostly produce consumer products. This is evidenced by the low private consumption expenditures (40%) in its GDP. The defense industry contributes a significant proportion of heavy industry and exports. In contrast, Turkey is a large importer in these items but is a net exporter in consumer products, inclusive of consumer durables.

Following the boom in trade relations, Turkey has been exporting to Russia mainly services and consumer products and importing from Russia products of heavy industry, inclusive of military equipment, in addition to fuel materials (*Moskova Ticaret* 1996-a). The economic structures of Russia and Turkey display strong complementarities that are likely to encourage strong trade relations.

MAJOR ITEMS IN ECONOMIC RELATIONS

Merchandise Trade

The expansion in the total volume of trade from 1987 onward calls for a brief look into the nature of the natural gas agreement since it has been acting as the major catalyzer. According to the stipulations of the agreement Turkey pays hard currency for natural gas imports; in turn, Russia pledges to spend 70% of the amount received for importing consumer products and contracting services from Turkey. Out of the total natural gas payments by the latter, 45.5% is paid back by the former via importing consumer products and 24.5% via importing contracting services; the remaining 30% is allocated to the repayment of Turkey's outstanding debt to the USSR.

Turkey's exports to the USSR remained stagnant between 1980 and 1987 but from then onward increased exponentially; by 1995, merchandise exports to Russia attained $1.2 billion. The same rapid increase is observed in imports, as shown in Table 8.2. As of this latter year, Russia came to contribute 6.5% of the total volume of trade and to rank as Turkey's fifth largest trading partner after Germany, the United States, Italy, and the U.K.

Table 8.2
Turkey's Exports to and Imports from the Former USSR and the Russian Federation: 1980–1995

Year	Million USD			%	
	Exports	Imports	Balance	Share in total exports	Share in total imports
1980	169.0	167.1	1.8	5.8	2.3
1981	193.7	151.1	42.6	4.1	1.8
1983	88.7	219.9	-131.2	1.6	2.6
1987	169.5	282.1	-112.6	1.7	2.2
1989	704.7	579.0	125.8	6.1	4.0
1991	610.6	1013.3	-402.7	4.5	5.2
1992 (*)	438.4	1040.4	-602.0	3.0	4.5
1993 (*)	499.0	1542.4	-1043.4	3.3	5.2
1994 (*)	820.1	1045.4	-225.3	4.5	4.5
1995 (*)	1238.2	2082.4	-844.2	6.4	6.6

(*) Figures refer to trade with the Russian Federation.

Source: State Institute of Statistics.

However, these official figures are far from telling the true importance of Russia in Turkey's exports, for unrecorded trade figures exceed by far recorded trade. Unofficial trade is carried out by petty traders, coming as tourists to major shopping centers with "empty suitcases" and undertaking their "on-the-spot" purchases.[5] Sales to such petty traders are estimated to attain between $5 billion and $10 billion annually, including sales to all tourists from Eastern Europe and the other CIS countries. This market is important not only for its large volume of sales but for other reasons as well. Equally important is the fact that goods traded in this market are rather low-quality products that Turkey cannot market elsewhere and that are sold at very low prices. Small firms, major producers of such products, can reach thereby an export outlet in a direct way, thus overcoming their export constraints. Additionally, the suitcase trade market has been the major catalyzer in reviving the economy of northeastern Anatolia, as one of its major shopping centers is centered in the city of Trabzon.

Official trade with Russia, however, is also of crucial importance because it has proved to be a ready market for many consumer products that face non-tariff barriers, such as "sensitive products" in Western markets. Some fresh fruits and vegetables, confectionary products inclusive of chocolates, soft drinks as well as alcoholic beverages, chewing gums, vegetable oils, cigarettes, pasta, and tea leaves rank as the most important items in the food-tobacco-beverages category of exports. The same is true of Turkey's apparel exports: Russia has rapidly moved up to third rank, after Germany and the United States, on the export list. Leather products, shoes, and other traditional export products, not easily exportable either because of their low quality or because of import barriers abroad, have found a major outlet thanks to the opening of the Russian market (*Moskova Ticaret* 1996 b: 1–7).

Even if the overall volume of official exports may not seem large, for these basic reasons Russia has become an indispensable trading partner for some provinces and for some producer categories. Suffice it to say, the number of exporters to Russia increased from 901 in 1993 to 1,786 in 1994 and the number of product varieties from 1,854 in 1993 to 2,465 in 1994 (*Moskova Ticaret* 1996 b: 4).

Service Trade

Three items in overall service trade can be distinguished as the most important in terms of their quantity as well as the indispensability of the Russian market as a crucial outlet: contracting, tourism, and transportation.

Turkish contracting firms entered Middle East Arab countries in the wake of the first oil crisis, starting with Libya, which had been shunned by Western contractors. They then moved on to other Arab countries and, to a much lesser extent, to some European countries, increasing their total contract awards to about $15 billion by the early 1990s. But the Gulf War and the ensuing embargo on Iraq almost put an end to their operations in the Middle East region. Thanks to the opening up of the Russian market they were saved from running into serious economic hardships. They could readily expand their operations in this market on account of their high performance ratings and competitive edge in terms of prices.

By the end of 1995, their total contract awards in Russia amounted to $6.9 billion, constituting about one-fourth of their total awards in the world and rapidly rising year by year in amount (*Moskova Ticaret* 1996b: 2–3). They have been engaged, by and large, in the construction or renovation of private housing, public, and commercial buildings, hotels, and cultural and sports centers, as well as other entertainment-related buildings. Noteworthy is the fact that contracts awarded to Turkish companies amount to 69% of the total undertaken in the CIS by foreign contractors and that Turkish contractors (about 76 in number) run their operations employing Turkish workers and Turkish personnel, so that, by the mid-1990s, several thousands of Turkish citizens were actively engaged in Russia.[6]

The second buoyant service trade is centered on tourism. Prior to the mid-1980s, tourists from the USSR hardly appeared on the list of foreigners visiting Turkey. With the commencement of cross-border trade and accompanied by suitcase trade, shopping centers located in Istanbul, Trabzon, and Izmir started to teem with tourists from the USSR. By 1993, the number of tourists coming from the CIS had reached 271,000, ranking as fourth after Germany, the U.K. and the United States. By 1994 and 1995, however, their numbers exploded to exceed 1.4 million and 1.3 million, respectively, and they shifted to the first rank in terms of numbers.[7]   Additionally, Turkey's summer resort centers on the Mediterranean coast attract rich tourists from Russia as well as other parts of the CIS, and the Russian language has come to be one of the three languages, after German and English, spoken in tourism centers.

On account of the social turmoil and economic hardships in Russia, however, it is far from being the first choice of Turkish tourists going abroad. But a large number of students, by and large those who have failed to be admitted to their preferred departments at the universities of their first or second choice, have started going to Russia or some other part of the CIS to get a degree. There are also "therapy tours" to Russia, in particular for the cure of ophthalmological diseases, organized by Turkish tourism companies.

In short, whereas the USSR and Turkey lived as contiguous, but completely isolated, countries with almost no direct human contact in the Cold War days, this is no longer valid.

Transportation is the third service industry that yields Turkey net export income in trade with Russia. The Russian market is distinguished as the first in terms of the overall benefits it confers on transport companies as well.

The EU has banned the entry into its territory of aged trucks; hence, there is the need to renew the fleet by way of undertaking new investments. Since no such bans exist in Russia or the CIS at large, Turkish transporters can go on using their aged trucks in trade relations with this region (UND June 1996: 28). This enables them to prolong the depreciation period of their overall truck fleet and, hence, to reduce average transport costs. They can, thus, sustain their competitive edge in the European market, notwithstanding the enormous costs of renewing their European-oriented truck fleet (UND June 1996: 28).

According to figures given by the Association of Land Route Transporters, the number of their runs to Russia amounted to 36,000 in 1994 and to 57,000 in 1995, whereas the number of runs by Russian carriers to Turkey was only 67 as of the latter year. The association estimates its export income to amount to $1.1 billion in 1995 (UND May 1996: 21 and June 1996: 28). This imbalance, however, turned out to be a major source of discontent on the part of Russian transporters, and both countries' governments came to be involved in the search for a satisfactory solution.

Capital Flows and Cooperation in Science and Technology

Some categories of capital flows, notably credits, between Russia and Turkey not only have been small in amount but also have given rise to intergovernmental conflicts rather than to the enhancement of economic relations. This is primarily because of the failure, on the part of one or the other, to duly honor debts on account of economic hardships. In the last few years, this has been mostly true for Russia in paying back its debts to Turkey (*Ticari ve Ekonomik İlişkiler* 1996: 5–11).

As of mid-1995, the number of direct investments undertaken by Russian firms in Turkey amounted to 64. They are, by and large, in the form of joint ventures with local firms and extremely small in amount. The largest, undertaken by Yukos, the oil company, hardly reaches $100,000. Direct investments by Turkish firms in Russia display similar characteristics; they numbered 105 in 1994, inclusive of two joint ventures in banking, and amounted to $13 million as of the same year (Aydın and Bekar 1995: 135–136).[8]

The Turkish Exim Bank extended $1.15 billion in credits to the USSR between 1989 and 1991; an additional $350 million investment credits were pledged as of mid-1990 for financing the construction works to be undertaken by Turkish contractors. On account of the failure of the USSR to pay back its debts on time, however, this project credit was not made available to the Russian Federation until the signing of the rescheduling agreement at the end of 1995.

Turkey has also been donating small sums to Russia in the last years: $313,000 in 1993, $709,300 in 1994, and $91,300 in 1995 (*Ticari ve Ekonomik İlişkiler* 1996: 4).

In contrast to the flourishing of trade relations in merchandise and services, capital flows have been very modest, as both countries suffer from capital shortages, and, in both, risk exposure of capital is high due to extreme economic instability. But the incipient effective cooperation in the field of science and technology between the relevant institutions seems to pave the way for further enhancing cooperation, in the same way as private enterprise has been doing. Such cooperation is likely, however, to bear fruit in the longer run.

The Turkish Scientific and Technical Research Organization (TÜBİTAK) has set up a joint commission with its peer in Russia, patterned after the agreement signed between the two governments, as of September 1992. Several seminars have been run since then in the fields of fundamental sciences and information technology; joint projects ranging from space research, to pollution control in the Black Sea, to high-energy astrophysics have been put on the agenda. An observatory is currently being set up on Turkey's Mediterranean coast by TÜBİTAK for joint research in astronomy. A program has been launched, under the auspices of TÜBİTAK, for setting up a computer network linking countries coastal to the Black Sea. Additionally, several scientists from Russia have been invited, in the context of advanced fellowship program run by TÜBİTAK (whereby travel and research grants in the fields of basic, applied and medical sciences are awarded to scientists who are citizens of a North Atlantic Treaty Organization (NATO) Cooperation Partner country) to give lectures and to participate in joint research projects. This covers all ex-Soviet republics and Eastern Europe, plus Slovenia and Albania.

The complementarity observed in the economic structures of the two countries is valid here as well. In contrast to Turkey's rather inadequate background in the fundamental sciences, Russia has a very rich scientific heritage. But Turkey, as opposed to Russia, is better versed in social sciences and modern management techniques.

PROSPECTS FOR THE NEAR FUTURE

Econometric estimates, projecting into future years the growth and composition of various types of economic relations (e.g., merchandise trade, service trade, capital flows, etc.) between Russia and Turkey, based on historical data, would hardly be meaningful. This 15-year historical survey should have helped show how political changes can introduce total changes in economic relations. Currently, political uncertainty and economic instability characterize both countries, in particular Russia. These two issues render it difficult to foresee the evolution of economic relations in the coming few years, let alone the period beyond the year 2000. If the continuing impoverishment at home encourages Russian leaders to revert to Russian nationalism, such a radical change would again evoke total changes in economic as well as overall relations. Similarly, major changes could occur if Islamic fundamentalism were to come to power in Turkey.

It is, however, also true that in both countries private agents have currently a greater say in political decision making and greater vested interests in each other's market than erstwhile. Not only are governments no longer the sole determinants of economic policies, but also there seems to be greater goodwill to produce sensible solutions to existing issues. This is a great asset that can be preserved and enhanced insofar as democratic governments remain in office in both countries.

Given the foregoing observations, we analyze the prospects for economic relations in the coming years.

First, the boom in economic relations between Russia and Turkey originated in the natural gas and related offset agreement. This agreement is to remain in effect for a period of 25 years, starting from 1987. It stipulates that Russia pledges to pump, and Turkey to buy each year, an agreed amount of natural gas. This agreement will, in the coming years, draw the bottom line in economic relations.

Second, the extent to which economic relations can be enhanced will be determined by the persistence of open markets. Restoration of strong protective measures is contradictory to this purpose. But its avoidance will depend, by and large, on the achievement of stability and economic growth in both economies.

There are at the present some signs that Russia is reverting to protection on imports. Beginning with 1 August 1996, Russia reduced the tax exempt amount in suitcase trade imports from $2,000 to $1,000; moreover, officials announced that soon this amount will be reduced to $500 (*Milliyet* 23 July 1996).[9] This is a serious blow not only to suitcase trade and the boom it spurred in the related industries and regions in Turkey but also to overall economic relations. Similarly, in the case of transportation, it has been announced that Russia will close frontier gates to Turkish transporters by 15 August 1996. The pending implementation aroused such ire in Turkish transporters and exporters that they had to resort to President Süleyman Demirel, who, in turn, sought a solution by taking the issue to President Yeltsin (*Cumhuriyet* 26 July 1996).

Third, there are also some institutional constraints, binding both countries, that will involve the introduction of some trade impediments in the coming years. As Turkey adopts the common external tariff under the customs union agreement with the EU, it will have to raise taxes on some imports from Russia as well as from third countries.

Similarly, the Russian Federation currently implements, under certain conditions, a concessionary tariff on merchandise imports from Turkey, whereas taxes on overall imports were raised as of 15 May 1996 (*Moskova Ticaret* 1996b: 7). Insofar as this concession remains in effect, it obviously confers a competitive edge on Turkey's exports in this market. But, as Russia comes under the mainstream of international rules and regulations in the process of integrating its economy with the global economy, this concession will have to be lifted. It will have to adopt General Agreement on Tariffs and Trade (GATT) rules that preclude such bilateral concessionary treatment.

Contracting activity also seems confronted with the slowing down effects of legal issues. The Duma, the lower house of the Russian Parliament, refused to pass a law in 1995 related to the avoidance of double taxation between the two countries in the operations of their companies (Aydın and Bekar 1995: 136). Additionally, confusing tax rules, the raising of tax rates in the employment of Turkish workers, and the reduction of the three-year tax exemption initially accorded to Turkish contractors to one year are some of such issues. Their result is to erode the competitive edge of Turkish contracting companies.

Finally, Turkey has largely benefited from the rapid expansion in economic relations with Russia. This expansion has definitely contributed to an amelioration in overall relations. The furthering of economic relations at the same rate as over the last decade, however, will be partly determined by the attainment of a cooperative solution in the "pipeline routes" issue discussed earlier and partly by the achievement of stability and growth in both economies. Also, political actions, on the part of each government, that evoke misgivings must be avoided if private agents are to be faced with lower risks in their economic operations in the other party's market.

NOTES

1. There are, however, signs of a thaw here as well. The advent to power of Islamic fundamentalists (from mid-1996 to mid-1997) in Turkey, even if as the major partner in a coalition government, has led Russian officials to tone down their indictments against Turkey. Similarly, on account of the indispensable interests of Turkish businessmen in the Russian market, Turkish officials try to produce pragmatic solutions to conflicts.

2. In the context of the customs union agreement, Turkey is integrated with only the economic community of the European Union. This latter comprises political bodies where Turkey is not represented.

3. The Duma defied Turkey by its decision to set up a working committee for settling the "Kurdistan issue." The contention was that by way of Russian support to Kurds, the latter can help enhance democracy in Turkey and, thus, eradicate the Turkish threat to Russia (*Milliyet* 27 June 1996).

4. Russia's ex-ambassador to Ankara, A. Chernyshev, argues that on account of the ambiguity of the legal status of the Caspian Sea, coastal countries thereto cannot explore and exploit natural resources before that issue is settled (*Milliyet* 1 July 1996).

5. The outstanding importance of suitcase trade for Turkish companies is also evidenced by their running special reduced-fare charter tours between the two countries (*Moskova Ticaret* 1996b: 3).

6. In 1995, the total number of workers going abroad stood at 61,145, of whom 39,870 went to Russia (TİKA 1996: 1).

7. Turkey's State Statistical Office does not distinguish between tourists from Russian and the CIS. Other sources show tourist numbers from Russia to stand at 830,000 in 1994 (*Moskova Ticaret* 1996b: 3).

8. The number of Turkish firms, inclusive of representative offices, company branches, and joint ventures, in Russia is estimated to exceed 200; adding firms not registered by Turkish authorities brings this figure to 300 (*Moskova Ticaret* 1996b: 4).

9. The chairman of the Russian committee on economic policy notes that Russia's primary economic task is "to conquer the domestic market and to defend domestic producers from the flood of imported goods" (Berger 1996). Suitcase imports to Russia in excess of $1,000 will henceforth be subject to 30% tax. The overvaluation in the Russian ruble noted in the text is a main factor in the emerging protective tendency.

9

Turkey and the Changing Oil Market in Eurasia
Meliha Altunışık

INTRODUCTION

The collapse of the Soviet Union and the emergence of new states in the Caucasus and Central Asia seemed to provide new opportunities for Turkey. A major Turkish role in the production and especially in the transportation of Eurasian oil was considered among those new opportunities. Hoping to reap both internal and external benefits of a possible Turkish involvement in this field, the Turkish government engaged in extensive "oil diplomacy." During this process the government actors sought to manipulate domestic and international politics simultaneously.

However, the oil saga has become a case of showing the limitations of Turkey's new role in the area. In fact, Ankara soon found itself in the midst of regional rivalries. By early 1993 especially Russia, within the context of its "near abroad" policy, made its continuing interests in Eurasia clear. The Turkish government was late to recognize this fact and for a long time based its policy on a zero-sum game with Russia. In the meantime, it trusted the support it could get from the United States as well as its "special relationship" with Eurasian countries. Yet, despite some minor gains, Turkey realized the limits of its role in the changing oil market in Eurasia.

INITIAL EUPHORIA

The disintegration of the Soviet Union in December 1991 presented Turkey with an opportunity to establish closer relations with the newly independent states especially, in the Caucasus and Central Asia.[1] It was hoped that common linguistic, ethnic, and religious ties with these states would provide a common ground from which the relations could flourish. More important, this development came at a time when Turkey was feeling isolated internationally. The country's possible membership into the European Community (EC) was seen as more and more problematic. Furthermore, there were serious concerns among the Turkish political elite that the collapse of the Soviet Union and the end of the Cold War could decrease Turkey's strategic importance within the Western alliance and, thus, erode its bargaining position.[2] In the meantime, right after the collapse of the Soviet Union, Western countries, especially the United States, also started to promote Turkey as the most influential regional actor in this area and as a counterweight to Iran.[3] There were also expected benefits for Ankara, especially in the area of economic cooperation with these states. Forging of relations with the countries in the Caucasus and Central Asia was hoped to open up new markets and investment areas for Turkey at a time when the country was facing an increasing foreign trade deficit.

Within this context a major area of interest that emerged was the vast oil and natural gas resources in three of these countries, namely, Azerbaijan, Kazakhstan, and Turkmenistan. Turkey wanted both to be involved in the exploitation of the Eurasian oil and to have it transported through its territory. Therefore, there were two issues involved: production and transportation of Eurasian oil. Especially the latter became a matter of intense bargaining and negotiation on the part of the Turkish government. The issue was brought up by Turkey in different forums as early as 1992. During the first Turkic Summit, which was convened in Ankara in October of that year, then-president Turgut Özal sought commitments from these countries to agree to the construction of oil and gas pipelines that would cross Turkey. However, the issue was not even mentioned in the Ankara Declaration, which was signed at the end of the summit.[4] The only achievement for Turkey, if one can call it such, was a protocol signed between Turkey and Turkmenistan which called for the construction of a natural gas pipeline from that country to Turkey. Even then the logistics of such a pipeline were not specified (Winrow 1995b: 19). However, in the Istanbul Declaration, which was signed after the Second Turkic Summit, which convened in Istanbul in October 1994, there were more specific references to the issue of oil pipelines. The declaration stated that the participant states "welcomed the work being carried out among interested countries on natural gas and oil pipelines to be built extending to European and the Mediterranean via Turkey" (*Turkish Daily News* 22 October 1994). However, Turkish oil diplomatic efforts intensified, especially in 1995. Tansu Çiller, then-prime minister, made the pipeline issue one of two major foreign policy priorities (the other being the signing of the customs union with the European Union [EU]) of her government. She appointed an oil pipeline coordinator, who became directly responsible to her and started an all-out effort for the realization of an oil pipeline through Turkey.

There were three policy goals for the Turkish government in pursuing an active role in production and, especially, distribution of Eurasian oil. First of all, there were obvious economic benefits involved. Such an involvement would decrease Turkey's dependence on Middle Eastern oil and Russian gas. Also, handsome royalties and transportation fees would accrue to state coffers if a pipeline was to be built through Turkey. Finally, benefits to the Turkish construction firms that could construct the pipeline and the employment opportunities that would be created, especially in the less developed eastern parts of the country, were considered other positive effects of such an involvement.

However, at least as important as the economic goals were the political and strategic considerations of the Turkish political elite.[5] It was believed that speedy marketing of Eurasian oil and especially doing so through Turkey would increase economic independence of these countries, consolidate their political independence, and thus decrease Russian influence in the area. As a corollary, Turkey would acquire a new voice in regional affairs and, thus, increase its strategic and political importance in the post-Cold War era.

Last but not least, domestic considerations played an important role in the active oil diplomacy that was pursued, especially during the Çiller administration. It was obvious that success would have increased the popularity of the Çiller government, which was facing elections. Throughout the oil saga, domestic concerns played a crucial role and determined the way the issues were presented to the public. However, the considerable fanfare that surrounded the government's diplomacy negatively affected the diplomatic process. Exaggerated expectations and untimely declarations of "success" in the oil game made Russia apprehensive.

PRODUCTION AGREEMENTS

Although less important for Turkish political elites when compared to the issue of pipelines, the initial bargaining process was about the partition of the oil fields for production. Turkey was a newcomer to the international oil production business and therefore had limited goals.

The most important development in terms of production agreements was experienced in Azerbaijan when the so-called deal of the century was signed.[6] After intense negotiations, the Azerbaijani national oil company, SOCAR, and foreign oil companies concluded a Product Sharing Contract (PSC) on 20 September 1994. This was followed by the formation of the Azerbaijan International Operating Company (AIOC), known as the International Consortium, to coordinate the activities of the contractors.[7] AIOC planned to develop Chirag, Azeri, and Guneshli fields in an $8 billion program phased in over three decades.[8]

The Turkish national oil company, TPAO (Turkish Petroleum Corporation),[9] became one of the 11 international companies that formed the International Consortium. TPAO initially had a share of 1.75%. When the Azerbaijani gov-

ernment, which was in financial difficulty, decided to sell a 10% share of
SOCAR, Turkey saw this as an opportunity to increase its share in the consortium. Initially, it seemed that the Turkish government would be successful in
achieving its aim. In fact, even before a final agreement was reached Prime
Minister Çiller and Minister of Energy Veysel Atasoy told the press that
TPAO's share in the AIOC would be increased to 6.75%. This was presented as
a major victory for Turkey and, of course, for the Çiller government. However,
soon it was understood that there was no agreement on the matter yet, and,
contrary to the claims made by the government, the Haidar Aliyev government
in Azerbaijan was perhaps approaching other players, including Iran, to sell its
share. Finally, in April 1996 Aliyev announced that SOCAR would sell 5% of
its share to Turkey and the remaining 5% to Exxon.[10] The fact that this announcement came after an unsuccessful coup attempt against Aliyev in 12–17
March raised suspicions about a possible Turkish role in the attempt.[11] It was
also argued that Aliyev took this decision as a result of pressures from the U.S.
government, which was adamantly against any Iranian participation in the
Caspian oil. In any case, Çiller went to Baku to sign the agreement on 12 April
1995, and TPAO's share in the consortium was increased to 6.75%. After that
the TPAO got a 15% share in the Shahdeniz field as well.

Turkish companies were also involved in oil production agreements in
Kazakhstan.[12] As a result of an agreement that was signed in June 1994, TPAO
started to carry out exploration and drilling activities in four different fields,
which have reserves of 4 billion barrels of oil and about 200 billion cubic meters of gas, in the western part of that country. Besides the TPAO, some private
Turkish oil companies also started exploration and production activities in both
Azerbaijan and Kazakhstan. However, Turkey's role in the production of the
Eurasian oil expectedly remained limited, parallel to its role in the world energy market.

ENTER RUSSIA

The Russian Federation was very much disturbed by the developments in
Caspian oil and especially by the signing of "the deal of the century." By then
Moscow was trying to reassert itself in the former Soviet republics.[13] The so-
called near abroad policy adopted by the Russian government emphasized Russia's vital political, economic, and military interests in these areas.[14] The developments in Eurasian oil were analyzed and interpreted within this framework. However, it appeared that two policy outcomes followed this logic, and
each was represented by different government agencies. The Russian state's
attitude toward the Azerbaijani oil deal underlined these differences. The Minister of Fuel and Energy and the Russian oil company LUKoil[15] argued that
Russia should participate in the Caspian oil deals and thus acquire benefits
from the oil bonanza. In line with this argument, in November 1993 Russia's
minister of fuel and energy and the president of LUKoil visited Baku. At the

end of this visit an agreement that gave LUKoil 10% share in the future contract on the Azerbaijani oil was signed.[16]

On the other hand, the Russian Foreign Ministry adopted a hard-line position and made it very clear that Russia was against any foreign investment in Caspian oil. These views were openly stated in Directive No. 396, "On Protecting the Interests of the Russian Federation in the Caspian Sea." Foreign Minister Andrei Kozyrev and the director of Russia's Foreign Intelligence Service, Yevgeny Primakov, persuaded Boris Yeltsin to sign this directive, "which made the standard Russian realist case for a Russian sphere of influence" (Barylski 1995: 223). Furthermore, in order to prevent any foreign encroachment and to consolidate its control and influence in the area, the Kremlin also raised the issue of the legal status of the Caspian Sea.[17] Russia started to argue that the Caspian was a lake, and as such there should be joint possession of the Caspian, including its mineral resources. Obviously, this argument was not accepted by other littoral states, except Iran. Newly independent states along the Caspian insisted that it was a landlocked sea and, thus, that each littoral state had rights to its territorial waters, continental shelf, and exclusive economic zone. However, this did not stop Moscow from continually raising the issue and using it as a Damocles' sword over the former Soviet republics. On 5 October 1994 Moscow asked the United Nations (UN) General Assembly to include the question of the legal regime of the Caspian Sea in the agenda of its winter session (Uibopuu 1995: 120). Later, in April 1994, the Foreign Ministry sent a threatening note to the British Embassy in Moscow stating the invalidity of oil deals in the Caspian Sea until the legal regime of that sea was determined.[18] The Russian Foreign Ministry also brought forward environmental concerns and stated that Russia was "worried about ecological impact of any agreement on Caspian resources" (Uibopuu 1995: 120).

A closed meeting was held in Moscow among the Caspian states on 12 October 1994 to consider these issues. Russia argued for the institution of a veto power for each littoral state over offshore oil development projects in the Caspian. However, these arguments were not accepted by the other participants. Later, under pressure from Russia, Kazakhstan took the initiative to convene a meeting in Almaty again to discuss the subject of the legal status of the Caspian Sea. In the first meeting, which was held in July 1995, the littoral states agreed to create a constantly functioning negotiating mechanism. At the following meeting, in September 1995, all participants in the conference agreed to reject the Russian idea for joint control (*Kazakh Radio First Program Network* 27 September 1995). Yet Moscow continued to raise this issue and challenge the legal status of the Caspian. Finally, in November 1996, in another meeting of the Caspian states, Russia proposed a compromise offer that called for 45-mile territorial waters for each littoral country, plus "pinpoint jurisdiction" for Azerbaijan over fields it had already started to develop. This offer seemed acceptable to Iran and Turkmenistan, and Kazakhstan accepted it as a basis of negotiation with some minor adjustments. However, the proposal was unacceptable for Azerbaijan which is hoping to develop other offshore oil fields within its territorial waters (*Economist* 11 January 1997: 27).

The differences of opinion among several actors of the Russian state and the consequent adoption of alternative policies in some ways complemented each other. Hard-line policies of the foreign ministry facilitated LUKoil's participation in all Caspian oil deals without a real financial contribution, since the Caspian states felt threatened by the declarations and moves of the Russian Foreign Ministry. After the signing of the "deal of the century" the Azeri government signed two other contracts: one on the Karabakh and the other on the Shahdeniz oil fields. LUKoil got handsome shares from both of these contracts as well.[19] After signing the contract for the Karabakh oil field, the Russian Minister of Fuel and Energy declared this "a serious victory of Russia's oil complex and diplomacy." For him "projects of this kind promote integration in the CIS [Commonwealth of Independent States]" and demonstrate "Russia's strengthening position in the region" (*Interfax* 10 November 1995). In fact, his words were a clear indication of the politicized nature of the Caspian oil and the way Russia perceived its interests in the area. In fact, after the signing of the agreement with Russia, the Azerbaijani president, Aliyev, openly stated that "the current contract has more political than economic significance" (*Turan* 10 November 1995).

PIPELINE POLITICS

The possible route for the marketing of the Caspian oil has become the subject of intense diplomatic and legal battles, especially between Russia and Turkey. Both countries wanted the pipeline to cross through their territories and, therefore, have presented alternative routes as the most viable ones and engaged in a bitter struggle to convince other parties.

Ankara, from the start, argued that Turkey was the ideal route to carry the Eurasian oil to the Western markets and, initially, using its very close relationship with the pro-Turkish Ebulfez Elchibey government in Azerbaijan, was making headway. An agreement was signed between Azerbaijan and Turkey on 9 March 1993. That agreement seemed to make Turkey the winner in the oil pipeline bonanza. However, before that agreement could be implemented, the Elchibey government was overthrown on 4 June 1993 by a military coup. It was replaced by a government headed by Haidar Aliyev, a previous member of Soviet Politburo.[20] This was one of the signs of increasing Russian influence in Eurasia. Soon after Aliyev came to power, Azerbaijan became a member of CIS in September 1993.[21] These developments meant that the pipeline agreement with Turkey was forgotten. Now alternative routes were proposed by Russia and Iran. The Baku-Persian Gulf route proposed by Iran became unattainable because of U.S. insistence to exclude Iran from both production and transportation of the Caspian oil. Therefore, the Russian and Turkish proposals became the main contenders. Figure 9.1 shows the various proposed oil pipeline routes.

Figure 9.1
Proposed Pipeline Routes for Caspian Oil

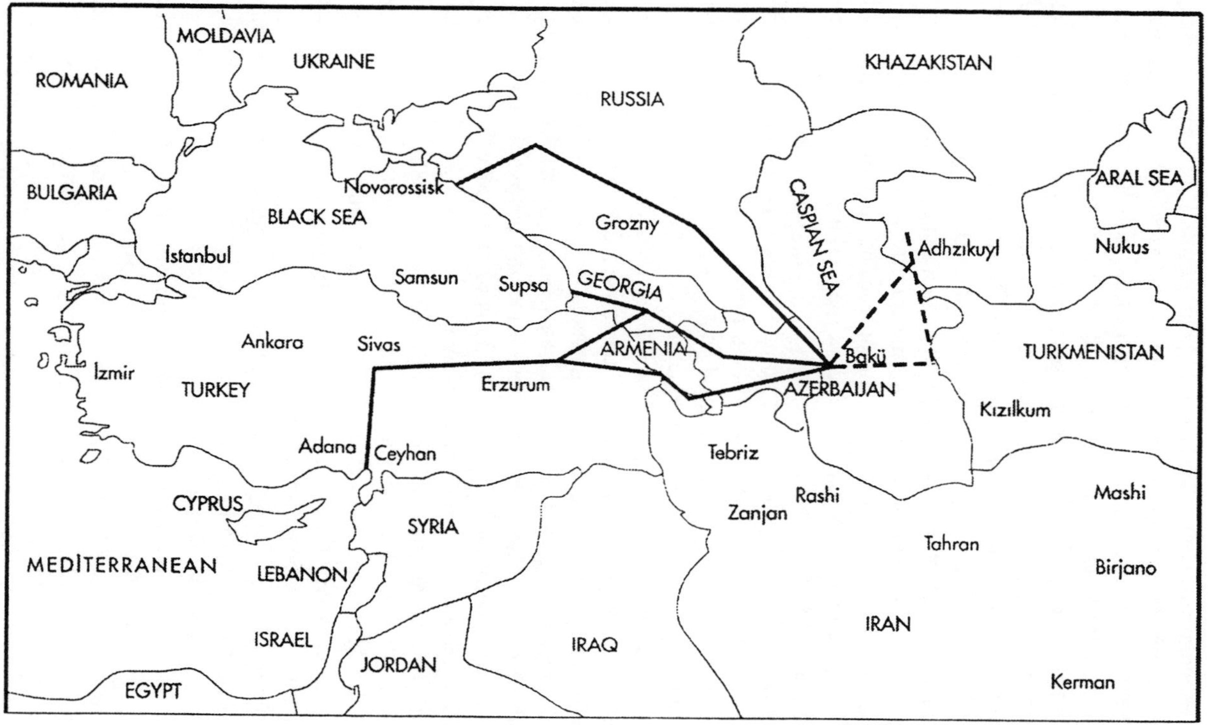

In December 1994 the Turkish government put forward a proposal called the "Caspian-Mediterranean Oil Pipeline Project." It aimed to carry the Kazak and Azeri oil through two interconnected pipelines from Tengiz and Baku overland from Turkey to the Ceyhan export terminal on the Mediterranean.[22] The Turkish position was based on the premise that Baku-Ceyhan pipeline would be more economical because Turkey would commit itself to finance the pipeline, would ask for the lowest transportation fee, and would offer to buy part of the oil. The Turkish government also guaranteed the security of the pipeline.

Realizing the place of the United States as a major player, the Turkish government tried to get Washington's support for its proposal. After intense diplomatic efforts, in January 1995, the U.S. government declared its support for a "pipeline through Turkey." However, this idea was presented in a general framework of U.S. policy of "multiple pipelines." The U.S. government did not want to alienate Russia altogether. On the other hand, for economic and political reasons Washington did not want one country to control the tap. This became the cornerstone of U.S. policy throughout the "pipeline politics." At times the U.S. government also put pressure on the Turkish government to negotiate with Russia as well. However, especially at the beginning, the Turkish government did not show any interest in doing so. Only later did Turkish officials start to emphasize that this project would not be an alternative to the northern route. On the contrary, it was argued that it would be designed to carry the over-capacity oil from the Russian pipeline.

In the beginning the exact route for the proposed Baku-Ceyhan pipeline was not clear. Coming from Azerbaijan, it could pass through Armenia or Georgia. Initially, an Armenian option, which would be the shortest route, was supported, especially by the U.S. government. It was also believed that this would contribute to the achievement of Azeri-Armenian peace. In January 1995, the U.S. undersecretary of foreign affairs, Richard Holbrooke, visited Turkey. He made it clear that the United States would support the Baku-Ceyhan option but that the Turkish government should look for ways of cooperating with the Armenians. After that the Turkish Foreign Ministry tried to work out a peace between the Azeris and Armenians. However, these efforts were not particularly welcomed by Aliyev (*Yeni Yüzyıl* 7 April 1995). As a result, it was decided that the pipeline would be built via Georgia.

In the meantime, Çiller visited Kazakhstan in August 1995, and a framework agreement for the building of the pipeline was signed. This was a more limited agreement than the Turkish government hoped for. Kazakh leader Nursultan Nazarbayev in the press conference made it clear that the Russian pipeline that already existed did not have enough capacity, so it was necessary to look for other ways to transport the Kazakh oil. However, being aware of Moscow's sensitivities, Nazarbayev made it clear that Russian partnership should also be sought in the Mediterranean pipeline (Çevik 1995: 7). This was not surprising, given Kazakhstan's dependence on Russia. The fact that about 40% of the

Kazakh population is Russian and that the bureaucracy is largely occupied by that minority largely explains this dependence.

The Turkish government, while continuing to promote the Baku-Ceyhan route, made several arguments against the Russian proposal, which aimed to bring the oil to the terminal at Novorossiisk, a Russian port on the Black Sea coast, and then carry it with tankers via the Turkish Straits.[23] First of all, Turkey made it clear that it would oppose the use of the straits in transporting the Caspian oil. It was stated that if all Caspian Sea oil passes through the Bosphorus, this would mean that each year 100 million tons of oil would pass instead of the current 32 million tons. This would put an additional strain on the traffic in this already overloaded, narrow waterway, create environmental problems, and present an increased health risk to Istanbul's 12 million inhabitants. To prevent this from happening, the Turkish government hastily adopted some new regulations concerning the passage of oil tankers through the straits on 1 July 1994. Russia protested these new regulations and accused Turkey of trying to get an upper hand in the tug of war for the oil pipelines.[24] The timing of these actions by the Turkish government gave the impression that, like the Russian ecological concerns for the Caspian Sea, Turkey had political reasons behind this decision as well. However, the threat to the Bosphorus and Istanbul is so real that eventually the Turkish arguments received at least an understanding, if not support, from different circles, including the Consortium. To counter this, Russia proposed an alternative route through Bulgaria and Greece. However, Turkey argued that the "Burgas-Alexandropolis" pipeline project was not economically viable, mainly because of the double-handling of oil.

Turkey also reminded of the limitations of the port of Novorossiisk. Since the current annual 30 million-ton capacity of the port would be inadequate to handle the export of Caspian oil, either an expansion or the building of a new port was needed, and both would add to the expenses. In addition, it was noted that this Black Sea port "is closed at least one third of the year because of the adverse weather conditions." Finally, as long as the Chechnian problem continued, there was the issue of the security of the Russian pipeline that was crossing Chechnya.[25]

On the other hand, Russia also tried to convince the consortium and the related governments that the Turkish proposal was much less attractive. First of all, it would cost more than the Russian proposal. Moreover, several Russian officials brought the Kurdish problem to the discussion very often and argued that the Turkish route was unsafe. Moscow openly "warned Almaty and Baku of a possible negative reaction on the part of the Kurds" (*Interfax* 28 February 1995).

The issue of security became an important part of the debate throughout the pipeline politics and both sides accused each other of fanning the flames in their problem areas. However, the head of the AIOC stated that the consortium was not very much concerned about these issues, and what was important was to provide security at the pumps (*32. Gün* [32nd Day], Show TV 16 July 1996).

Apparently, the consortium had already accepted the instabilities in the region as a given. Yet the Kurdish question and the problems in Chechnya continued to be used by both sides to further their arguments.

THE POLITICS OF "EARLY OIL"

Unlike the oil-producing countries of Eurasia and Turkey, other players are not necessarily in a hurry to market the Eurasian oil. The softness of the world oil market and the possible diverse effects of an influx of large amounts of oil into the world market on the other oil-producer states, like Saudi Arabia, are of major concern to the multinational oil companies especially and to the U.S. government. However, in the meantime, Eurasian oil producers are in dire need of cash. As a result of these considerations a compromise solution called "early production" was worked out for Azerbaijan. The consortium decided to produce about 5 tons of oil per year maximum, totaling 20 tons over a 10-year period. Again the selection of the export route for this relatively small quantity of oil, the so-called early oil, to be produced by the consortium became an issue. Eventually the AIOC reduced the options to two possibilities [26]: the northern route to transport oil from Baku through Chechnya to the Russian port of Novorossiisk on the Black Sea or the western route to the port of Soupsa on the Black Sea coast of Georgia.

This decision put the Turkish government in a difficult position. The Baku-Ceyhan route was not even considered viable for the "early oil." But what should be the position of the Turkish government vis-à-vis the two proposals? At this point divisions occurred among the several government actors that had been involved in pipeline politics. The Turkish Foreign Ministry believed that Turkey should support the Soupsa route. This was also the position of Prime Minister Çiller and her oil pipeline coordinator Emre Gönensay. It was argued that if that route was chosen, that would end the domination by Moscow of the transportation infrastructure of the region. This would, it was believed, increase the chances of the Turkish project. It was also claimed that part of the Baku-Soupsa route, namely, the Baku-Tbilisi section, could easily became part of the main route to the Turkish port of Ceyhan. The Ministry of Energy and especially BOTAŞ (Turkish State Pipeline Agency), on the other hand, argued that Turkey should concentrate its efforts on the main route and try to win support for its own proposal as soon as possible (*Yeni Yüzyıl* 19 October 1995). Hayrettin Uzun, then general manager of BOTAŞ, claimed that Soupsa was an alternative to Ceyhan, and thus, by supporting the Georgian option, Turkey would be supporting a rival project (*32. Gün* [32nd Day], *Show TV* 16 July 1996).

In the end, the government opted to actively support the Baku-Soupsa route for the "early production." In spring 1995 Prime Minister Çiller declared Turkish support for the Georgian port. In the meantime, the Turkish Foreign Ministry made concrete proposals toward the financing of the Baku-Soupsa line. It pledged also to buy the Soupsa route oil. However, from the beginning, the Turkish government made it clear that this support for the western route was linked to the ultimate realization of the Baku-Ceyhan pipeline. Moreover, "the financing proposals were conditional on limiting the capacity of the Baku-Soupsa line to maximum six million tons with the expectation that a future expansion of only the Baku-Tbilisi section will be the first part of the main export pipeline to the Mediterranean" (İskit 1996: 79). Following this decision Turkey engaged in intensive diplomacy, especially in Washington and Baku, to win the support for the Soupsa route.[27]

However, criticisms continued against Turkey's support for the western route and the government's handling of the issue in general. In addition to the press, there were critical voices coming from even Çiller's coalition government. The Ministry of Energy raised the issue of whether the country should spend that much money on financing the Soupsa line. Another area of concern was the competitive mode of Turco-Russian relations as a result of the pipeline issue. It was argued that before the United States, the government should have negotiated with the Russian Federation first. Finally, the way in which the oil diplomacy was conducted became a target of criticism. It was claimed that the issue was the subject matter of the Ministry of Energy and BOTAŞ, and others should not be involved in it.[28] There were even alternative proposals, like the Samsun-Yumurtalık pipeline linking Turkey's Black Sea coast to Yumurtalık on the Mediterranean. This project was defended on the grounds that it would require both Russian and Turkish participation and facilitate cooperation between the two countries. The company that proposed the project even got credits from the Treasury. However, the credits were canceled when the Ministry of Energy intervened (*Yeni Yüzyıl* 6 July 1995). The project was criticized by the Foreign Ministry on two grounds. First, it was considered non-economical because of the problem of double-handling. Second, such a pipeline would "still leave the control of Caspian oil in Russian hands" (İskit 1996: 68). Such arguments made by the supporters of the Soupsa route made it clear that one of the main policy aims of the Turkish government was to prevent Russia from increasing its influence in the region. Therefore, it was feared that if Turkey would not support the Soupsa route, the Consortium could opt for the northern line, and this would be a major blow to the Turkish policy.

Ankara submitted its proposal to the AIOC in August. It consisted of the rehabilitation of the existing pipeline and the financing of a new 13-kilometer one. It was stated that Turkey would partly finance the $250 million project and commit itself to buy all of the early oil. The proposal also stipulated that the pipeline and the terminal could be built by Turkish contractors and guaranteed to be finished on time. In addition, Turkey committed itself to charge low transportation fees (*Yeni Yüzyıl* 31 August 1995). Of course, in return for all this, Turkey wanted the consortium to choose the Baku-Soupsa option for early oil. If the consortium were to choose both of the proposals, then the Turkish government made it clear that it would finance the Baku-Soupsa pipeline only under two conditions: that the amount of oil that would flow from both pipelines should be the same and that the construction should start simultaneously (*Yeni Yüzyıl* 4 October 1995).

Following the submission of the proposal, a Turkish delegation headed by Gönensay went to Azerbaijan in August 1995. After that, it was announced that the same group would go to Moscow as well. If realized, this would have been the first high-level visit to Moscow to discuss the issue of oil pipelines (*Yeni Yüzyıl* 23 August 1995). However, the meetings were canceled. In the meantime, SOCAR's general manager, Natik Aliyev, was invited to Moscow to discuss the Russian proposal for early oil. These developments disturbed Turkish officials (*Yeni Yüzyıl* 31 August 1995).

After months of difficult negotiations, on 9 October 1995 the AIOC decided to use two pipeline routes to export the early production oil from three Caspian Sea fields to the world markets: both the northern and the western routes. How the oil would be divided between the two routes was to be announced later as a result of technical negotiations that would be held later.

Economically, the decision did not make much sense, but apparently, politically, it was seen as necessary. Three immediate factors were important in the decision. The most crucial one was the attitude of the U.S. government. The Bill Clinton administration had adopted a policy that called for the building of "multiple pipelines" for the transportation of the main oil. At the last minute they adopted the same approach as regards to the "early oil." In this, the diplomatic efforts by the Turkish government probably played some role. The U.S. government made its policy openly known when the U.S. ambassador to Baku, Richard Kauzlarich, gave a press conference a few days before the international consortium was to make public the route for the transportation of early oil. He reiterated the U.S. support for multiple lines since the U.S. government believed that the more oil pipeline routes there were, the greater the chances to ensure the safety of oil transportation and investments.[29] In addition, President Clinton called President Aliyev and restated Washington's desire for multiple pipelines.[30] It is safe to argue that concerns for regional balance of power played an important role in this support.

Another factor was the Chechen conflict. Being aware of the fact that continuation of that conflict was decreasing the chances of the northern route, the Russian government was trying to do something about it. In fact, the situation in the Chechen conflict was cited as a reason for the delay in the decision of the Consortium (Bagirov 1996: 47). Only after a declaration of a cease-fire did the consortium announce its decision for the transportation of "early oil."

Finally, Turkish support for the western route and the proposal that was submitted by the Turkish government were decisive in the decision of the consortium. In fact, after the announcement of their decision, the vice president of the AIOC, Art MacHaffie, said that the consortium initially preferred the Russian route but then, when Turkey said that it would finance the Georgian route and decrease the transportation rate considerably, the western route also became economical. "In the final analysis," he said, "the northern route which requires about $50 million investment but a high transportation rate and the southern route which requires about $250 million investment but has lower transportation rates have equal economic value." MacHaffie also added that, in addition to economic considerations, the consortium did not want to rely on one route for the reasons of political risks (*Yeni Yüzyıl* 19 November 1995).

Çiller's adviser responsible for the conduct of "pipeline diplomacy," Gönensay, declared the decision of the AIOC as a victory for Turkey. He argued that this decision signaled the realization of the Baku-Ceyhan route. Turkey could now turn its attention to Kazakhstan (*Yeni Yüzyıl* 6 October 1995). It was true that Turkey's support for the Georgian route had played a major role in the decision of the consortium. Yet the question remained as to whether or not this decision was really a signal of a pipeline through Turkey. In fact, soon there were new developments that signaled that Turkey was on square one in terms of the realization of Baku-Ceyhan. The vice president of the AIOC made it clear that it was too early even to talk about a Baku-Ceyhan route.

In the meantime, there were important developments as far as the Kazakhstan oil was concerned. The Caspian Pipeline Consortium (CPC) signed an agreement with Russia in April 1996 for the transport of the Kazakh oil to the world market. Ironically, in August 1995 Çiller in her visit to Almaty had signed a "framework agreement" with Nazarbayev for the transportation of oil from the Tengiz oil field. However, this final agreement with Russia put an end to the hopes of the Turkish government for Kazakh oil.

As far as the "early oil" was concerned, the developments were also not encouraging for Turkey. The AIOC concluded agreements with Georgia and Russia concerning early oil shipments through these states. As expected, however, the Russian route was commissioned first, as it demanded little construction. An agreement on the transportation of Azeri oil was signed between Azerbaijan and Russia in January 1996. It is interesting to note that while signing the agreement, a statement of the Russian government was adopted that noted that the signing of the agreement could not be interpreted as "changing the positions of the parties concerning the status of the Caspian Sea" (*Snark* 19 January 1996). This showed that the Kremlin was not yet ready to give up its leverage.

In the meantime Turkey's proposals concerning the construction of the Baku-Soupsa oil pipeline were discussed at a meeting in Baku. Representatives from Azerbaijan, Georgia, and the oil consortium companies attended the meeting, headed by the new chief adviser to the Turkish prime minister's office and oil pipelines coordinator, Bilsel Alisbah. Turkey submitted two proposals at the meeting, both of them calling for the speedy implementation of the western line. The proposal that foresaw Turkey's providing the financing of the western route was supported by the participants. However, the final decision was left to the following meeting, which was to be convened later.[31] The developments seemed to put the Turkish government in an awkward position. The AIOC did not accept Turkey's preconditions about the financing of the Baku-Soupsa line. However, apparently to continue the viability of the Mediterranean

option, the Turkish government would like to be involved in the financing of
the western route. The danger is that without the support of Ankara, this route
might not even be realized, at least not in the near future. Even then the government has not been very active in this regard. It seems that since the elections
and the downfall of the Çiller government, the pipeline issue has been put onto
the back burner. The volatility of the domestic political scene in Turkey could
have played a role in this indifference.

CONCLUSIONS

In the last few years Turkey has been greatly involved in the complex relationships that characterized the political economy of Caspian oil. Throughout
this process there were some successes. Turkey participated in the production of
Caspian oil. This participation seemed to open up new venues for the Turkish
oil industry which used to be largely domestic-oriented. Furthermore, Ankara
became one of the key players of the politics of Caspian oil and was accepted as
such by all the parties involved. All this was achieved through the active diplomacy of the Turkish government.

However, there were disappointments for Turkey as well, especially as far as
pipeline politics were concerned. The initial euphoria was finally replaced by a
more pragmatic look at the issue at hand. This meant the realization of the
Russian influence in the area. From the beginning the Turkish political elite
acted more with political motives and aimed to limit the Russian presence in
the Caucasus and Central Asia. A corollary of this policy was heightened hopes
for a new regional role for Turkey. The Caspian-Mediterranean pipeline project
was put forward as an element of this new role. Nevertheless, Moscow had already changed its plans for the CIS countries by then. It seems that at least
some of the Turkish policy-makers were slow to recognize the implications of
Russia's "near abroad" policy. Part of the reason for this misperception was the
preoccupation with the domestic spillover of "pipeline politics." Eventually,
Turkey began to state that the Baku-Ceyhan route was not an alternative to the
Russian proposal, but rather a complement to it. However, this came as too little too late, especially for the hard-liners in the Kremlin, who were determined
to reintegrate former Soviet republics into Russia.

Since the announcement of the early oil decision, there seem to be some
changes in this respect in the policy of the Turkish state. A few weeks after that
announcement, Turkey and Russia held talks in Moscow on ways of cooperating for the Caspian oil exports (*Turkish Daily News* 25 October 1995: A5).
Later, President Süleyman Demirel, in his visit to Azerbaijan in December
1995, reassured Moscow that "Turkey has no intention of competing with other
states for influence in the region" (*Nezavisimaya Gazeta* 15 December 1995).
Finally, Foreign Minister Çiller's visit to Moscow in December 1996 proved
that Turkey was trying to establish closer relations with Russia. In this visit, the

message was given to the Kremlin that, among other things, Ankara was ready to cooperate with Russia in the field of oil pipelines.[32]

Whether or not all this could change the Russian opposition to the Baku-Ceyhan pipeline is not certain and remains to be seen.[33] However, it is clear that deterioration of Turco-Russian relations would benefit neither country. Economic relations between the two countries are already satisfactory. In 1994 the trade volume between the two countries was about $2 billion (State Institute of Statistics February 1994: 33). In addition to that, unofficial trade amounts to more than twice that figure. Finally, the value of work undertaken by Turkish contractors in Russia is around $6 billion (İskit 1996: 72). There are also political benefits of cordial relations between the two countries. Therefore, as far as pipeline politics are concerned, Turkey should try to enlist Russian support for its project. This could be realized by encouraging Moscow's participation in the financing and construction of the Baku-Ceyhan pipeline. In this respect Ankara could get the support of those elements within the Russian state that are in favor of Russia's participation in oil ventures in the area. As mentioned before, there are signs that the Turkish government has started to implement a policy that aims to cooperate with Russia. However, the success of this policy also depends on the attitude of the Kremlin and domestic developments in Russia. If the Russian government continues its zero-sum policies, the prospects of the Baku-Ceyhan project grow dimmer.

There are other problems for the realization of this pipeline. First of all, the Caspian Pipeline Corporation, which would build a pipeline to the port of Novorossiisk to carry the Kazakh oil, decided to expand the facilities in that terminal. That would ease the problems related to the port of Novorossiisk and weaken one of the arguments of Turkey. Furthermore, the fact that Turkey's concerns for the Bosphorus were not particularly taken into consideration caused concern for the Turkish political elites (*Milliyet* 31 December 1996). It seems that, recently, the pressures on Turkey for the use of the Turkish straits have intensified. The representatives of both the Russian government and the AIOC have stated several times that this route is much more economical. Although the AIOC states that it finds the Turkish government's environmental concerns legitimate, these could be at least partly solved through some technical arrangements.[34] On the other hand, the problems in Chechnya no longer seem to be an obstacle for the northern route. Moscow reached an agreement with the newly elected Chechen government of Aslan Mashadov for the rehabilitation of that part of the pipeline. The Chechen government, which badly needs the windfall earnings of the pipeline, has been giving assurances for its security.

A related problem is that the realization of both routes for early oil might eventually make the Baku-Ceyhan proposal obsolete. It is estimated that, even during periods of peak production, the extra amount of oil that will be exported will not be more than the capacity of the northern and the southern routes combined (Bagirov 1996: 48).

In the meantime Turkey seems to continue its efforts for the realization of the pipeline. A feasibility study for this project was started by the World Bank on the request of Turkey (*Cumhuriyet* 2 July 1996). However, the current Welfare Party government did not seem to place a high priority on this issue, and the diplomatic efforts toward the realization of Baku-Ceyhan appear to have subsided. On the other hand, at times the consortium gives encouraging signs to the Turkish government that Ceyhan is the most suitable proposal for the main Azeri oil and that the Turkish concerns about the straits are well understood (İskit 1996: 80; *Yeni Yuzyıl* 2 June 1996). More important, the interests of the other parties could increase the chances of the Baku-Ceyhan route. Actors involved in the Caspian oil, except Russia, have an interest in the realization of alternative routes in order to decrease their dependence on one route. In fact, these complex and sometimes conflicting interests of the main actors involved in this oil saga create possibilities and room for maneuvering, especially for the weaker parties. For instance, the Azerbaijani government recently signed its fourth big Caspian development contract with a consortium of foreign partners for a new offshore field. The fact that for the first time the Russian LUKoil company was excluded from such a contract could be a sign that the balance is slipping somewhat in the pipeline politics. Azerbaijani president Aliyev's visit to Washington in the summer of 1997 was a further sign of that shift. During that visit, the U.S. government once more, but in a stronger tone, voiced its support for multiple pipelines. After that, the Yılmaz government in Ankara, formed in mid-1997, decided to use the opportunity to launch what is being labeled as an "energy offensive." The first sign of this new effort was high level visits paid to Azerbaijan and other former Soviet republics in September 1997. Given the complexity of interests and the intensity of power politics that surrounded the issue from the beginning, it is hard to predict how the consortium will decide. If the chances of the Baku-Ceyhan route have increased, this does not owe much to the policies of the Turkish governments. However, one thing that seems clear is that the oil saga has required a redefinition in Turkey's new role in the region.

NOTES

1. See Fuller (1993b); Robins (1993); Sayarı (1994); Winrow (1995b).
2. See Hunter (1993: 5).
3. Turkey was promoted as a "model" to these countries. For instance, during a trip to several Central Asian states, then U.S. secretary of state James Baker "recommended to the political leaders of the new republics the adoption of the Turkish model for their political and economic development". See the *Wall Street Journal* (14 February 1992: 12); Kramer (1996).
4. Contrary to the high hopes, the first Turkic Summit was in general a failure. See Winrow (1995: 18).
5. Document from the Turkish Foreign Ministry.
6. For the terms of the agreement see Bagirov (1996).

7. Initial shares of the participants were as follows:

BP/Statoil (UK/Norway)	25.5%
SOCAR (Azerbaijan)	20%
Amoco (United States)	17%
LUKoil (Russia)	10%
Pennzoil (United States)	9.8%
Unucol (United States)	9.5%
McDermott (United States)	2.45%
Ramco (UK)	2%
TPAO (Turkey)	1.75%
Delta (Saudi Arabia)	1.68%

8. Combined reserves in the PSC area are estimated at $4–5 billion. See *Oil and Gas Journal* (16 October 1995: 38, 48).

9. Established according to the Petroleum Law of 1954.

10. Since then there have been other changes in the participants of the consortium. In early 1996 the Japanese company Itochu joined the consortium with its purchase of a 2.45% share previously held by McDermott and another 5% from Pennzoil.

11. See, for instance, *Yeni Yüzyıl* (7 April 1995).

12. In April 1993 U.S. Chevron Oil and Kazak government established a joint venture for the exploitation of Kazakhstan's Tengiz oil field. Later, the Caspian Pipeline Consortium was set up by Russia, Kazakhstan and Oman to construct a pipeline for the exportation of Kazak oil. After considerable efforts Kazakhstan convinced Chevron to participate in the consortium.

13. For an analysis of different stages in Russian policy toward the former Soviet republics, especially in the Caucasus and Central Asia, see Barylski (1995).

14. For a very strong argument that Russia's energy policies vis-à-vis the CIS countries amounted to an "outright coercion and colonialism," see Blank (1995).

15. As a part of privatization efforts in Russia, LUKoil became a joint company. Yet the government still holds a controlling block of shares.

16. See Bagirov (1996: 40); *Turan* (22 November 1993: 71).

17. The legal regime of the Caspian Sea has been governed by two treaties that were signed between the Soviet Union and Iran, first in 1921 and again in 1940. Since the breakup of the Soviet Union three new states emerged along the Caspian shores. Soon the Russian Federation started to argue that these treaties were no longer valid and that the legal status of the Caspian had to be negotiated among the littoral states. On the legal issues concerning the Caspian Sea, see Uibopuu (1995: 119–123).

18. British Petroleum was the first company to sign an agreement with the Azerbaijani government.

19. The Azeri government signed a contract on the Karabakh oil field on 10 November 1995. Parties to the contract are LUKoil (Russia) 32.5%, Agip (Italy) 30%, Pennzoil (United States) 30%, SOCAR 7.5%. The contract territory covers 427 square kilometers, which will be developed for 25 years. The Karabakh oil field is located in the northern part of the Azeri section of the Caspian Sea and contains approximately 40 million tons of oil. A contract was also signed for the Shahdeniz oil field. The participants to that contract were BP/Statoil, TPAO, SOCAR, and LUKoil. The field's recoverable stocks are estimated at 230 million tons of oil and 530 billion cubic meters of gas. Azerbaijan has been pressuring Iran to join the consortium on the exploitation of

the Shahdeniz oil field. However, Tehran was hesitant, arguing that the legal regime of
the Caspian was debatable. See Bagirov (1996: 50–52); *Interfax* (29 September 1995, 2
October 1995: 68–69); *Rossiyskaya Gazeta* (6, 11 January 1996).

20. A possible Russian role in the coup was rumored at that time. Later, right before
the signing of the "deal of the century," Aliyev himself became a target of an unsuccessful coup attempt. After he survived the coup, Aliyev openly made a connection with
oil deals and indicated Russian involvement in the unrest. In his appeal to the public he
asked for their "loyalty against the conspirators who cooperated with the 'outside
forces' that aimed to prevent the implementation of the oil agreement" (*Azerbaycan
Radio Televiziyasi* (4, 5 October 1994).

21. However, Aliyev did not invite Russian troops to Azerbaijan like other CIS members in the region (Swietockowski 1994: 132).

22. According to the project, the pipeline was to have a capacity of 45 million tons
(20 million tons Kazakh and 25 million tons Azeri oil) and an approximate length of
2,500 km to 2,700 km.

23. See İskit (1996).

24. Passage through the Turkish Straits is governed by the Montreux Convention of
1936. According to Russia this one-sided act violated the Montreux Convention and
other international conventions on straits. However, the Turkish government stated that
the new regulations were prepared in accordance with the principles and recommenda-
tions of International Maritime Organization, and the studies for such a regulation
started in 1968, long before the "pipeline wars."

25. Reportedly, Chechen leaders declared that they would not permit the construction
of a pipeline through their territories as long as their independence was not recognized
(*Turan* 31 July 1995–1 August 1995: 77).

26. AIOC also had been considering a plan to export Caspian oil by way of a pipeline
to be laid across Iran. But that plan was dropped later mainly for political reasons
(opposition of the U.S. government).

27. Gönensay went to Washington in July 1995, and Çiller went to Baku on 10–12
July 1995. Çiller also sent a letter to President Clinton.

28. For example, see the press conference of the minister of state, a member of the
Social Democratic Party, and the head of the Turkish-Russian Joint Economic Commission, Onur Kumbaracıbaşı, who openly argued that Turkey had been following a wrong
policy in Eurasian oil. See *Yeni Yüzyıl* (7 September 1995).

29. Reported in *Segodnya* (30 September 1995: 3, 6 October 1995: 71–72).

30. Apparently, the Turkish government was disappointed that the U.S. support the
western route came in the last minute. İskit writes, "The U.S. government, which was
bound by its policy of 'multiple pipelines' still did not decide to put its weight in favor
of the western option until the last moment" (İskit 1996: 79).

31. The other proposal called for the implementation of the build-operate-transfer
principle (*TRT TV Network* 24 January 1996: 74).

32. During this visit the two countries also signed an agreement "to cooperate in
fighting terrorism." For Çiller's visit see *Milliyet* (16, 19 December 1996); *Yeni Yüzyıl*
(18 December 1996).

33. There are already some signs that this would not be very easy to achieve. A few
weeks after Çiller's visit a new crisis broke out between Ankara and the Kremlin when
the latter announced a deal with the Greek Cypriots for the selling of S-300 missiles.
With the U.S. intervention, that crisis was postponed, but it showed again that, as far as

Turco-Russian relations are concerned, the Kremlin has other cards to play to put pressure on Ankara on issues like the passage rights from the Bosphorus.

34. See, for instance, *Yeni Yüzyıl* (26 January 1997); *Milliyet* (26 February 1997).
which was bound by its policy of 'multiple pipelines' still did not decide to put its weight in favor of the western option until the last moment (İskit 1996: 79).

31. The other proposal called for the implementation of the build-operate-transfer principle (*TRT TV Network* 24 January 1996: 74).

32. During this visit the two countries also signed an agreement "to cooperate in fighting terrorism." For Çiller's visit see *Milliyet* (16, 19 December 1996); *Yeni Yüzyıl* (18 December 1996).

33. There are already some signs that this would not be very easy to achieve. A few weeks after Çiller's visit a new crisis broke out between Ankara and the Kremlin when the latter announced a deal with the Greek Cypriots for the selling of S-300 missiles. With the U.S. intervention, that crisis was postponed, but it showed again that, as far as Turco-Russian relations are concerned, the Kremlin has other cards to play to put pressure on Ankara on issues like the passage rights from the Bosphorus.

34. See, for instance, *Yeni Yüzyıl* (26 January 1997); *Milliyet* (26 February 1997).

Turkey's Emerging Relationship with Other Turkic Republics

Oral Turan and Ilter Turan

INTRODUCTION

The demise of the Soviet Union came at a time when major shifts in the international environment in which Turkey had been operating were already taking place. The relations characterized earlier by hostility between the members of the Western and the Soviet blocs had given way to more temperate relationships, culminating in the disappearance of the Warsaw Pact and the growth of security cooperation through a series of treaties and organizational instruments during the 1980s. Turkey had been a participant in this process as a member of the Western defense system. New economic opportunities also seemed to be opening up both in Eastern Europe and in the Soviet Union from which Turkey anticipated to benefit. However, none had expected the Soviet Union to break up so easily and smoothly into its "constituent units." The emergence of countries to the east that had Turkic origins was rather sudden and caught all parties unprepared. Yet, a feeling of euphoria swept Turkey. Finally, other countries of Turkic origins with which a partnership could be established had come into being.

HISTORICAL BACKGROUND

Despite the reality of common cultural roots, historically, Turkey's relations with the Turkic regions of Central Asia have been limited. The ruling elite of the Ottoman Empire had not traditionally seen themselves as being Turkish, a term reserved for the Anatolian peasants. Only toward the end of the nineteenth century, when Pan-Turkist ideologies had begun to penetrate the political thinking of the intellectual and the military-bureaucratic elites of the empire

Turkey's Emerging Relationship with Other Turkic Republics

Gül Turan and İlter Turan

INTRODUCTION

The demise of the Soviet Union came at a time when major shifts in the international environment in which Turkey had been operating were already taking place. The relations characterized earlier by hostility between the members of the Western and the Soviet blocs had given way to more temperate relationships, culminating in the disappearance of the Warsaw Pact and the growth of security cooperation through a series of treaties and organizational instruments during the 1980s. Turkey had been a participant in this process as a member of the Western defense system. New economic opportunities also seemed to be opening up both in Eastern Europe and in the Soviet Union from which Turkey anticipated to benefit. However, none had expected the Soviet Union to break up so easily and smoothly into its "constituent units." The emergence of countries to the east that had Turkic origins was rather sudden and caught all parties unprepared. Yet, a feeling of euphoria swept Turkey. Finally, other countries of Turkic origins with which a partnership could be established had come into being.

HISTORICAL BACKGROUND

Despite the reality of common cultural roots, historically, Turkey's relations with the Turkic regions of Central Asia have been limited. The ruling elite of the Ottoman Empire had not traditionally seen themselves as being Turkish, a term reserved for the Anatolian peasants. Only toward the end of the nineteenth century, when Pan-Turkist ideologies had begun to penetrate the political thinking of the intellectual and the military-bureaucratic elites of the empire, had the term gained widespread acceptance. Enver Pasha, the general who led the empire into the First World War, was a dedicated Pan-Turkist. His policies to restore the empire to its former prominence by allying with the Germans, however, ended in total failure. The nationalist leadership that organized an effort to build a Turkish nation-state from the remnants of the empire by conducting a successful independence effort against the Allies was committed to consolidating the new state and shied away from trans-nationalist ideologies and movements. In the case of Azerbaijan and other Turkic parts of the Soviet Union, there were compelling reasons to disavow interest. The new republic wanted to maintain friendly and peaceful relations with its neighbors, especially its more powerful neighbor to the north, with which it shared an anti-imperialist orientation.

From the early years of the republic, Pan-Turkist movements were generally suppressed. Although they became somewhat more assertive during the Second World War under German prodding, they were never so strong as to influence foreign policy. During the late 1960s, a Pan-Turkist party was finally established. This party, which excelled more in street politics than with the electorate, managed to gain representation in the Turkish Grand National Assembly and became a partner in a series of governments known as "Nationalist Front" coalitions, which ruled Turkey intermittently between 1974 and 1978. While the party may have had some, though limited, non-public links with persons and underground movements in the Turkic parts of the Soviet Union, most notably in Azerbaijan, there is no evidence that its Pan-Turkist ideology constituted an important input to foreign policy-making or implementation. Rather, Pan-Turkism became manifest in its anti-communist rhetoric where references were made to "captive Turks under the Soviet yoke."

The presence of a political movement avowedly taking an interest in the "Turks" of the Soviet Union did not mean that there existed major academic or other expertise on Turkic peoples of the East. Although the history of the Turks constituted a specialization within the departments of history at a number of Turkish universities, there were very little information and, consequently, expertise available about contemporary Azerbaijan and Central Asia. The existing historical literature was often characterized by romanticism and a yearning for a distant and not so well known past.

Another source that kept the idea of the Central Asian connection alive was the multifarious émigré associations. There was a considerable Azeri population in eastern Turkey, particularly in areas bordering Iran and Armenia. Almost all Central Asian groups were present, if not in large numbers, in various parts of Turkey. These communities were often organized into cultural and/or mutual assistance associations. The successive Turkish governments would not allow these organizations to engage in activities aimed at influencing foreign policy, but they were free to work toward the preservation of culture and traditions. If there was a political value to these émigré associations, it was that they were anti-communist, an orientation that rested well with the center-right parties that usually formed the governments in Turkey. It is not unlikely that some associations as well as some individuals had links with the Turks of the Soviet Union, but these were not significant enough to belie the generalization that linkages between these populations and Turkey were almost nonexistent.

The relations with the Turkic republics were established through Moscow. Contacts were usually limited to the cultural domain. Occasionally, a Turkish singer or actor would visit some cities in Azerbaijan or Central Asia, and, similarly, Soviet artists might come for a visit. Except for a few contracts in the Turkic republics won by Turkish companies just prior to the breakup of the Soviet Union, economic relations were almost nonexistent.

These facts and the expectation that the Soviet Union would continue to function in some form meant that Turkey had no well-planned strategy to give it direction in its foreign policy actions when Azerbaijan and the Turkic states of Central Asia became independent. What existed was a romantic notion of distant cousins yearning to be in some kind of political community with the Turkish Republic, a desire that had so far been thwarted by the Soviets. True, as the Soviet Union lost its ability to provide for the economic well-being of the constituent republics, it had been forced to allow the latter to engage in direct economic relations with other countries, a situation that had made it possible for Turkey to sign some economic agreements with such countries as Azerbaijan and Kazakhstan (see, e.g., Smolansky 1994: 293; Zviagelskaya 1994: 137), but whether these were temporary or would be long-lasting could not be easily judged. However, now that the Soviet Union was no more, linkages on all fronts could quickly be established.

STAGES OF EVOLUTION IN THE TURKEY-TURKIC REPUBLICS RELATIONSHIP

Having the benefit of hindsight, it may now be proposed that the relations between Turkey and Azerbaijan and the Turkic states of Central Asia went through three stages. These stages are not marked by specific events in the instance of all countries; rather they reflect transformations of the outlooks that have given direction to the relationship. Therefore, they should be construed not as being discrete but as fluctuations on a continuum. The first stage is marked by high levels of optimism and expectations about the future. The second comprises the period of the mutual discovery of constraints that helped define the limits of the relationship. The third stage can be described as the routinization of the relationship. We use these stages as an organizational scheme in the following analysis.

THE PERIOD OF OPTIMISM

As the constituent republics of the Soviet Union began to declare their independence from the center in the fall of 1991, a feeling of excitement swept Turkey. It was felt that the coming of independence to the Central Asian states would open the way to the construction of a Turkic world in which Turkey would occupy a leading role. Accordingly, Turkey was the first state to extend diplomatic recognition to Uzbekistan, Kazakhstan, Kyrgyzstan, Turkmenistan, and Azerbaijan. Shortly afterward, starting with Nursultan Nazarbayev of Kazakhstan in September 1991, within a short interval, the presidents of the Turkic republics all paid visits to Ankara. Saparmurad Niyazov (now Turkmenbashi) of Turkmenistan, Islam Kerimov of Uzbekistan, and Askar Akaev of Kyrgyzstan stopped in Ankara in December, while Ayaz Muttalibov of Azerbaijan came in January 1992 (Çandar 1992: 63–64).

The optimism regarding the evolution of a Turkic world as an important region and an autonomous actor in the world system was reflected in the speeches of Turkish political leaders and in the official statements made by the government. For example, President Turgut Özal frequently alluded to the idea that the twenty-first century would be a "Turkic century" (Çandar 1992: 64), while the then prime minister Süleyman Demirel pointed to the birth of a Turkic world that extended from China to the Adriatic Sea, intimating that Turkey was ready to take on major responsibilities in this region (Smolansky 1994: 283). On their part, the leaders of the newly independent states of the Turkic world also appeared to be interested in developing links with Turkey, as evidenced by their visits to Turkey and their willingness to respond favorably to Turkish offers of cooperation.

Diplomatic Cooperation

Some areas of cooperation immediately came to the fore. The newly born states did not have well-developed diplomatic services, since external relations were not a responsibility of the constituent republics during the Soviet era. For the same reason, they did not have a corps of diplomats trained under the Soviets who might assume responsibility for developing a ministry of foreign affairs. Yet, the new countries were hard-pressed to become involved in the workings of the international system, not only to consolidate their newly won independence but also in order to reach sources of economic assistance and support that they desperately needed. In this context Turkish offers of diplomatic guidance and support were, therefore, welcome. For example, very quickly a training program for diplomats was initiated by the Turkish Foreign Ministry. Turkey assumed the role of guide in promoting the participation of the Central Asian states in international forums such as the Conference on Security and Cooperation in Europe (CSCE) and the United Nations. Through Turkish efforts, Azerbaijan was included in the Black Sea Economic Cooperation (BSEC), which came into being in February 1992 (Elekdağ 1992: 125). Similarly, Turkish efforts were indispensable in getting the five Turkic states to join (Kazakhstan as an observer) the Economic Cooperation Organization (ECO), which was originally established to promote economic, cultural, and technological cooperation between Turkey, Iran, and Pakistan at the end of 1992.

Turkey soon became aware that some institutional capability was needed to promote and coordinate closer, multidimensional relations between itself and the new Turkic states. The recently established Turkish Cooperation and Development Agency (TİKA), operating under the auspices of the Ministry of Foreign Affairs, was given this responsibility. This agency has been one of the driving forces in the development of relations.

Communications and Transportation

Another area where the need for cooperation was immediately felt was in the field of communications. Although there were high hopes on the part of Turkey to become a builder and a key member of the Turkic world, it soon became apparent that communications with the new states were very difficult, impeding from the start the realization of such an aspiration. Before extensive new communications systems could be established, which would inevitably take a long time, the Turkish government proceeded to donate digital telecommunication exchanges to each of the five Turkic republics. These had the capacity to accommodate 2500–3500 subscribers (Arık 1993: 35–36), which facilitated communications between Turkey and these countries, as well as communications of the latter with the rest of the word. Based in part on this experience, Turkish telecommunication companies later won contracts to improve and develop further the telecommunication systems in some of these countries.

When Azerbaijan and the Central Asian Turkic republics became independent, there was no way to reach them by air except through Moscow. In anticipation of meeting growing needs as well as demonstrating the political importance Turkey was according to its linkage with the new states, Turkish airlines initiated direct flights, first, to Baku, Tashkent, and Almaty in mid-1992 (Robins 1993: 604). Later, while these were rendered more frequent, new flights were added to Ashgabad and Bishkek. Even today, some of the most convenient and reliable connections to Baku and the Turkic capitals of Central Asia are served by the Turkish airlines. As these states have developed their own national air carriers, all have started to offer flights to Istanbul, such that air travel to and from them to Turkey is easy and frequent.

Land transport, in contrast to air transport, could not be improved with similar ease. With the opening of the East, Turkey opened a border crossing at Sarp into the Ajaristan region of Georgia and improved the road leading to it. This made it possible for trucks to go through Georgia into Azerbaijan, where they would then take the truck ferry from Baku to Krasnovodsk (now Turkmenbashi) in Turkmenistan. From there, all points in the Central Asian republics could be reached. There also existed a sea-land combination going through Russia. Shipments could be made by boat to Novorossisk on the Black Sea coast, where the loads would be transferred to trains that would go to such places as Almaty and Bishkek. The port of Novorossisk was overcrowded, however, and there were complaints that Turkish exports were given low priority in rail transport. A third way of reaching the Central Asian markets was through Iran. Here again, the roads were not good, and Iranian cooperation was less than satisfactory. Rail links between Iran and Turkmenistan, on the other hand, did not exist until 1996. Finally, it would have been possible to have highway access into Azerbaijan and then on to Central Asia through Armenia, but the use of this option could not be entertained until the Azeri-Armenian dispute over Nagorno-Karabagh and the termination of the Armenian occupation of 25% of Azeri territory was settled to the satisfaction of both parties. In the initial years, all routes, whether they were highways or railways, suffered from security problems. Merchandise was often stolen or damaged, and security had to be purchased by paying fees to local gangs. Although conditions have somewhat improved, transportation of goods to Central Asia continues to be difficult.

Helping Develop Manpower Resources

Aware of the importance of elite ties in the development of long-lasting relationships between countries and recognizing that well-trained individuals, particularly in the fields of economics, banking, management, accounting, diplomacy, and other similar fields, were needed in the new countries in order for them to develop a reliable public service system while, at the same time, making the transition to market economies, Turkey initiated a program through which a total of 10,000 students, 2000 from each of the five republics, would be awarded scholarships to study at Turkish universities. Already in early 1993, 7557 students from Turkic states had enrolled at a variety of Turkish educational institutions, a majority of them at universities (Arık 1993: 34). Though not without problems, such as insufficient preparation on the part of the incoming students to pursue university studies in the Turkish system and insufficient scholarship money on the part of the Turkish government, the scholarship program is continuing and will soon be producing its first graduates.

Turkey also undertook to open an elite public high school in each of the republics, a commitment that has already been achieved. These schools, modeled after elite public schools in Turkey, in addition to teaching students standard Turkish, which would enable them to "connect with" Turkey, teaches English, which constitutes the critical instrument through which these countries can relate to the world without the intermediation of Russia. The schools have now been in operation for three years. In recent years, a proliferation of private institutions of Turkish origins, offering secondary education, has also occurred. These also offer both English and Turkish to their students, filling a foreign languages gap that the local educational system is, apparently, not able to provide (see Alpay 1996: 20; Bayramoğlu 1996: 5).

A number of other educational activities were also initiated by Turkey in the early stages of relations. For example, a program for training Quran readers, which had been started in 1990 before the breakup of the Soviet Union, was continued after Turkic republics became independent. In 1992, a Kazakh university in the city of Turkestan, the Hodja Ahmed Yesevi University, was reorganized into a Turkish-Kazakh University, aiming to offer education to young people from the region.

Enhancing Cultural Linkages

Helping train and develop manpower resources, in addition to providing professional training and the acquisition of skills, has, from the very beginning, inevitably served as a channel of cultural interaction and transmission. Since the Turkish affinity to these states was based on historical ties, a common language, and common culture, developing cultural links was given attention in the first years of relations. As early as November 1991, the Institute of Turkish Studies of the Marmara University in Istanbul had convened a "Contemporary Turkish Alphabets Symposium" to examine the possibility of developing a standard alphabet for Turkish languages. A meeting with a similar theme was organized by the Turkish Ministries of Culture and Education in 1992 and the Ministry of Foreign Affairs in 1993 (Devlet 1993: 17). There seems to be a consensus that if a common alphabet is to be adopted, it is going to be based on Latin characters. So far, first Azerbaijan, then Turkmenistan and Uzbekistan have adopted the Latin alphabet. The transition to the new alphabet is planned to be completed by the year 2000. In most towns, street names have already been changed. But more comprehensive changes are impeded by costs deriving from the changes of the printing presses, typewriters, and so on. The presence of a high percentage of Russians appears to have kept Kazakhstan and Kyrgyzstan away from considering changing their alphabets at this time.

In a different arena of cultural interaction, Turkey initiated television broadcasts to the Turkic republics via satellite during 1992 (Haghayegi 1994: 261) A new channel, called the Eurasian Channel, was established by the Turkish Radio and Television, a state company, which began to broadcast programs that would presumably be of interest to Turkish-speaking audiences in the Caucasus and Central Asia. The programs, which contain depictions of life and society in modern Turkey, would also be designed to convey a sense of community among the Turkic peoples. While it was apparently not easy at the initial stages to watch this channel in Azerbaijan or Central Asia, nowadays it has begun to reach larger audiences.

The emphasis the Turkish government has placed on the development of multifaceted relations with the Turkic republics of the Caucasus and Central Asia has led to the establishment of an international organization called Turksoy. Established in 1994, the goal of this organization is to promote cultural interactions between the Turkic republics. Under the rules of this organization, the ministers of culture of the respective republics meet regularly to evaluate ongoing cultural activities and plan for future cooperation.

Economic Relations

As shall be elaborated later, independence came to the Turkic republics in the middle of an economic crisis, which was one of the major forces that also brought about the undoing of the Soviet Union. The new states all had socialist economies closely integrated with that of the Russian Federation. Therefore, the independent Turkic states, much like others that came into being after the dissolution of the union, faced the double problem of meeting the immediate economic needs of their populations and making a transition to market economies. The exporting of products to the world markets for cash was constrained in several ways. First, such products were limited in quantity and kind. Second, most of the marketable products had to be allocated for export to the Russian Federation in return for much needed amenities, which, under the difficult economic circumstances, could be procured only from that country. Furthermore, because of the lack of a transport system outside the Russian Federation through which these landlocked countries could reach international markets, Russia had significant leverage in influencing their economic decisions and behavior.

Turkey's economic relations with the Turkic states began to develop under the influence of these constraints. One of the first actions of TİKA, for example, was to extend humanitarian aid, comprising almost exclusively foodstuffs, to the newly independent countries. But TİKA has also constituted one of the prime forces in facilitating economic relations between Turkey and the Turkic republics, organizing technical assistance programs, and encouraging private entrepreneurs to pursue trade opportunities and to make investments. Economic relations have been promoted by a number of public and private organizations, such as the Turkish Exim Bank and the Foreign Economic Relations Board (DEİK), of which more will be said later.

The Turkish Model

In this early stage of optimism and high expectations, there were often allusions to the idea that the newly independent Turkic states could pursue the Turkish model of development. Many observers noted that Turkey possessed certain characteristics that might appeal to the leaders of the new Turkic societies. These included "a relatively dynamic market economy, secular government, a respect for Islamic traditions, and a democratic system" (Fridman 1994: 35). Similar ideas were expressed by some of the leaders of the Turkic states, such as Islam Kerimov of Uzbekistan (Smolansky 1994: 299) and Ebulfez Elchibey of Azerbaijan (Demir 1996: 227–228), and seem to have had an appeal both in the Turkic states and in Western countries with which Turkey had close links (Blank 1994: 273; Sander 1994: 40; Israeli 1994: 19, 22).

The interest shown in the Turkish model of development was prompted by a number of considerations. First, the Turkish experience was thought to have relevance in that Turkey had made a transition to a more market-oriented economy from an economy in which the state was the major actor, and the state economic enterprises accounted for most of the industrial production in the economy. Second, the Turkish experience was emphasized as a way of saying that the Turkic states were not interested in Islamic formulas that were being proposed by such countries as Iran and Saudi Arabia. Third, Turkey was thought to have better connections and more access to the Western world, from which economic assistance, investment capital, and new technology were expected to come. Finally, Western countries themselves felt that the Turkish model was a preferable model to follow than those being advocated by others (Vassilev 1994: 132). Turkish political leaders such as President Turgut Özal and, later, President Demirel also emphasized the relevance of the Turkish model for the Turkic states (Olcott 1996: 25–26).

The Emergence of Linkage Infrastructure

If one were to characterize the major developments during the period of optimism that began with the independence of Azerbaijan and the Turkic states of Central Asia in late 1991 and lasted through 1992, one can argue that this is a period of infrastructural development on various fronts. First, Turkey had to develop its own instruments to establish multidimensional linkages with the new states. These included bolstering institutional capabilities and financial resources of government agencies such as TİKA and the Exim Bank such that they would have the means to promote economic and cultural relations with the Turkic states as well as creating non-governmental organizations like the bilateral business councils established under the umbrella of DEİK. Second, Turkey helped bring the new states into regional organizations such as the Black Sea Economic Cooperation and ECO. Third, communication links and transportation between Turkey and the new Turkic republics were improved. Fourth, cultural and educational programs, such as the opening of high schools in the new countries and the training of university students, that would lead to long-term ties were initiated. Finally, Turkey entered the cognitive maps of the political leaders and the populace of these states as a country that was interested in their fate and to which they could turn for cooperation and assistance. Similarly, both the governments and the business communities of the countries of Western Europe as well as the United States became aware of Turkey's special interest in the new republics and its skills in establishing relations with them.

DISCOVERING THE LIMITATIONS

As optimism was continuing to characterize the relationships between Turkey and the Turkic states of the former Soviet Union, indications that there might be significant constraints in the development of more comprehensive relationships became apparent. Ironically, the initial signal came in the midst of an event that might be viewed as symbolically critical in the development of relations—the Ankara Summit, held in the Turkish capital in October 1992. The multiple intentions of the meeting included enhancing a sense of community, emphasizing the mutual benefit to be derived from operating as a community, and discussing specific projects. The declaration signed at the end of the summit did not entail very specific commitments. It contained loose political statements about strengthening security in the region and supporting peaceful resolution of conflicts and expressed economic aspirations such as cooperation in the field of communications and the realization of joint projects in oil and gas production and processing. (See also Zviagelskaya 1994: 138.) The lack of specific commitments owed much to Nursultan Nazarbayev of Kazakhstan, who, in addition to not making commitments, made it clear that such ties as would develop among the Turkic states would be pursued only to the extent they did not undermine his country's relations and commitments to the CIS, by which he clearly meant Russia (see Robins 1993: 599).

More generally, as relations between Turkey and the Turkic states began to intensify, a process of mutual discovery commenced. Within a year, all parties gradually became aware of the limitations and constraints to which their relationship would be subject. During the initial wave of optimism that a Turkic world might emerge, the importance of such constraints had not been sufficiently appreciated. As these societies began to interact, however, the presence of forces and conditions that impeded the evolution of closer relations began to become clear.

The Russian Presence

Although the breakup of the Soviet Union had meant a reduction in Russian influence in the affairs of the new republics, it was far from gone. The Russian Federation has continued to view the Turkic republics primarily as its special domain and has worked to maintain a special relationship, using a variety of means. One such means is the presence of ethnic Russians in the new republics (37.8% in Kazakhstan, 21.5% in Kyrgyzstan, 6% in Azerbaijan, 9.5% in Turkmenistan, and 8.3% in Uzbekistan). In the case of Kazakhstan and Kyrgyzstan, the numbers are sufficiently large that the preferences of the ethnic Russian population for having reasonably close relations with their mother country cannot be ignored. That may be why Nazarbayev even today feels compelled to make sure that his actions are not misconstrued as moving away from Russia. In the case of the others, ethnic Russians are often situated in important jobs. Governments want to make sure that not all Russians leave quickly, vacating jobs that cannot be filled easily by non-Russians, despite some signs that the presence of ethnic Russians may not always be appreciated.

Because the breakup of the union is relatively recent, the Russians are quite familiar with the internal politics of the new states. There also continue to exist individuals and groups interested in, or willing to collaborate with, the Russians to advance their own standing in domestic politics. In Azerbaijan, for example, the coup that brought the strongly pro-Turkish Ebulfez Elchibey down was realized, allegedly with Russian help from pro-Russian agent Suret Husseinov, who rebelled against the government. Prior to this coup, the Russians had given military aid to Armenia in its eventually successful effort to wrest territory from Azerbaijan, thereby weakening the government that Husseinov brought down (Demir 1996).

Economic Dependence on Russia

The fact that the new states are tied economically to Russia is too well known to elaborate on here once again. The high degree of complementary and regional specialization that took place during the Soviet era had resulted in a high share of intra-regional trade. Prior to 1990, the share of intra-regional trade was never below 80%. Trade among the member states of the CIS has continued to be high. In 1995, for example, the exports of the Turkic states plus Tajikistan to the CIS were 50% of the total, and imports were 59%. Such trade dependency impedes developing economic relations with others in interesting ways. For example, as has already been mentioned, the few exportable commodities the new countries possess are usually committed for export to the Russian Federation in order to get much needed imports in return. Such economic integration and dependence have impeded the realization of the full potential that Turkey has expected from economic relations.

The Turkic states have also had great difficulty paying for their trade with Turkey either in cash or, in some instances, when prearranged, in kind. Even in instances when economic opportunities have been perceived, the question of obligations to Russia has stood in the way. One of the authors, through business contacts, knows of an instance in Uzbekistan where plans for a significant investment in textile, yarn, and cottonseed oil production were not seriously entertained after the authorities indicated that they could not ensure supplying the minimum amount of cotton needed for economical production after their commitment to Russia was met.

The dependence on Russia is not necessarily a relationship that only the Russians would like to maintain. Having small economies, lacking familiarity with the world of market economies, and not possessing the institutional structures that would enable them to be integrated to the world economic system, the Turkic republics of the former Soviet Union have themselves been reluctant to initiate policies that would put their special relationship with Russia in jeopardy. For example, while all countries at first tried to reduce the inflow of Russian goods by initiating barriers so that they could reduce the deficit in their balance of payments, Kazakhstan and Kyrgyzstan have recently joined a customs union with Russia, something in which Uzbekistan has also expressed an interest (Kubicek 1996). Interestingly, Russia has, at times, demonstrated less interest in this economic linkage to the extent that it might impose hardships on the Russian economy. A case in point is Russian disinterest in supporting the use of the ruble as domestic currency in these countries and its reluctance in including the interested countries in the ruble zone (Kubicek 1996).

The economic dependence on Russia, which the leaders would like to maintain, constrains the current leaders in making moves that would threaten their economic relationship with Russia. Such an orientation may change in the long run as the political and economic cadres of the Turkic states become more confident in operating in a market environment and as institutions of a market economy are better developed. Furthermore, the gradually transforming economies may, in time, generate more hard-currency income. Of particular importance in this regard are oil and gas exports, which are expected, in the long run, to generate substantial hard-currency income for Kazakhstan, Azerbaijan, and Turkmenistan.

Conflicts of Interest among the Turkic States

There had been, initially, a tendency on the part of Turkey to view other Turkic states as constituting a reasonably homogeneous whole, not harboring significant conflicts of interest among themselves. This exaggerated perception of unity derived, on one hand, from earlier lack of familiarity with the region and, on the other hand, from projections of hopes and aspirations. Turkey soon enough discovered, however, that it was dealing with five different states each of which had its own political leaders and its own national interests to pursue. By way of example, while it is true that cultures and languages of the Turkic peoples are related, it is equally true that there are enough differences among them that a Turk and an Azeri cannot understand a Kyrgyz or a Kazakh. More broadly, as a skeptical observer has put it, "while Turkey and the rest of the Central Asian countries...may feel euphoric about being Turkic, there is virtually no guarantee that it alone could become a basis for cooperation" (Ahrari 1994: 536). In addition, since the new countries have existed as units for quite some time now, each has developed its own distinct sense of identity, its own political institutions, and its own political cadres and leaders, a fact that only reinforces whatever ethnic and cultural differences may exist.

The ethnic compositions of the new republics are different, such that, for example, the presence of Uzbeks in Kyrgyzstan (which has generated inter-ethnic conflict in the past) is seen as a security problem by the latter. Some observers have also noted that Uzbekistan, which has the largest population, feels itself to be the natural leader of the Central Asian republics, a role that the others have not been willing to acknowledge. Or, while Turkey tends to think that they all belong in the same group, the Central Asian states do not feel Azerbaijan belongs to the same world as they.

Furthermore, each of the Turkic republics has different security concerns and, therefore, different ideas about how it should conduct its relations with the Russian Federation. Azerbaijan, for example, has tried to keep the Russian military out for fear that it will act more as a domestic force than one that would remain within the confines of an alliance relationship. Turkmenistan has also resisted reestablishing close relations with Russia for fear that it would easily fall under Russian domination once again. Kazakhstan, on the other hand, has maintained a much more cooperative attitude toward Russia, if for no other reason than the fact that, as has already been noted, it has a sizable Russian population, and the Kazakh nature of some of its territory has already been questioned by Russian nationalists.

All countries, with the possible exception of Kyrgyzstan, are run by authoritarian regimes. Each leader has devised different formulas for legitimating his power, but nationalism has been a common theme in all. Nationalism in this case means local nationalism. Nationalism of a transnational kind is viewed negatively by all leaders as a force that might undermine their own authority. Similarly, just as the political leaderships of these countries are trying to build their new states, references to collectivities that transcend the nation-state are seen as detrimental to the state-building effort. Although Central Asian leaders have come together to discuss possibilities of economic cooperation, the creation of a common economic space, and so on (Kubicek 1996), the discussion of political union has been absent. Under the circumstances, the talk of a greater union by one leader may be perceived as an attempt to dominate them by the others.

In short, the differences among the Turkic republics have been a constraint in Turkey's interaction with them. Turkey has had to devise specific policies for each of the countries and has had to be careful that what it does with one country does not generate reaction in others. But more important, Turkey has become aware that the Turkic world for which it had hoped to lay the foundations during the initial period of optimism that swept the country would not, in the short run, be easy or practicable.

Conflicts of Interest between Turkey and the Turkic States

Although Turkey has given, and continues to give, high priority to the Turkic republics in its foreign policy, there are other important linkages that it has had to take into consideration in its relations with the latter. Similarly, as the discussion of the Russian influence in the region and the economic dependence of Turkic republics on the Russian Federation has already demonstrated, each state may have policy preferences that deviate from those of Turkey.

Ankara has an important economic relationship with the Russian Federation that it aims to retain and develop. Turkish construction companies have had, and continue to have, major contracts in various parts of Russia. Tourism trade is large, with Russians coming to Turkey for vacations and shopping. There is extensive "suitcase trade," that is, tourists taking goods back with them from Turkey to Russia to sell, which may total $7–8 billion, according to the higher estimates. In developing and implementing its policies in the Caucasus and Central Asia, Turkey is always compelled to make sure that these do not generate significant losses in its relations with Russia. Turkey's trade with Russia, after all, is as much as 10 times its trade with the Central Asian republics (Olcott 1996: 171). In practice this means that Turkey's policies can aim at political and economic cooperation and not security cooperation. As Olcott notes, for Turkey's leaders "to challenge Russia's special security relationship with all the CIS states is to risk sharp deterioration in their own relations with Russia" (Olcott 1996: 171).

Currently, there is only limited security cooperation, mainly in the form of Turkey's training some military officers, and there appears to be no immediate interest, particularly on the part of the Central Asian states, to have common security activity with Turkey. The Russians have, nevertheless, found Turkey's interest in the Turkic republics to be a reason for concern and want to make sure that this does not conceal any Pan-Turkish aims. Frequently, Ankara has had to give assurances that it has no such aims.

There are some specific areas where Turkey's interests and its policies contain elements of conflict in its relations with both Russia and some of the Turkic republics. One such area is Turkey's support for Azerbaijan in its conflict with Armenia. The Russians have generally been more supportive of the Armenians and have tried to use the Armenian occupation of Azeri territory as leverage against the Azeris, who have resisted Russian offers of sending Russian troops back into their country. The plight of the Azeris does not seem to generate the compassion and support in the other Turkic republics that it does in Turkey, for a variety of reasons. Actually, the opposite may describe the situation a little better. Turkey's active involvement in the support of Azerbaijan against the Armenians may invite a Russo-Turkish confrontation (Vaughn 1994: 310), in which the Central Asian countries would not like to be involved. While we do not need to belabor the reasons behind these differences of approach and policy, it is important to note that the unity that Turkey had hoped would exist in a community of Turkic states is simply not there.

Another specific area where differences of preference and approach are manifest is in getting the natural gas and oil of Azerbaijan, Kazakhstan, and Turkmenistan to the world markets. As regards oil, from the very beginning, Turkey has argued that the best way to transport the fuel to the world market is through a system of pipelines that will go through Turkey, to the Mediterranean port of Ceyhan (Yumurtalık). While a line through Azerbaijan and Armenia seems to be more direct, because of the ongoing Azeri-Armenian conflict, proposals for a slightly longer route going through Georgia have been developed. When it became apparent that the construction of such a long pipeline would have to await substantial increases in production, Turkey encouraged a pipeline that would reach the Georgian Black Sea port of Soupsa, a counteroffer to the Russian proposals of shipping the so-called early production from Azerbaijan to Novorossisk. The international consortium that is producing the oil has proposed dividing the shipment between the northern (Novorossisk) and the southern (Supsa) lines. Because some shipment capacity already existed on lines remaining from the Soviet Union, the opening of the northern route has received priority and is closer to being operational at the time of this writing.

Turkey has tried to get the Turkic republics to make a commitment to support the construction of a pipeline that would carry Central Asian and Azeri oil to the Mediterranean. Support, however, has been low-key and usually not specific, despite the fact that such a development would generate high income for the producer countries as well as for those through which the lines will transit, rendering them less dependent on Russia. Just as the Turkish anxiety to have a pipeline go through Turkey as quickly as possible is understandable, so is the hesitation of the Turkic republics to make a clear and irrevocable commitment, due to fear of Russian reprisals. The Russian presence and influence, as well as the economic dependence of these states on Russia, constitute sufficient explanation of the latter's hesitation. Suffice it to point out that the Azeri president Haidar Aliyev, who has tried to accommodate Russia, has experienced no less than two, very likely Moscow-fomented coup attempts to oust him from power (as well as attempts on his life) because he has not totally given in to Russian demands and has tried to pursue a somewhat independent line (Cohen 1996: 5).

Finally, there may be a difference of perspective between Turkey and the Turkic states on the nature of their relationship. While Turkey has tried to view itself as a magnet for the newly independent countries, a leader that would help them get integrated into the world economic system, offer guidance in their transformation to market economies, and serve as an intermediary between them and Western countries, the Turkic republics have been reluctant to accept exclusive Turkish leadership. Although this reluctance can be explained, in part, by what we have already talked about (Russian influence and economic dependence on Russia) and, in part, by what is to follow (a recognition of the limitations of Turkey in playing the role that it has shown an interest in playing), a third factor has also to be recognized: the newly independent republics have just left a heavy-handed union and are still trying to loosen the entanglements remaining from that association. They are probably not interested in acquiring a new big brother but "aim at greater diversification of their foreign relations" (Zviagelskaya 1994: 140; Olcott 1996: 27 for a similar observation).

Mutual Awareness of Each Other's Limitations

It appears, in retrospect, that, initially, Turkey overestimated its ability to extend assistance and support to the new republics and also misjudged the ability of the republics to bring about the necessary changes in their administration and politics so as to become integrated to the world system. Similarly, the new republics made judgments both about themselves and about Turkey that turned out to be not terribly accurate.

It may be best to explicate the problem by some examples. When the Turkic states first became independent, Turkey promised economic aid, both as grants and credits, to finance Turkish exports and investments. While these were all realized, and Turkey devoted substantial financial resources to that end, the sums involved did not reach nearly the levels initially promised. One observer, for example, argues that the Turkish financial promises in 1992 corresponded to 80% of the country's hard-currency reserves, a sum so high that it was necessary to renege on the promises (Goble 1994: 3). In the instance of the export credits to be made available by Turkish Exim Bank, to cite one example, the credits made available did not reach the amounts promised. Part of the problem derived from the fact that many a Turkish governmental leader, in the excitement of visiting one or more of the Turkic republics for the first time, would make promises on the spot, that had to be forgotten later, since the means to implement the promise did not exist.

The Turkish businessmen who were expected to lead the investment effort in the newly independent countries soon discovered that they were less easily accessible and that it was harder to do business in them, than initially anticipated (Olcott 1996: 26). These polities, in contrast to the impression held by Turks that they had well-developed administrative systems, appeared less capable of delivering on their promises than was judged at first. From the perspective of the Turkic republics, Turkish investments were sufficient neither in their speed nor in their magnitude. A Kazakh academic research report, for example, judged that the relations between Turkey and Kazakhstan "remained limited because Ankara proved reluctant to invest money in the Kazakh economy" (as quoted in Smolansky 1994: 295).

After more frequent contacts with the outside world, the leaders of the Turkic republics have come to feel that "the Turkish model lagged behind that of other economies" (Olcott 1996: 27). Furthermore, it has also appeared to them that Turkey's access to European decision-making centers is not as facile as they had initially come to believe.

While more examples may be offered, the point is already clear. Both parties became aware that they did not have the resources to raise the relations to the levels that might have been desired at the early stage, characterized by optimism. Policy adjustments had to be made.

ROUTINIZATION: PREVALENCE OF ECONOMIC RELATIONS

The area of interaction between Turkey and the Turkic republics in which there is currently more intense activity than others is the field of economics. We therefore now turn to an examination of the economic links. We may begin our analysis by noting that the Turkish government has been one of the driving forces in the development of economic relations between the newly independent Turkic countries and Turkey. Implementation of policies along targets set by the government has helped the Turkish private sector become familiar with the new markets and move into them. With government encouragement private organizations such as the Istanbul Chamber of Commerce (ITO) and the Foreign Economic Relations Board (DEİK) have worked to facilitate and promote the further development and the deepening of economic relations.

The Evolution of Institutional Structures

Shortly after the Turkic republics declared their independence in 1991 and were immediately extended diplomatic recognition by Turkey, Turkey proceeded, on one hand, to establish a formal basis for economic cooperation and, on the other hand, to build private institutional bases for enhanced nongovernmental linkages. The formal bases on which economic relations would be grounded were Economic and Commercial Cooperation Agreements, which were signed with Azerbaijan (1992), Kazakhstan (1991), Kyrgyzstan (1991), Turkmenistan (1995), and Uzbekistan (1995). A similar agreement had also been signed with the Russian Federation in 1992. These agreements call for annual meetings of Joint Economics and Trade Committees in order to evaluate past performance, identify problems, and make future plans to expand relations. Those who participate in the meetings include high-ranking bureaucrats usually representing the respective treasuries, the ministries responsible for economic affairs, and the foreign ministries. Following a practice that was initiated in the late 1980s by joint committees established with other countries, private businesses or organizations representing them have also been allowed to sit in on these meetings and present their point of view. In this way, an opportunity is provided for bureaucrats of each country to get to know their counterparts and representatives of private business from the other side. In addition, interested business representatives use these occasions to develop links with other countries. The meetings are usually held toward the end of the year and try to put together an indicative list of items that can be exported and imported during the next year. Questions regarding how to organize, sponsor, or participate in regional and or international fairs and other similar matters are also discussed. Often documents and information are also exchanged. The results of these meeting are usually published in the *Turkish Official Gazette*.

The Turkish Cooperation and Development Agency (TİKA), which has been described earlier, although not oriented exclusively toward the Turkic republics and with activities not confined exclusively to economic matters, nevertheless needs to be mentioned here once again, since much of its activities and resources are expended for enhancing economic cooperation between Turkey and the Turkic republics. Similarly, the Turkish Exim Bank, though not exclusively oriented toward the new republics, has been one of the major public economic agencies that have been active in helping expand economic relations with the latter.

The private institutional basis for cooperation has usually been the bilateral business councils. These had been initiated after 1986 with a number of countries to promote economic relations. The Turkish side of these bilateral councils operates under the aegis of the Foreign Economic Relations Board (DEİK), an active, nonprofit organization responsible for improving economic relations between member countries by bringing together trade and investment partners. DEİK was founded in 1986 by nine private organizations, among them, the Turkish Union of Chambers of Commerce, Industry, Commodity Exchanges and Maritime Chambers of Commerce, the Union of Turkish Chambers of Agriculture, the Turkish Industrialists and Businessmen's Association, and the Foreign Investors Associations. It provides information for interested parties and helps organize bilateral business councils. The founding members of the councils on the Turkish side are generally companies that already have economic relations with the country with which a business council is to be established. Others join if they are interested in developing economic relations with a specific country. The counterpart organizations in the newly independent Turkic republics are usually either state trading organizations or ministries of foreign economic relations. These institutions usually have close contacts with both the private and public sectors in their respective countries.

A Turkish-Soviet Business Council was established as early as 1986. It started with 35 member companies, but membership had grown to 180 by 1991. This was a time when Turkish-Soviet trade was expanding rapidly. With the assistance of this business council, Turkish businessmen had an opportunity to get acquainted with how the economy operated in Russia, Ukraine, Georgia, and Azerbaijan. The representatives of the Turkish-Soviet Business Council also participated in the annual meetings of the intergovernmental Turkish-Russian Joint Economic Committee and contributed to the planning of trade and the devising of investment projects. They often traveled along with official delegations on state visits and attended official conferences. With the dissolution of the Soviet Union, the council was renamed the Turkish-CIS Business Council to reflect the new political reality.

Shortly after Azerbaijan declared its independence and before the Turkish government recognized it in November 1991, a Turkish-Azerbaijan Business Council was quickly established. Others followed suit in due time. Turkmen, Kazakh, and Kyrgyz councils were established in 1992, and the Uzbek council in 1993.

Good Intentions, Difficult Relations

While the independence of the Turkic republics appeared to present economic opportunities for Turkey, Turkish businessmen got further confirmation of what they had learned during their experience with the Soviet Union. The transition from a planned, socialist economy to a more decentralized capitalist economy was proving problematical, rendering foreign entry to these markets difficult. These countries had been spared from the great politico-economic transformation waves that had swept Eastern Europe and some parts of the Soviet Union and had therefore been able to avoid the turmoil experienced by countries that had broken away abruptly from state guidance and control. But they continued to experience extreme economic difficulties in adjusting to the new economic realities. The rate of inflation in all countries tends to be high. Their economies, for the most part, are in a decline. The contribution of foreign direct investments to their economies is negligible. Public ownership of enterprises is still widespread, allowing for old work habits and practices to survive. Competitiveness of enterprises is feeble. The role of the state in the economy continues to be critical, and it has been sluggish in bringing about the required changes for transition to a market economy.

Not unfamiliar with these hazards, Turkish businesses have tried to reduce their risks by obtaining support or coverage from the Turkish government. An example is credits from the Turkish Exim Bank to finance projects and trade. As of the end of 1995, a total of $936 million had been allocated by the Turkish Exim Bank, but only 55% of this total, or $514.8 million, had been disbursed. Of this sum, $322.1 million, or 62.5%, has gone to finance the purchase of goods, while $192.7 million, or 37.5%, has been used to finance various projects. Important sums had been made available to Uzbekistan ($154.3 million), Kazakhstan ($128.3 million), Turkmenistan ($89.2 million), and Azerbaijan ($89.6 million) (Turkish Exim Bank 1996: 22). The bank has been criticized for the slowness in its disbursements. In response, bank officials have argued that delays have stemmed from lack of modern commercial practice and modern accounting techniques in these countries. One could also add to this the fact that while the government is generous with allocations, it does not make the funds available to the bank on time for prompt disbursement.

Neither of the parties is punctual and effective in dealing with the problems that arise in the economic relationship. Decision-making processes in both Turkey and the Turkic republics operate slowly. Although agreements have been reached to remove double taxation and to offer some guarantees as well as other incentives for investments, neither Turkey nor those countries with which agreements have been signed have been able to complete all procedures necessary to put these measures into force.

Trade Relations

Turkey's trade with the Turkic states is seen to have long-term potential, but currently it is limited. One of the reasons for the modest amount of trade has already been indicated. The high interdependency of trade between countries of the former Soviet Union leaves little room for other countries to enter the market. But a second reason is equally important. The volume of external trade of the new Turkic states is very modest indeed. This area of the world with its 60 million people (including Tajikistan) generated in 1995 around $11 billion worth of exports of which only $6 million went to non-CIS countries. During the same period, they imported more than $9 billion worth of goods, of which only $3.5 million came from the non-CIS countries. The non-CIS trade is led by the European Union (Germany, Italy, France, and U.K., in that order).

Turning to Turkey's trade with the Turkic republics, in 1992, Turkey's exports to these countries totaled $154 million. It jumped to $455.3 million in 1993, $484 million in 1994, and $551.2 million in 1995. In terms of percentages, the 1992 and 1995 figures correspond, respectively, to 1% and 2.5% of Turkey's exports. Turkey's imports, on the other hand, were only $96 million in 1992, or less than 0.5% of Turkey's total. They rose to $196.8 million in 1993, receded to $191.9 million in 1994, and went up again to $293.6 million in 1995. So in a matter of four years, from 1992 to 1995, the share of the Turkic republics in Turkey's imports had risen from 0.4% to 0.8% in 1995. Trade and other data are summarized in Table 10.1.

The modest level of Turkey's trade with the Turkic republics becomes clearer when it is compared with its trade with the Russian Federation. The Turkish trade with Russia expanded initially during the mid-1980s as Turkey began to import substantial amounts of natural gas from the Soviet Union. After the dissolution of the Soviet Union and the collapse of the socialist system, trade expanded such that by 1995, exports totaled $1.3 billion while imports reached $2.1 billion, accounting for 5.7% of exports and 5.8% of imports, respectively (Undersecretariat of Foreign Trade 1997). If only Turkey's trade with the CIS is taken as the criterion, then Russia takes 60% of Turkey's exports and provides 63% of its imports. There exists between all countries of the former Soviet Union and Turkey the so-called suitcase trade, which is not reflected in government statistics, suggesting that the trade between these countries and Turkey may be more substantial than what statistics would indicate. But observers all feel that the bulk of this trade, which is estimated to be $5–8 billion, is with the Russian Federation.

These figures indicate that the significance to Turkey of trade with the Turkic republics continues to be modest. But due to the low volume of their external trade, the Turkic republics do not occupy an important place in the external trade of any non-CIS country. As indicated, they have some trade with the countries of the EU. Both the United States and Japan, on the other hand, have been rather slow in entering these markets. In addition to the two large hegemonic powers, Russia and China, a group of sub-regional powers, including Iran, Pakistan, Korea, India, and Turkey, have taken an interest in trade in the region, with Turkey and Iran being most active. In this context, their imports from Turkey are far from being negligible, accounting for 5.9% of their total imports in 1995 or 14.5% of imports from outside the CIS. We may conclude that, in the long run, there is reason to expect that trade relations between

Turkey and the Turkic republics will grow in parallel with the growth these economies may register.

As shown in Table 10.2, Turkish exports to the area currently comprise mainly processed foods, textiles, machinery, and transport equipment. Turkish imports from the area, on the other hand, mainly comprise textiles and metal products. (See Table 10.3.) As the energy resources in these countries are developed, and the products begin to reach world markets, Turkey's imports of energy from the region will inevitably increase.

But more generally, future trade patterns will depend not only on how quickly these countries will be able to generate income but also on which trading routes will become available to them. Landlocked as they are, trade patterns will be closely affected by how relations with neighbors translate into access routes to world markets. Links to the East and to the West, by rail or by road, will, in the end, depend more on political, than on economic, factors.

Investment and Finance

Entry and penetration into the markets of the new republics seem to have followed an identifiable pattern. In the first stage, trading has been the primary type of economic activity. At that stage, the Turkish Exim Bank extended credit to exporters to promote trade. After the exporting firms achieved credibility and recognition, to sustain their trade, branching and the establishment of service networks became necessary. At this second stage, Turkish firms began to feel the need for financing to expand their businesses. Initially, the Turkish Exim Bank made credits available to serve this end. But later, both public and private Turkish banks have begun to operate in these markets. Sometimes establishing partnerships with local banks, these banks have offered investment loans (see Table 10.4). Finally, in the third stage, firms have become interested in investing in sole or joint ventures. Here, firms have faced both economic and political risks. To encourage investments, Turkish Exim Bank has moved to offer guarantees against political risk. Currently, it is also seeking the help of the Multilateral Investment Guarantee Agency of the World Bank to co-insure the bank's investment risk and to help it develop model contracts (Ida 1997).

Turkish companies have been active as investors in the Turkic republics. Currently, after Russia, Turkey has become the chief investor in the Central Asian republics. As of 1996, Turkish investments in Turkmenistan totaled $1.6 billion, and in Kazakhstan $1.5 billion, to be followed by Uzbekistan with $928.4 million and Kyrgyzstan with $279 million (Sezerler 1997: 12). The major initial investments have been in the field of hotels, food, and textiles. But there are literally hundreds of Turkish firms established and operating in the new Turkic republics about which no reliable information is available.

Table 10.1
Major Economic Indicators, Turkic Countries

Country	Population million (1995)	Area (1000 square Km)	Inflation (annual in %)		GDP growth rate (%)		Per Capita income (dollars)		Total Exports (TE) of (million $) 1995		Share of Exports to Turkey in TE of … in 1995 % of.		Total Imports (TI) of (million $) 1995		Share of Imports from Turkey in TI of … in 1995 % of.	
			1992	1995	1992	1995	1992	1995	Total	Non-CIS	Total	Non-CIS	Total	Non-CIS	Total	Non-CIS
Azerbaijan	7.5	86.6	1350	412	-22.6	-17.2	2228	1223	547	330	4.0	6.6	632	403	25.5	40.0
Kazakhstan	16.6	2717.3	1513	176	-13.0	-8.9	3612	2271	4974	2343	1.8	3.7	3742	1172	4.0	12.9
Kyrgyz Rep.	4.7	198.5	855	43	-15.9	-6.9	2014	1228	409	167	1.3	3.3	522	166	7.3	2.3
Tajikistan	5.2	143.1	1157	884	-30.0	-12.4	1287	815	749	497	0.9	1.3	799	321	0.8	1.9
Turkmen.	4.1	488.1	493	1262	5.3	-9.3	2683	1610	1736	564	6.4	19.8	720	92	7.8	61.2
Uzbekistan	22.5	447.4	4671	305	-10.6	-1.2	2068	1989	3100	1825	2.0	3.4	2900	1650	4.8	8.4
C.Asia (5)									10968	5396	2.5	5.0	8683	3401	4.5	11.5
ALL 6	60.6	4081.0							11515	5726	2.6	5.1	9315	3804	5.9	14.5

Source : Compiled from various Issues of the EIU s (Economist Intelligence Unit) *Country Reports*, and IMF's *Direction of Trade Statistics Yearbook* and State Statistical Institute of Turkey's Annual *Statistical Yearbooks*.

Table 10.2
Commodity Composition of Turkey's Exports to the Region (1995)

	Major Sectors	Exports to Azerbaijan	Exports to Kazakhstan	Exports to Kyrgyzstan	Exports to Turkmenistan	Exports to Uzbekistan
1	Agricultural raw materials, livestock and animal products	13,979,674	636,532	156,517	763,658	712 296
2	Food industry tobacco	35,486,400	35,691,223	9,472,915	6,640,320	55,532,905
3	Mineral manufactures	34,095,107	3,866,047	1,862,332	250,492	1,784,784
4	Chemical industrial goods	853,459	380,036	172,052	314,010	357,161
5	Chemical industrial goods	8,671,955	11,887,252	1,809,440	3,207,511	16,495,797
6	Rubber and related products	3,766,847	4,678,544	903,391	1,998,416	3,358,362
7	Hides and leather	1,376,102	4,176,685	141,838	1,962,748	706,226
8	Saw mill and lumber industry, furniture	680,172	1,202,550	63,310	903,097	141,497
9	Paper, and related products	2,952,204	2,945,039	223,668	955,280	2,175,718
10	Textiles, clothing	6,603,801	37,151,655	6,753,157	9,650,201	35,596,709
11	Ceramics, glasswork, stones	4,209,940	3,.15,970	1,220,737	3,141,997	2,391,620
12	Metal products	6,988,292	7,778,113	1,652,009	6,500.,73	3,810,380
13	Machinery and Transportation Equipment	30,151,507	30,844,478	12,770,693	13,842,731	13,038,269
14	Miscellaneous manufactured articles, and others	11,525,349	5,191,395	1,020,312	6,67,204	1,837,480
	TOTAL VALUE	161,344,248	150,145,519	38,222,374	56.352.938	137,939,204
	Sectors with highest share	2, 3, 13	10, 2, 13	13, 2, 10	13, 10, 2	2, 10, 5

Source : Calculated from raw data given by TÜSIAD (Turkish Industrialists and Businessmen's Association) (In dollars).

199

Table 10.3
Commodity Composition of Turkey's Imports from the Region (1995)

	Major Sectors	Imports from Azerbaijan	Imports from Kazakhstan	Imports from Kyrgyzstan	Imports from Turkmenistan	Imports from Uzbekistan
1	Agricultural raw materials, livestock and animal products	370,503	1,639,702	616,293	117,447	113,209
2	Food industry tobacco	73,582	20,219	0	0	0
3	Mineral manufactures	0	0	0	0	0
4	Chemical industrial goods	0	0	90	0	0
5	Chemical industrial goods	414,767	31,209	56,973	5,365	914,177
6	Rubber and related products	2,771,814	2,279,764	17,087	0	0
7	Hides and leather	2,240,758	20,359,700		5,873,290	1,037,198
8	Saw mill and lumber industry, furniture	90,248	108,116	3,327,734	0	0
9	Paper, and related products	102,133	182,008	0	0	0
10	Textiles, clothing	10,540,231	918,048	1,027,811	104,052,762	58,680,226
11	Ceramics, glasswork, stones	11,424	0	535	0	0
12	Metal products	4,920,940	61,035,023	397,729	1,735,631	383,793
13	Machinery and Transportation Equipment	235,840	57,697	60,576	41,306	395,753
14	Miscellaneous manufactured articles, and others	4,841	0	386	0	0
	TOTAL VALUE	21,777,081	86,631,486	5,505,214	111,852,801	61,524,356
	Sectors with highest share	10, 12, 6	12, 7, 6	8, 10, 12	10, 7, 12	10, 7, 5

Source : Calculated from raw data given by TÜSIAD (Turkish Industrialists and Businessmen's Association) (In dollars).

Table 10.4
Participation of Banks from Turkey in Banks in the Turkic Republics (December 1995)

Bank	Azerbaijan	Kazakstan	Turkmen.	Uzbeksitan
Ziraat Bankası	Azerbaycan-Türkiye Birge Sehimdar Kommers (Azer Turk Bank), Baku, 1995.	Kazkommerts-Ziraat International Bank (KZI Bank), Almaty, 1993	Turkmen-Turkish Commercial Bank (T.T.C. Bank), Ashkabat, 1993	Uzbekistan-Turkish Bank (U.T. Bank), Tashkent, 1993.
Emlak Bank		Türkiye Kazakhstan International Bank, Almaty, 1992		
Halk Bankası			Uluslararası Türkmen-Halk Kalkınma Bankası	
Ege Bank	Baybank, Baku, 1995			

Source: The Banks Association of Turkey, *Bankalarımız 1995*, no. 1996 (May 1996): 550–551.

Barring major political downturns, Turkish investments and financial activity in the new republics are likely to continue into the future. It may be anticipated that when the Turkic states begin to receive higher income from oil and gas exports, Turkish firms will assume a more active role in the expanding economies of these states.

Multilateral Relations

Turkey has also tried to enhance its relations with the Turkic republics by working through international organizations and by trying to develop for itself a role as the leading country with which others should cooperate in developing their economic relations with the Turkic republics.

Reforms for strengthening economic management and programs of stabilization and structural reforms in the Turkic republics are, in most cases, supported by public and, occasionally, private multilateral donors/creditors, such as the Tacis Committee of the European Union, the European Bank of Reconstruction and Development (EBRD), and the United Nations Development Program (UNDP). The International Monetary Fund (IMF) and the World Bank, which the new republics joined within a year of their independence, have helped them formulate economic policy frameworks. Turkey has sought opportunities for cooperation with these agencies in the implementation of their economic programs, including the delivery of technical assistance. For example, in a cooperative effort between the EU, EBRD, the Turkish Treasury, and the Banks Association of Turkey, a Regional Bank Training Center has been established in Tashkent in order to train bankers from the Kyrgyz Republic, Tajikistan, and Uzbekistan. There appears to be room for similar projects offering training in the fields of accounting, customs management, tax systems, compiling of economic statistics, computer programming, and the development of cadastral surveys, among others.

Turkey has also tried to impress upon the international business community that Turkey would be a good partner to work with in these markets in trade, services, or investments. To that end, DEİK and others have organized tours to the Turkic republics in which Turkish and foreign businessmen traveled together. The expression coined to describe the role Turkey would like to play between major economic actors and the Turkic republics is "bridge." The impact of this approach is not easy to measure. Turkish construction companies have, for example, been partners in consortia that have won contracts in the new republics, but that kind of cooperation between Turkish and foreign companies has existed for some time in the Soviet Union and in Russia. There is not enough joint investment yet to infer that these have been inspired by Turkey's self-prescribed role.

Turkish businessmen have certain advantages over their Western counterparts that may expand the role of Turkey as a bridge in the future. To begin with, they have greater familiarity with an environment in which the state has been a major and an interventionist actor in the economy. Second, Turkish workers and professionals are more willing to accept the relative deprivation that foreigners experience when working in these republics. Finally, Turks adapt to local life and customs more easily, in addition to learning the local language more quickly.

CONCLUSION: MAIN FEATURES OF CONTEMPORARY TURKISH POLICY

After the flurry of excitement about a rapid formation of a politically and economically integrated Turkic world dwindled in the face of harsh political and economic realities, the policy of Turkey toward the Turkic republics has become stabilized. Closer political cooperation and more developed economic relations are maintained as long-range goals. It is recognized that significant transformation has to take place within the Turkic republics on the economic, political, and cultural fronts in order to come close to achieving the long-term goal. But to move in the desired direction, cultural linkages are promoted, and the intensification of linkages with the non-Russian world is supported. Educational exchange programs, training young people in Turkey, and the work toward the spread of Turkish and English as the first international languages are manifestations of this policy.

In the medium term, policies that would reduce the reliance of the economies of the new countries on Russia are promoted. These include the promotion of Turkish investments in the region as well as attempts to bring in other Western capital. The efforts to have as much of the Azeri and Central Asian oil and gas reach the world markets as possible without the intermediation of Russia can also be cited as part of an effort to reduce the ties between these economies and that of Russia.

In the immediate future, the policy is to conduct relations in a variety of fields, but most importantly in the economic domain. Without the continual links that the economic relationships provide, longer-term changes cannot be brought about.

Turkey has become increasingly aware that Russian security concerns should be taken into consideration in the making and implementation of policy. Accordingly, Turkey has emphasized not only that it has no Pan-Turkish intentions in the long run but also that it values its relations with Russia. In fact, there also appears to be a subtle shift taking place in policy, though not always reflected in rhetoric. As the recognition that Russia continues to be in a position to thwart Turkey's policies toward the Turkic states becomes more widely shared, the need for cooperating with the Russians in the Caucasus and Central Asia is beginning to appear as a more rational policy. So, in the short and medium terms, we may more often observe cooperative relationships than competitive ones between the two countries. The Turkic republics may also find this suitable since, in this way, they would escape the pressures the Russo-Turkish competition brings them.

Bibliography

Ad-Hoc Commission on Turkey–BSEC Relations. *Türkiye–Karadeniz Ekonomik İşbirliği İlişkileri* (Turkey–BSEC Economic Relations). Ankara: Turkish State Planning Organization (TSPO), 1995.

Ahrari, M. E. "The Dynamics of the New Great Game in Muslim Central Asia." *Central Asian Survey* 13, no. 4 (1994): 525–39.

Alpay, Şahin. "Türkiye'nin Orta Asya da Kozu Eğitim." *Milliyet*, 1 November 1994a.

———. "Cennetten Cemiyete." *Milliyet*, 2 November 1995b.

Arık, Umut. "Türkiye'nin Azerbaycan ve İç Asya Devletleri İnsani, Ekonomik ve Teknik Yardım Politikaları." In Erol Manisalı, ed., *Türk Cumhuriyetleri Arasında Politik ve Ekonomik İşbirliği*. Istanbul: Kıbrıs Araştırmaları Vakfı, 1993.

Asbeghian, J. *International Economics*. Minneapolis, West, 1995.

Aydın, Mustafa. "Turkey and Central Asia: Challenges of Change." *Central Asian Survey* 15, no. 6 (1996): 157–77.

Aydın, T., and O. Bekar. *Türkiye'nin Orta ve Uzun Vadeli Çıkarları: Türk-Rus İlişkileri*. Istanbul: TESEV, 1995.

Azerbaycan Radio Televiziyası (Baku). In Azeri 1914 GMT 4 October 1994 [FBIS-SOV 5 October 1994].

Bagirov, Sabit. "Azerbaijani Oil: Glimpses of a Long History." *Perceptions* (Ankara) 1, no. 1 (1996): 22–52.

Balassa, Bela. "Trade Liberalization and 'Revealed' Comparative Advantage." *The Manchester School of Economic and Social Studies* 33 (1965): 9–23.

Balkır, Canan. "Turkey and the European Community: Foreign Trade and Direct Foreign Investment in the 1980s." In Canan Balkır and Allan M. Williams, eds., *Turkey and Europe*. London: Pinter, 1993a.

———. *Karadeniz Ekonomik İşbirliği (KEİB)–Ekonomik bir Değerlendirme*. Istanbul: TÜSİAD, 1993b.

Balkır, Canan, and Allan M. Williams, eds. *Turkey and Europe*. London: Pinter, 1993.

Banks Association of Turkey. *Bankalarımız 1995*.

Bibliography

Ad-Hoc Commission on Turkey—BSEC Relations. *Türkiye-Karadeniz Ekonomik İşbirliği İlişkileri* (Turkey—BSEC Economic Relations). Ankara: Turkish State Planning Organization (TSPO), 1995.

Ahrari, M. E. "The Dynamics of the New Great Game in Muslim Central Asia." *Central Asian Survey* 13, no. 4 (1994): 525–39.

Alpay, Şahin. "Türkiye'nin Orta Asya'da Kozu Eğitim." *Milliyet,* 1 November 1996a.

———. "Cemaatten Cemiyete." *Miilliyet,* 2 November 1996b.

Arık, Umut. "Türkiye'nin Azerbaycan ve İç Asya Devletlerini İnsanı, Ekonomik ve Teknik Yardım Politikaları." In Erol Manisalı, ed., *Türk Cumhuriyetleri Arasında Politik ve Ekonomik İşbirliği.* Istanbul: Kıbrıs Araştırmaları Vakfı, 1993.

Asheghian, P. *International Economics.* Minneapolis: West, 1995.

Aydın, Mustafa. "Turkey and Central Asia: Challenges of Change." *Central Asian Survey* 15, no. 6 (1996): 157–77.

Aydın, T., and O. Bekar. *Türkiye'nin Orta ve Uzun Vadeli Çıkarları Açısından Türk-Rus İlişkileri.* Istanbul: TESEV, 1995.

Azerbaycan Radio Televiziyasi (Baku). In Azeri 1914 GMT 4 October 1994 (FBIS-SOV 5 October 1994).

Bagirov, Sabit. "Azerbaijani Oil: Glimpses of a Long History." *Perceptions* (Ankara) 1, no. 1 (1996): 22–52.

Balassa, Bela. "Trade Liberalization and 'Revealed' Comparative Advantage." *The Manchester School of Economic and Social Studies* 33 (1965): 9–23.

Balkır, Canan. "Turkey and the European Community: Foreign Trade and Direct Foreign Investment in the 1980s." In Canan Balkır and Allan M. Williams, eds., *Turkey and Europe.* London: Pinter, 1993a.

———. *Karadeniz Ekonomik İşbirliği (KEİB)—Ekonomik bir Değerlendirme.* Istanbul: TÜSIAD, 1993b.

Balkır, Canan, and Allan M. Williams, eds., *Turkey and Europe.* London: Pinter, 1993.

Banks Association of Turkey. *Bankalarımız 1995.*

Barings, Ing. *Russia: Better the Devil You Know?* London: Eastern European Research, 1996.

Barkey, Henri J. "Iran and Turkey: Confrontation across an Ideological Divide." In Alvin Rubinstein and Oles M. Smolansky, eds., *Regional Power Rivalries in the New Eurasia: Russia, Turkey and Iran.* New York: M. E. Sharpe, 1995.

Barro, Robert J. "Are Government Bonds Net Wealth?" *Journal of Political Economy* 82 (1974): 1095–1117.

Barylski, Robert V. "Russia, the West, and the Caspian Energy Hub." *Middle East Journal* 49, no. 2 (1995): 217–232.

Bayar, Uğur. "Developments in the Privatization Arena, Valuation Methods, Like Privatization Targets, Policy Developments at the Privatization Agency, Privatization Experiences in Other Countries." Paper presented at Euromoney Conference, Istanbul, 15 May–16 May 1996.

Bayramoğlu, Ali. "Orta Asya'daki Türk Misyonerleri." *Yeni Yüzyıl,* 31 October 1996.

Berger, M. "Protectionism as Economic 'Moderation.'" *Moscow Times,* 28 May 1996.

Bilge, S. "Bağımsız Devletler Topluluğu ve Türkiye." *Avrasya Etüdleri.* Winter 1995. Ankara: TİKA, 1995.

Birand, Mehmet Ali. *Türkiyenin Ortak Pazar Maceras 1959–1985.* Istanbul: Milliyet Yayınları, 1985.

Blank, Stephen. "Russia, the Gulf and Central Asia in a New Middle East." *Central Asian Survey* 13, no.2 (1994): 267–281.

———. "Energy, Economics and Security in Central Asia: Russia and Its Rivals." *Central Asian Survey* 14, no. 3 (1995): 373–406.

BSEC. *KEİB: Mevcut Durum ve Gelecek* (The BSEC: The Present and the Future). Istanbul: BSEC Permanent International Secretariat, 1994.

Calvo, Guillermo A., and Carlos A. Vegh. "Exchange Rate-Based Stabilization under Imperfect Credibility." Working paper 91/77, International Monetary Fund, Washington, D.C., August 1991.

Çandar, Cengiz. "Değişmekte Olan Dünyada Türkiye'nin Bağımsızlığını Yeni Kazanan Yeni Türk Cumhuriyetleriyle İlişkileri." In Şen Sabahattin, ed., *Yeni Dünya Düzeni ve Türkiye.* Istanbul: Hava Harp Okulu, 1992.

Carley, Patricia M. "Turkey and Central Asia: Reality Comes Calling." In Alvin Rubinstein, and Oles M. Smolansky, eds., *Regional Power Rivalries in the New Eurasia: Russia, Turkey and Iran.* New York: M. E. Sharpe, 1995.

Çevik, İlnur. *Yeni Yüzyıl,* 16 August 1995.

Chase, Robert S., Emily B. Hill, and Paul Kennedy. "Pivotal States and U.S. Strategy." *Foreign Affairs* 75, no. 2 (1996): 33–51.

Cohen, Ariel. "The New 'Great Game': Oil Politics in the Caucasus and Central Asia." *The Heritage Foundation Backgrounder,* no. 1065. Washington, D.C.: Heritage Foundation, 1996.

Commission of the European Communities. *Commission Opinion on Turkey's Request for Accession to the Community.* Brussels (SEC 89, 2290 fin./2, plus annex), 20 December 1989.

Coppieters, Bruno, ed., *Contested Borders in the Caucasus.* Concord: Paul and Company Publishers Consortium, 1996.

Cumhuriyet (Istanbul). 4 August 1995; 5 April 1996; 9 May 1996; 23 June 1996; 2 July 1996; 26 July 1996; 2 August 1996; 10 September 1996.

Da, İlhan D. "Türkiye-Avrupa Birliği İlişkilerinde İnsan Haklar Sorunu." In A. Eralp, ed., *Türkiye ve Avrupa: Batılaşma, Kalkınma ve Demokrası*. Ankara: İmge Kitabevi Yayınları, 1997.

Deardorff, A.V. "Testing Trade Theories and Predicting Trade Flows." In R. W. Jones, and P. B. Kenen, eds., *Handbook of International Economics*, vol. 1. Amsterdam: North Holland, 1984.

DEİK (Dış Ekonomik İlişkileri Kurulu). *Bülten: 1992 Faaliyetleri*. Istanbul: DEİK, 1993.

De Melo, Martha, Cevdet Denizer and Alan Gelb. "From Plan to Market: Patterns in Transition." Working paper 1564, World Bank, Washington, D.C., January 1996.

Demir, Ali Faik. "SSCB'nin Dağılmasından Sonra Türkiye-Azerbaycan İlişkileri." In Faruk Sönmezoğlu, ed., *Değişen Dünya ve Türkiye*. Istanbul: Bağlam, 1996.

Devlet, Nadir. "Yeni Türk Cumhuriyetleri Açısından Türkiye ile (Politik, Ekonomik, ve Kültürel Sahalarda) İşbirliğinin Önemi." In Erol Manisalı, ed., *Türk Cumhuriyetleri Arasında Politik ve Ekonomik İşbirliği*. Istanbul: Kıbrıs Araştırmaları Vakfı, 1993.

Donges, Juergen. *The Second Enlargement of the European Community: Adjustment, Requirements and Challenges for Policy Reform*. Philadelphia: Coronet Books, 1982.

Donges, Juergen, and Klaus-Werner Schatz. "Muster der Industriellen Arbeitsteilung im Rahmen Einer Erweiterten Europaischen Gemeinschaft." *Die Weltwirtschaft*, no. 1 (1980): 160–186.

Dornbusch, Rudiger, Ilan Goldfjan, and Rodrigo O. Valdes. "Currency Crisis and Collapses." *Brookings Papers on Economic Activity* 2 (1995): 219–70.

Easterly, William and Klaus Schmidt-Hebbel. "Fiscal Adjustments and Macroeconomic Performance: A Synthesis." In W. Easterly, C. A. Rodriguez, and K. Schmidt-Hebbel, eds., *Public Sector Deficits and Macroeconomic Performance*. Oxford: Oxford University Press, 1994.

Economic Development Foundation. "Avrupa Birliği Bütünleşmesinin Vard Nokta: 1996 Hükümetlerarası Konferans ve Türkiyenin Bu Gelişimdeki Yeri." *Economic Development Foundation*, no. 137 (1996): 45–48.

Economist (London). 14 December 1991 (survey); 1 June 1996; 8 June 1996; 11 January 1997.

Economist Intelligence Unit. *Country Reports*. Various issues.

Elekdağ, Şükrü. "Karadeniz Ekonomik İşbirliği." In Şen Sabahattin, ed., *Yeni Dünya Düzeni ve Türkiye*. Istanbul: Hava Harp Okulu, 1992.

Eralp, A. "The Second Enlargement Process of the European Community and Its Possible Effects on Turkey's External Relations." *Yapı Kredi Economic Review* 11, nos. 2–3 (1988): 3–24.

———. "The Politics of Turkish Development Strategies." In Andrew Finkel and Nükhet Sirman, eds., *Turkish State, Turkish Society*. London: Routledge, 1990.

———. "Turkey and the EC in the Changing Post-War International System." In Canan Balkır and Allan M. Williams, eds., *Turkey and Europe*. London: Pinter, 1993.

———. "Turkey and the European Community: Forging New Identities along Old Lines." In Max Haller and Rudolph Richter, eds., *Toward a European Nation?* Armonk, N. Y.: M. E. Sharpe, 1994.

Erguvenç, S. "Turkey: Strategic Partner of the European Union." *Foreign Policy Quarterly* 20, nos. 1–2 (1995): 3–22.

Ertan, Nazlan. "Troubled Partners of the Black Sea." *Turkish Probe*, no. 131 (1995): 11.

Ferhatoğlu, Hakan. "Prospects for Institutional Investing in Turkey." Paper presented at Euromoney Conference. Istanbul 15–16 May 1996.

Financial Times. 29 October 1996.

Finger, J. Michael, and Dean A. DeRosa. "Trade Overlap, Comparative Advantage and Protection." In Herbert Giersch, ed., *On the Economics of Intra-Industry Trade.* Philadelphia: Coronet Books, 1979.

Finger, J. Michael, and Mordechai E. Kreinin. "A Measure of Export Similarity and Its Possible Uses." *The Economic Journal* 89 (1979): 905–12.

Fridman, Leonid A. "Economic Crisis as a Factor of Building up Socio-Political and Ethnonational Tensions in the Countries of Central Asia and Transcaucasia." In Vitaly Naumkin, ed., *Central Asia and Transcaucasia: Ethnicity and Conflict.* London: Greenwood, 1994.

Fuller, E. "Turkish-Russian Relations: 1992–1994." *RFE-RL Research Report* 3, no. 18 (1994).

Fuller, Graham E. "Conclusions: The Growing Role of Turkey in the World." In Graham E. Fuller and Ian O. Lesser, eds., *Turkey's New Geopolitics.* Boulder, Colo.: Westview, 1993a.

———. "Turkey's New Eastern Orientation." In Graham E. Fuller and Ian O. Lesser, eds., *Turkey's New Geopolitics.* Boulder, Colo.: Westview, 1993b.

Garih, Ü. "Turkey, Europe and the Black Sea Cooperation Organization Countries." *Turkish Daily News,* 9 December 1995.

Gavin, Michael, Ricardo Hausmann, and Ernesto Talvi. "Saving, Growth and Macroeconomic Vulnerability: Lessons from Asia and Latin America." *Development Policy* 5, no. 2 (1996): 1, 4–7.

Gençkaya, Ö. F. "The Black Sea Economic Cooperation Project: A Regional Challenge to European Integration." *International Social Science Journal* 138 (November 1993): 549–557.

Goble, Paul A. "The 50 Million Muslim Misunderstanding: The West and Central Asia Today." In Anoushiravan Ehteshami, ed., *From the Gulf to Central Asia: Players in the Game.* Exeter: University of Exeter Press, 1994.

Gruen, George E. "Turkey's Emerging Regional Role." *American Foreign Policy Interests* 17, no. 2 (1995): 13–24.

Gültekin, N. B., and A. Mumcu. "Black Sea Economic Cooperation." In Vojtech Mastny and R. C. Nation, eds., *Turkey Between East and West: New Challenges for a Rising Regional Power.* Boulder, Colo.: Westview, 1995.

Gürbey, G. "Özal Dönemi Dış Politikası (Foreign Policy during Özal Years)." *Dış Politikası* 6, no. 2 (1995): 47–62.

Haghayeghi, Mehrdad. "Islamic Revival in the Central Asian Republics." *Central Asian Survey* 13, no. 2 (1994):. 249–66.

Hale, William. "Turkey, the Black Sea and Transcaucasia." In Richard Schofield, John F. Wright, and Suzanne Goldenberg, eds., *Transcaucasian Boundaries.* New York: St. Martin's, 1996.

Halefoğlu, V. "Türkiye'nin Dış Politikası Kolay Değişmez." Interview. *Cumhuriyet,* 26 July 1996.

Harrison, Glenn W., Thomas F. Rutherford, and David G. Tarr. "Economic Implications for Turkey of a Customs Union with the European Union." Working paper 1599, World Bank, Washington, D.C., May 1996.

Hufbauer, C. Gray, and John C. Chilas. "Specialization by Industrial Countries: Extent and Consequences." In Herbert Giersch, ed., *The International Division of Labor: Problems and Perspectives.* Philadelphia: Coronet Books, 1974.

Hughes, Kirstly. "The 1996 Intergovernmental Conference and EU Enlargement." *International Affairs Journal* (1996): 1–8.

Hunter, Shireen. "Transcaucasia and the Middle East: Patterns of Mutual Impact." Paper presented at the MESA 27th Annual meeting, Research Triangle Park, N.C., 11–14 November 1993.

Hürriyet (Istanbul). 9 September 1993; 18, 19 October 1994.

Ida, Akira. 1997. Lecture on MIGA delivered on 21 February 1997 at the Asia-Pacific Research Center of the Faculty of Economics of Istanbul University.

Interfax (Moscow). In English 1632 GMT 29 September 1995 (FBIS-SOV 95-190, 2 October 1995); In English 1643 GMT 10 November 1995 (FBIS-SOV 95-218, 13 November 1995); 28 February 1995 (FBIS-SOV 95-040, 1 March 1995).

İskit, Temel. "Turkey: A New Actor in the Field of Energy Politics?" *Perceptions* (Ankara) 1, no. 1 (1996): 58–82.

Israeli, Raphael. "Return to the Source: The Republics of Central Asia and the Middle East." *Central Asian Survey* 13, no. 1 (1994): 19–31.

Kabaalioğlu, Haluk. "Turkey and the European Community." Forum European Conference, Belgium 1992.

Karaosmanoğlu, Ali L. *NATO Enlargement: Does It Enhance Security? Turkey and the European Union: Nebulous Nature of Relations.* Ankara: Foreign Policy Institute, 1996a.

———. "Europe's Geopolitical Parameters." Paper presented at the Seventh International Antalya Conference on Security and Cooperation. Antalya, 10–14 October 1996b.

Kazakh Radio First Program Network. In Russian 1500 GMT 27 September 1995 (FBIS-SOV 95-188, 28 September 1995).

Kazgan, G. "External Pressures and the New Policy Outlook." In Canan Balkır and Allan M. Williams, eds., *Turkey and Europe.* London: Pinter, 1993.

———. "Büyük Güçlerin Türkiye'yi Çevreleyen Alana ve Türkiye'ye Yaklaşmasındaki Değişmenin Türkiye'ye Ekonomik Etkileri; 1990 ve Sonrası." In Erol Manisalı, ed., *Balkanlar Kafkasya ve Ortadoğu'da Gelişmeler ve Türkiye.* Istanbul: KAV, 1994.

———. "Prospects for Cooperation versus Integration in the Middle East: Turkey's Political Choice." Paper presented at Social Science Research Council Workshop on New Regionalism and the Middle East, New York, 1995.

Keynes, J. Maynard. "A Tract on Monetary Reform" In *The Collected Writings of J M. Keynes,* vol. 4. London: Macmillan, 1971.

Kissinger, H. "Beware: A Threat Abroad." *Newsweek,* 17 June 1996.

Klodt, Henning. "Technologietransfer und Internationale Wettbewerbsfahigkeit." *Aussenwirtschaft* 45, no. 1 (1990): 57–79.

Kramer, Heinz. "EC-Turkish Relations: Unfinished Forever?" In Peter Ludlow, ed., *Europe and the Mediterranean.* London: Brassey's, 1994.

———. "Turkey and the European Union: A Multi-Dimensional Relationship with Hazy Perspectives." In Vojtech Mastny and R. C. Nation, eds., *Turkey between East and West: New Challenges for a Rising Regional Power.* Boulder, Colo.: Westview, 1995a.

————. "Resolution Dated March 6th, regarding the Customs Union and the Association between EU-Turkey." Paper presented at the meeting of the CHP-SDP, June 1995b.

————. "Will Central Asia Become Turkey's Sphere of Influence?" *Perceptions* (Ankara) 1, no. 1 (1996): 112–27.

Kubicek, Paul. "Regional Cooperation in Central Asia: Economic Imperatives, Local Nationalism, and the Shadow of Russia." Paper presented to the Joint JAIR/ISA Conference, Makuhari, Japan, 20–22 September 1996.

Kumcu, Ercan. "Exchange Rate Regime, Balance of Payments, and Economic Stability." In Hasan Ersel, ed., *Towards a New Medium Term Stabilization Program for Turkey* (in Turkish). Istanbul: TÜSIAD, 1995.

Kut, Ş. "Karadeniz Ekonomik İşbirliğinin Boyutları (The Scope of Black Sea Economic Cooperation)." *Strateji*, no. 3 (1995): 93–105.

Lafay, Gerard. "The Measurement of Revealed Comparative Advantages." In M. G. Dagenais and P. A. Muet, eds., *International Trade Modeling*. London: Chapman and Hall, 1992.

Leicester, Graham. "Turkey and the European Union: The Case for a Special Relationship." University of Reading Discussion Papers in European and International Social Science Research, no. 55 (October 1995).

Lieberman, Ira. "Chairman's Introduction." Paper presented at Euromoney Conference, Istanbul 15–16 May 1996.

MacFarlane, S. N. "The Structure of Instability in the Caucasus." *Internationale Politik und Gesellschaft* 4 (1995).

Mastny, Vojtech, and R. Craig Nation, eds. *Turkey between East and West: New Challenges for a Rising Regional Power*. Boulder, Colo.: Westview, 1996.

McCallum, John. "Government Spending and National Saving." In Mario Baldassarri, Robert Mundell, and John McCallum, eds., *Debt, Deficit, and Economic Performance*. New York: St. Martin's, 1993.

Milliyet (Istanbul). 28 May 1996; 15, 16, 27 June 1996; 1, 6, 23 July 1996; 16, 19, 31 December 1996; 26 February 1997.

Moskova Ticaret Müşavirliği. *Rusya Federasyonu: Temel Göstergeler*. Moscow, 1996a.

————. *Türkiye ile Rusya arasındaki Ekonomik ve Ticari İlişkiler*. Moscow, 1996b.

Nezavisimaya Gazeta (Moscow; in Russian). 15 December 1995 (FBIS-SOV 96-001-S, 2 January 1996).

Nugent, Neil. "The Deepening and Widening of the European Community: Recent Evolution, Maastricht and Beyond." *Journal of Common Market Studies* (September 1992): 311–328.

————. "Redefining Europe." *Journal of Common Market Studies* (August 1995).

OECD. *OECD Economic Survey 1994–1995, Turkey*. Paris: OECD, 1995.

Official Journal of the EC, no. 271 (29 December 1964), no. 293 (27 December 1972).

Oil and Gas Journal (16 October 1995).

Olcott, Martha Brill. *Central Asia's New States: Independence, Foreign Policy and Regional Security*. Washington, D.C.: U. S. Institute of Peace Press, 1996.

Öniş, Ziya. "Turkey in the Post-Cold War Era: In Search of Identity." *Middle East Journal* 49, no. 1 (1995): 48–69.

Öniş, Ziya, and James Riedel. *Economic Crisis and Long Term Growth in Turkey*. Washington, D.C.: World Bank, 1993.

Permanent International Secretariat of BSEC. *BSEC Handbook on Documents* Vol. 1. Istanbul: BSEC, 1995.

Przeworski, Adam. *Democracy and the Market: Political and Economic Reforms in Eastern Europe and Latin America.* New York: Cambridge University Press, 1991.

Roberts, John. *Caspian Pipelines.* London: Royal Institute of International Affairs, Former Soviet South Project, 1996.

Robins, Philip. 1993. "Between Sentiment and Self Interest: Turkey's Policy Toward Azerbaijan and the Central Asian States." *Middle East Journal* 47, no. 4 (1993): 593–610.

Robson, P. *The Economics of International Integration.* London: George Allen and Unwin, 1987.

Rodrik, Dani. "Some Policy Dilemmas in Turkish Macroeconomic Management." In Tosun Arıcanl and Dani Rodrik, eds., *The Political Economy of Turkey: Debt Adjustment and Sustainability.* New York: St. Martin's, 1990.

Rossiyskaya Gazeta (Moscow, in Russian). 6 January 1996 (FBIS-SOV 96-008 11 January 1996).

Rubinstein, Alvin, and Oles M. Smolansky, eds., *Regional Power Rivalries in the New Eurasia: Russia, Turkey and Iran.* New York: M. E. Sharpe, 1995.

Sabah (Istanbul). 14 October 1996.

Sander, Oral. "Turkey and the Turkic World." *Central Asian Survey.* 13, no. 1 (1994): 37–44.

Saraçoğlu, Rüşdü. "The Role of Real Exchange Rates in Stabilization Policies: The Case of Turkey." Paper presented at a colloquium for the executive director of the World Bank, Washington, D.C., 8 November 1985.

———. "Closing Address." Paper presented at Euromoney Conference, Istanbul, 15–16 May 1996.

Sargent, Thomas J., and Neil Wallace. "Some Unpleasant Monetarist Arithmetics." *FRB of Minneapolis Quarter Review* (1981): 1–17.

Sayan, Serdar. "The Importance of Transportation and Communications Infrastructure for BSEC Members." Discussant's comments, BSEC-Bosphorus University Workshop on the Black, Caspian and Mediterranean Seas: A Turntable between Three Continents. Istanbul, 5–6 December 1996.

Sayarı, Sabri. "Turkey, the Caucuses and Central Asia." In A. Banuazizi and M. Weiner, eds., *The New Geopolitics of Central Asia and Its Borderlands.* New York: St. Martin's, 1994.

Segodnya (Moscow, in Russian). 28 September 1995 (FBIS-SOV 95-193 5 October 1995); 30 September 1995 (FBIS-SOV 95-194, 6 October 1995).

Selcuk, Faruk. "Seigniorage and Dollarization in a High Inflation Economy: Evidence from Turkey." Bilkent University Department of Economics Working Paper 96(11), 1996a.

———. "Consumption Smoothing and Current Account: Turkish Experience 1987–1995." Bilkent University Department of Economics Working Paper 96(12), 1996b.

———. *Perpetual Motion Machine: The Turkish Economy 1994–1996* (in Turkish). Ankara: Imge Press, 1997.

Selcuk, Faruk, and Anjariitta Rantanen. *Government Expenditures and Public Debt in Turkey* (in Turkish). Istanbul: TÜSIAD, 1996.

Şen, F. "Turkish Communities in Western Europe." In Vojtech Mastny and R. Craig Nation, eds., *Turkey between East and West: New Challenges for a Rising Regional Power.* Boulder, Colo.: Westview, 1995.

Sezerler, Didem. "Türkiye Orta Asya'nın Yatırım Şampiyonu." *Yeni Yüzyıl,* 13 February 1997.

Smolansky, Oles. "Turkish and Iranian Policies in Central Asia." In Hafeez Malik, ed., *Central Asia: Its Strategic Importance and Future Prospects*. New York: St. Martin's, 1994.
Snark (Yerevan; in English). 1411 GMT 19 January 1996 (FBIS-SOV 95-015, 23 January 1996).
Snyder, Jack. "International Security in the Black Sea Region: A Systems Perspective." *Boğaziçi Journal: Review of Social, Economic and Administrative Studies* 9, no. 1 (1995): 41–46.
Spaventa, Luigi. "The Growth of Public Debt." *IMF Staff Papers* 34 (1987): 374–399.
State Institute of Statistics. *Foreign Trade Statistics*. Ankara: State Institute of Statistics, February 1994.
State Planning Organization. "Turkey-EU Relations." Photocopy. Ankara: State Planning Organization, EU Relations Directorate, November 1996.
———. *Main Economic Indicators*. Ankara: State Planning Organization, December 1996.
Swietockowski, Tadeusz. "Azerbaijan's Triangular Relationship: The Land between Russia, Turkey, and Iran." In A. Banuazizi and M. Weiner, eds., *The New Geopolitics of Central Asia and Its Borderlands*. New York: St. Martin's, 1994.
Tekeli, İlhan, and Selim İlkin. *Türkiye ve Avrupa Topluluğu* (Turkey and the European Union), 2 vols. Ankara: Ümit Yayıncık, 1991.
Tezel, Yahya S. *Economic History of the Republic Era* (in Turkish). Ankara: Economic and Social History Foundation of Turkey, 1994.
32. Gün [32nd Day]. Show TV 16 July 1996.
Ticari ve Ekonomik İlişkiler. *Rusya Federasyonu ile Ticari ve Ekonomik İlişkilerimiz hakkında Not*. Ankara: Ticari ve Ekonomik İlişkiler, 1996.
TİKA. *Note on Technical Cooperation between Russia and Turkey*. Ankara: TİKA, 1996.
Tinbergen, J. *Shaping the World Economy*. New York: The Twentieth Century Fund, 1962.
Togan, Sübidey. *Turkish Foreign Trade in the 1980s and Liberalization of Foreign Trade*. Ankara: Turkish Exim Bank, 1993.
———. "Black Sea Economic Cooperation, Economic Cooperation Organization, Turkic Republics and Turkey: Possibilities for Regional Economic Integration." Photocopy. Ankara: Bilkent University, 1994.
Toksöz, Mina. "International Capital Raising for Projects and Issuers." Paper presented at Euromoney Conference, Istanbul, 15–16 May 1996.
Tovias, Alfred, and Eyal Inbar. "Potential Effects of Turkey's Membership in the EC on Israel's Economy." Photocopy. 1991.
Trenin, Dmitri. "Russia's Security Interests and Policies in the Caucasus." In Bruno Coppieters, ed., *Contested Borders in the Caucasus*. Concord: Paul and Company Publishers Consortium, 1996.
TRT TV Network (Ankara, in Turkish). 2200 GMT 23 January 1996 (FBIS-SOV 96-016, 24 January 1996).
Tsoukalis, Loukas. *The European Community and Its Mediterranean Enlargement*. London: George Allen and Unwin, 1981.
TÜBİTAK. *Not*. Ankara: Başbakanlık Dış Ticaret Müsteşarlığı Anlaşmalar Genel Müdürlüğü, 1996.
Turan (Baku; in English). 1254 GMT 20 November 1993 (FBIS-SOV 93-223, 22 November 1993); in English 1043 GMT 31 July 1995 (FBIS-SOV 95-147, 1 August

1995); in English 1220 GMT 10 November 1995 (FBIS-SOV 95-218, 13 November 1995).

Turk Exim Bank. *Faaliyet Raporu*. Ankara: Turk EximBank, 1996.

Turkish Daily News (Ankara). 22 October 1994; 25 October 1995; 19 September 1996; 7 October 1996; 5 December 1996; 1, 3 January 1997.

Turkish Industrialists' and Businessmen's Association (TÜSIAD). *Turkish Economy '96*. Istanbul: TÜSIAD, 1996.

Uibopuu, Henn-Juri. "The Caspian Sea: A Tangle of Legal Problems." *The World Today* 51 (June 1995): 119–123.

UND. *Uluslararası Nakliyatçılar Derneği Dergisi*, May, June 1996.

Van Bergeijk, P.A.G., and H. Oldersna. "The Effects of German Unification on World Trade Flows." *Kyklos* 43 (1990): 599–609.

Vassiliev, Alexei. "Turkey and Iranian Trancaucasus and Central Asia." In Anoushiravan Ehteshami,ed., *From the Gulf to Central Asia: Players in the Game*. Exeter: University of Exeter Press, 1994.

Vaughn, Bruce. "Shifting Geopolitical Realities between South, Southwest and Central Asia." *Central Asian Survey*. 13, no. 2 (1994): 305–315.

Vegh, Carlos A. "Stopping High Inflation, An Analytical Overview." *IMF Staff Papers* 39, no. 3 (1992): 626–92.

Verney, Susannah. "Greece and the European Community." In Kevin Featherstone and Dimitrios K. Katsoudas, eds., *Political Change in Greece: Before and after the Colonels*. New York: St. Martin's, 1987.

Viner, Jacob. *The Custom Union Issues*. New York: Carnegie Endowment for International Peace, 1953.

Wall Street Journal (New York). 14 February 1992; 27 March 1997.

Winckler, Georg, Eduard Hochreiter, and Peter Brandner. "Deficits, Debt and European Monetary Union: Some Unpleasant Fiscal Arithmetic." University of Vienna Department of Economic Working Paper 9615, 1996.

Winrow, Gareth M. "Discussion of Jack Snyder's Article." *Boğaziçi Journal: Review of Social, Economic and Administrative Studies* 9, no. 1 (1995a): 47–50.

———. *Turkey in the Post-Soviet Central Asia*. London: Royal Institute of International Affairs, 1995b.

World Bank. *World Development Report: 1994*. New York: Oxford University Press for the World Bank, 1994.

Yeni Yüzyıl (Istanbul). 4, 7 April 1995; 9 May 1995; 6 July 1995; 4, 23, 31 August 1995; 7, 12 September 1995; 4, 6, 19 October 1995; 19 November 1995; 4 August 1996; 18, 20 December 1996; 26 January 1997.

Yıldırım, Zekeriya. "Direct and Portfolio Investment Opportunities and New Financial Services." Paper presented at Euromoney conference, Istanbul 15–16 May 1996.

Zaman (Istanbul). 25 June 1996; 25 September 1996.

Zviagelskaya, Irina. "Central Asia and Transcaucasia: New Geopolitics." In Vitaly Naumkin, ed., *Central Asia and Transcaucasia: Ethnicity and Conflict*. Westport, Conn.: Greenwood, 1994.

Index

Index

216 Index

About the Contributors

MELIHA ALTUNIŞIK was a Fulbright Scholar at Harvard University in 1988–89 and received her Ph.D. in political science from Boston University in 1994. She is currently an assistant professor in the Department of International Relations at Middle East Technical University in Ankara, Turkey. Her area of specialization is the political economy of oil in the Middle East.

CANAN BALKIR received her Ph.D. from Aegean University and is currently a lecturer in the Department of Economics at Dokuz Eylül University in Izmir, Turkey. Previously she has served as a Fulbright scholar at North Carolina State University, as a research fellow at the Institute of Development Studies in Brighton, UK, and as a British Council Scholar and, more recently, an Honorary Visiting Professor at the University of Exeter, UK. She is the author of numerous articles and books, including the edited volume *Turkey and Europe*.

ATILA ERALP holds his B.S. degree from Middle East Technical University in Ankara, Turkey and M.A. and Ph.D. degrees from the University of Southern California. He is currently chair of the Department of International Relations at Middle East Technical University.

GÜLTEN KAZGAN retired from the Faculty of Economics of Istanbul University in 1994. She then joined the Istanbul School of International Studies which has recently evolved into Istanbul Bilgi University, where she became the founding president. She is the author of numerous books and articles and writes a weekly column on economics and finance for the Turkish newspaper, *Yeni Yüzyıl*.

LIBBY RITTENBERG is a professor of economics at Colorado College. She received her Ph.D. from Rutgers University in 1980 and served as a Fulbright Lecturer at Bosphorus and Marmara Universities in Istanbul, Turkey in the mid-1980s. She has published articles on various aspects of the Turkish economy in the post-liberalization period and on transition issues in east/central Europe.

SERDAR SAYAN is an assistant professor in the Department of Economics as Bilkent University in Ankara, Turkey. He was awarded a Fulbright grant for graduate studies in the U.S. and received his Ph.D. from Ohio State University in 1992. His research focuses on policy analysis with computable general equilibrium models of the U.S. and Turkish economies and on international economics relations of Turkey with neighboring countries and with the European Union.

FARUK SELCUK holds a Ph.D. degree from the Graduate School of the City University of New York and is currently an assistant professor at Bilkent University in Ankara, Turkey. Before joining the faculty at Bilkent University in 1992, he taught at Baruch College, Queens College, and Hunter College. He has published books and articles on the macroeconomic situation of Turkey.

GÜL TURAN, professor of economics at Istanbul University, specializes in international monetary economics, international political economy, and banking and financial institutions. She received her B.A. from the American University in Cairo and her Ph.D. from Istanbul University.

İLTER TURAN is currently a professor of political science at Koç University in Istanbul. He received his B.A. from Oberlin College, his M.A. from Columbia University, and his Ph.D. from Istanbul University. He is the author of numerous publications on Turkish politics and Turkish foreign policy.

GARETH WINROW was Associate Professor in the Department of Political Science and International Relations at Bosphorus University until 1997. He has written extensively on Turkish foreign policy, regional security issues in the Transcaucasus and Central Asia, and problems of European security in general. Recent books include *The Kurdish Question and Turkey: An Example of a Trans-State Ethnic Conflict* and *Turkey in Post-Soviet Central Asia*. His articles have appeared in such journals as *Central Asian Survey*, the *Oxford International Review*, the *Journal of South Asian and Middle Eastern Studies*, and *European Security*.

BAHRI YILMAZ did graduate work at the University of Cambridge and received his Ph.D. in economics from the University of Bonn. He has taught at numerous universities in Turkey and Germany and is currently in the Department of Economics at Bilkent University in Ankara, Turkey. He is the recipient of several research fellowships, including the Alexander von Humbolt Stiftung research fellowship, an Oxford University research fellowship, and a Korean Development Institute fellowship. He is the author of many articles on political and economics relations of Turkey in Turkish, English, and German.

OSMAN ZAIM received his Ph.D. in 1989 from Washington State University and is currently on the economics faculty at Bilkent University in Ankara, Turkey. His main research interests include topics in applied microeconomics and production efficiency.

ISBN 0-275-95596-6

HARDCOVER BAR CODE